"Society Must Be Defended"

MICHEL FOUCAULT

"Society Must Be Defended"
LECTURES AT THE COLLÈGE DE FRANCE, 1975-76

Edited by Mauro Bertani and Alessandro Fontana
General Editors: François Ewald and Alessandro Fontana

English Series Editor: Arnold I. Davidson

TRANSLATED BY DAVID MACEY

PICADOR
NEW YORK

"SOCIETY MUST BE DEFENDED". Copyright © 1997 by Éditions de Seuil/Gallimard. Edition established, under the direction of François Ewald and Alessandro Fontana, by Mauro Bertani. Translation copyright © 2003 by David Macey. Introduction copyright © 2003 by Arnold I. Davidson. All rights reserved. Printed in the United States of America. No part of this book may be used or reproduced in any manner whatsoever without written permission except in the case of brief quotations embodied in critical articles or reviews. For information, address Picador, 175 Fifth Avenue, New York, N.Y. 10010.

www.picadorusa.com

Picador® is a U.S. registered trademark and is used by St. Martin's Press under license from Pan Books Limited.

For information on Picador Reading Group Guides, as well as ordering, please contact the Trade Marketing department at St. Martin's Press.
Phone: 1-800-221-7945 extension 763
Fax: 212-677-7456
E-mail: trademarketing@stmartins.com

ISBN 0-312-20318-7 (hc)
ISBN 0-312-42266-0 (pbk)

10 9 8 7 6 5 4 3

CONTENTS

FOREWORD

THIS VOLUME IS THE first in a series devoted to the lectures given at the Collège de France by Michel Foucault.

Michel Foucault taught at the Collège de France from January 1971 until his death in June 1984—with the exception of 1977, when he enjoyed a sabbatical year. His chair was in the History of Systems of Thought.

The chair was established on 30 November 1969 at the proposal of Jules Vuillemin and in the course of a general meeting of the professors of the Collège de France. It replaced the chair in the History of Philosophical Thought, which was held until his death by Jean Hyppolite. On 12 April 1970, the general meeting elected Michel Foucault to the chair.[1] He was forty-three.

Michel Foucault gave his inaugural lecture on 2 December 1970.[2]

Professors teaching at the Collège de France work under specific rules. They are under an obligation to teach for twenty-six hours a year (up

---

1 The candidacy presentation drawn up by Michel Foucault ends with the formula "[I]t would be necessary to undertake the history of systems of thought." "Titres et travaux," in *Dits et écrits*, ed. Daniel Defert and François Ewald (Paris: Gallimard), vol. 1, p. 846; trans., "Candidacy Presentation: Collège de France," in *Ethics: Subjectivity and Truth*, ed. Paul Rabinow, *The Essential Works of Michel Foucault, 1954-1984* (London: Allen Lane, The Penguin Press, 1994), vol. 1, p. 9.
2 It was published by Éditions Gallimard in March 1971 under the title *L'Ordre du discours*. The English translation by Rupert Swyer, "Orders of Discourse," is appended to the U.S. edition of *The Archaeology of Knowledge;* it does not appear in U.K. editions.

to half the hours can take the form of seminars).[3] Each year, they are required to give an account of the original research that they have undertaken, which means that the content of their lectures must always be new. Anyone is free to attend the lectures and seminars; there is no enrollment, and no diplomas are required. The professors do not award any diplomas.[4] In the vocabulary of the Collège de France, its professors do not have students, but *auditeurs* or listeners.

Michel Foucault gave his lectures on Wednesdays from the beginning of January to the end of March. The very large audience, made up of students, teachers, researchers, and those who attended simply out of curiosity, many of them from abroad, filled two of the Collège de France's lecture theaters. Michel Foucault often complained about the distance this could put between him and his "audience" and about the way the lecture format left so little room for dialogue.[5] He dreamed of holding a seminar in which truly collective work could be done. He made various attempts to hold such a seminar. In his last years, he devoted long periods after his lectures to answering questions from his listeners.

This is how Gérard Petitjean, a journalist on *Le Nouvel Observateur*, captured the atmosphere:

When Foucault quickly enters the arena with all the resolution of someone diving into the water, he scrambles over bodies to get to his dais, pushes the microphones aside to put his papers down, takes off his jacket, switches on a lamp and takes off at a hundred kilometers an hour. His loud, effective voice is relayed by loudspeakers, which are the sole concession to modernity in a room that is only dimly lit by the light that comes from the stucco lamp-holders. There are three hundred seats, and five

---

3 Michel Foucault did so until the early 1980s.
4 In the context of the Collège de France.
5 In 1976, Michel Foucault changed the time of his lecture from 5:45 P.M. to 9:00 A.M. in a vain attempt to reduce the numbers present. Cf. the beginning of the first lecture (7 January 1976) in the present volume.

hundred people are crammed into them, taking up all the available space ... No oratorical effects. It is lucid and extremely effective. Not the slightest concession to improvisation. Foucault has twelve hours to explain, in a series of public lectures, the meaning of the research he has carried out over the year that has just ended. So he crams in as much as possible, and fills in the margins like a letter writer who has too much to say when he has reached the bottom of the sheet. 19.15. Foucault stops. The students rush to his desk. Not to talk to him, but to switch off their tape recorders. No questions. Foucault is alone in the crush. Foucault comments: "We ought to be able to discuss what I have put forward. Sometimes, when the lecture has not been good, it would not take a lot, a question, to put everything right. But the question never comes. In France, the group effect makes all real discussion impossible. And as there is no feedback channel, the lecture becomes a sort of theatrical performance. I relate to the people who are there as though I were an actor or an acrobat. And when I have finished speaking, there's this feeling of total solitude."[6]

Michel Foucault approached his teaching as a researcher. He explored possibilities for books in preparation, outlined fields of problematization, as though he were handing out invitations to potential researchers. That is why the lectures given at the Collège de France do not reduplicate the published books. They are not outlines for books, even though the books and the lectures do sometimes have themes in common. They have a status of their own. They belong to a specific discursive regime within the sum total of the "philosophical acts" performed by Michel Foucault. Here he quite specifically outlines the program for a genealogy of the relations between power and knowledge. From the early 1970s onward, it is this, and not the ar-

6 Gérard Petitjean, "Les Grands Prêtres de l'université française," *Le Nouvel Observateur*, 7 April 1975.

chaeology of discursive formations that had previously been his dominant concern, that provides the framework for his discussion of his
own work.[7]

The lectures also had a contemporary function. The *auditeurs* who
followed them were not simply captivated by the narrative that was
being constructed week after week; they were not simply seduced by
the rigor of the exposition; they found that they were also listening
to a commentary on current events. Michel Foucault knew the secret
of how to use history to cut through current events. He might well
have been speaking of Nietzsche or Aristotle, of psychiatric appraisal
in the nineteenth century or of Christian pastoralism, but his audience
was also learning about the present day and contemporary events. It
is this subtle interplay among erudite scholarship, personal commitment, and work on current events that gives Michel Foucault's lectures their great power.

⚜

The 1970s saw the development and the refinement of cassette tape
recorders. Michel Foucault's lecture theater was quickly invaded by
them. It is thanks to them that the lectures (and some of the seminars) have been preserved.

This edition is based upon the words pronounced in public by
Michel Foucault. It gives the most literal transcription possible.[8] We
would have liked to publish his words exactly as they were spoken.
But the transition from the oral to the written does require some
editorial intervention. At least some punctuation has to be introduced,
and paragraph breaks have to be added. The principle has always

---

7 Cf. in particular "Nietzsche, la généalogie, l'histoire," in *Dits et écrits*, vol. 2, p. 137. English
translation by Donald F. Brouchard and Sherry Simon, "Nietzsche, Genealogy, History," in
James Faubion, ed., *Aesthetics, Method, and Epistemology: Essential Works of Foucault, 1954-1984,
Volume II* (London: Allen Lane, 1998), pp. 369-92.
8 Particular use has been made of the recordings made by Gilbert Burlet and Jacques La-
grange. These have been deposited at the Collège de France and in the Fonds Michel Foucault
held by Institut Mémoires de l'Édition Contemporaine.

been to remain as close as possible to the lecture that was actually given.

When it seemed absolutely essential, repetitions have been cut; sentences that break off have been completed, and incorrect constructions have been rectified.

Ellipses indicate that the tape recording is inaudible. In the case of obscure phrases, brackets indicate a conjectural interpolation or addition.

Asterisks indicate significant variations between the notes used by Michel Foucault and what he actually said.

Quotations have been checked, and references to the texts used have been supplied. The critical apparatus is restricted to the elucidation of obscure points, the explanation of certain allusions, and the clarification of critical points.

For the reader's benefit, each lecture is preceded by a brief summary indicating its main articulations.

The text of the lectures is followed by the course summary published in the *Annuaire du Collège de France*. Michel Foucault usually wrote his course summaries in the month of June, or in other words some time after the end of his lecture course. He saw them as an opportunity to use the benefit of hindsight to clarify his own intentions and objectives. They are the best introduction to the lectures.

Each volume ends with a "situation" written by the editor: this is designed to provide the reader with contextual, biographical, ideological, and political information that situates the lectures in relation to Michel Foucault's published works. It situates the lectures in relation to the corpus used by Michel Foucault so as to facilitate an understanding of it, to avoid misunderstandings, and to preserve the memory of the circumstances in which each lecture was prepared and delivered.

⚜

This edition of the lectures given at the Collège de France marks a new stage in the publication of the "works" of Michel Foucault.

These are not unpublished texts in the strict sense of the word, as this edition reproduces words that were spoken in public by Michel Foucault, but not the written—and often very sophisticated—support he used. Daniel Defert, who owns Michel Foucault's notes, has allowed the editors to consult them. They are extremely grateful to him.

This edition of the lectures given at the Collège de France has been authorized by Michel Foucault's heirs, who wished to meet the great demand for their publication both in France and abroad. They wished this to be a serious undertaking. The editors have attempted to prove themselves worthy of the trust that has been placed in them.

FRANÇOIS EWALD AND ALESSANDRO FONTANA

INTRODUCTION

Arnold I. Davidson

THIS VOLUME INAUGURATES THE English-language publication of Michel Foucault's extraordinary courses at the Collège de France.

Claude Lévi-Strauss recounts that after he was elected to the Collège de France, an usher, who had grown old in his job, took him from room to room so that he could choose the room in which he would give his yearly course. After Lévi-Strauss had chosen a room the usher bluntly warned him: "Not that one!" to which Lévi-Strauss expressed surprise:

"You see," [the usher] explained, "it is laid out in such a way that in order to reach the rostrum you have to make your way through the entire audience, and, you have to do likewise while leaving." "Does it really matter?" I said. Whereupon he shot back this response with a peremptory look: "Someone could speak to you." I stood by my choice, but, in the tradition of the Collège, it is indeed a matter of the professor dispensing his words, and not receiving them or even exchanging them.[1]

And Lévi-Strauss goes on to talk about the "mental concentration and nervous tension" involved in giving a course at the Collège de France.[2]

In a 1975 interview Foucault himself noted the strange particularity of "teaching" at the Collège de France, remarking that he liked not having "the impression of teaching, that is, of exercising a relationship of power with respect to an audience."[3] The traditional teacher first makes his audience feel guilty for not knowing a certain number of

things they should know; then he places the audience under the obligation to learn the things that he, the professor, knows; and, finally,
when he has taught these things, he will verify that the audience has
indeed learned them. Culpabilization, obligation, and verification are
the series of power relations exercised by the typical professor.[4] But,
as Foucault points out, at the Collège de France, courses are open to
anyone who wishes to attend: "If it interests him, he comes; if it
doesn't interest him, he doesn't come."[5] At the Collège a professor is
paid to present his work, and "it is up to the audience to say or to
show whether or not it is interested":

> In any case when I am going to give my courses at the Collège,
> I have stage fright (*trac*), absolutely, like when I took exams,
> because I have the feeling that, really, people, the public, come
> to verify my work, to show that they are interested or not; if
> they don't have an interested look, I am very sad, you know.[6]

Nowhere were culpabilization, obligation, and verification less present
than in Foucault's lectures at the Collège de France, and the interested
public often gave way to an excited, enthusiastic public that made
the very idea of presenting lectures a difficult task. Rather than an
atmosphere of sadness, Foucault's courses produced a kind of frenzy,
a frenzy of knowledge, that was intellectually and socially electrifying.

In an exceptional essay on Foucault, Gilles Deleuze has distin-
guished two dimensions of Foucault's writings: on the one hand, the
lines of history, the archive, Foucault's analytic; on the other, the lines
of the present, of what is happening now, Foucault's diagnostic: "In
every apparatus, we have to disentangle the lines of the recent past
and those of the future at hand."[7] According to Deleuze, the majority
of Foucault's books establish "a precise archive with exceedingly new
historical means," while in his interviews and conversations, Foucault
explicitly confronts the other half of his task, tracing lines of actu-
alization that "pull us toward a future, toward a becoming."[8] Ana-
lytical strata and diagnostic contemporaneity are two essential poles
of Foucault's entire work. Perhaps nowhere more clearly than in Fou-

cault's lectures at the Collège de France do we see the balancing, the alternation, and the overlapping of these two poles. At one and the same time, these lectures exhibit Foucault's relentless erudition and his explosive force, giving further shape to that distinctive history of the present that so changed our twentieth-century landscape.

✤

One of the most emblematic, and often cited, lines of the first volume of Foucault's history of sexuality, *La Volonté de savoir*, published in 1976, the year of this course, is the trenchant remark "In thought and political analysis we have still not cut off the head of the king."[9] In studying the historico-political discourse of war in this course, Foucault shows us one way to detach ourselves from the philosophico-juridical discourse of sovereignty and the law that has so dominated our thought and political analysis. In an important lecture given in Brazil in 1976, and unfortunately still not translated into English, Foucault underscores his claim that "the West has never had another system of representation, of formulation, and of analysis of power than that of the law, the system of the law."[10] Many of Foucault's writings, lectures, and interviews of the mid- to late 1970s are responses to this conceptual impasse, are attempts to articulate alternative ways of analyzing power.

Foucault's concern during this period was both with the representation of power and with the actual functioning of power. The focus of this 1976 course is on one alternative conceptualization of power, a mode of thought that analyzes power relations in terms of the model of war, that looks for the principle of intelligibility of politics in the general form of war. Foucault himself, discussing the use of the notion of "struggle" in certain political discourses, posed the following question:

[S]hould one, or should one not, analyze these "struggles" as the vicissitudes of a war, should one decipher them according to a grid which would be one of strategy and tactics? Is the relation of forces in the order of politics a relation of war? Personally, I do not feel myself ready for the moment to respond in a definitive way with a yes or no.[11]

"Society Must Be Defended" is Foucault's most concentrated and detailed historical examination of the model of war as a grid for analyzing politics.

If this course is an answer to the question of who first thought of politics as war continued by other means, we must put it in the context of the development of Foucault's own thought with respect to this substantive claim. If in 1975, just before the lectures published here, Foucault seemed himself to take up the claim that politics is the continuation of war by other means,[12] by 1976, just after this course, Foucault had subtly but significantly modified his own attitude:

Should one then turn around the formula and say that politics is war pursued by other means? Perhaps if one wishes always to maintain a difference between war and politics, one should suggest rather that this multiplicity of force-relations can be coded—in part and never totally—either in the form of "war" or in the form of "politics"; there would be here two different strategies (but ready to tip over into one another) for integrating these unbalanced, heterogeneous, unstable, tense force-relations.[13]

As this quotation makes clear, Foucault's preoccupation with the schema of war was central to his formulation of the strategic model of power, of force-relations, a strategic model that would allow us to reorient our conception of power.

Although it is widely recognized that the articulation of this strategic model—with its notions of force, struggle, war, tactics, strategy, et cetera—is one of the major achievements of Foucault's thought during this time, the full scope and significance of this model has not been fully appreciated. Although a full study of the emergence of this strategic model in Foucault's work would have to begin with texts written no later than 1971,[14] his course summary published here leaves no doubt that the examination of the historico-political discourse of war was an essential stage in the formulation of a model of analysis that is presented at greatest length in part 4 of *La Volonté de savoir*. Rather than trace the changing forms of this model, I want at least to outline a few aspects of it that deserve further attention in the study of Foucault's writings during this period.

In *La Volonté de savoir*, Foucault's strategic model takes as its most central field of application power relations (and resistances), that is to say, nondiscursive practices or the social field generally. It provides a model of strategic coherence, intelligibility, rationality that answers to what Foucault sometimes called the *logic* of strategies.[15] Arrangements of relations of forces have a strategic intelligibility, and their rationality, as well as the transformation of these arrangements into other coherent arrangements, obeys a logic distinct both from the logic of epistemic coherence and transformations studied by Foucault in his archaeological works, and from the logic of the model of sovereignty and the law that is the direct object of Foucault's criticisms here.

Although this strategic model is, first of all, intended to provide an alternative system of representation of the nondiscursive social field, a mode of representation that does not derive from the juridical conception of power, in order to assess its significance we must not forget that as early as 1967 Foucault recognized that the form of strategic intelligibility could also be applied to discursive practices. In an unpublished lecture, "Structuralisme et analyse littéraire," given in Tunisia in 1967, Foucault, invoking among others the name of J. L. Austin, argued that the description of a statement was not complete when one had defined the linguistic structure of the statement, that the analysis of discourse could not be reduced to the combination of elements according to linguistic rules, that therefore "discourse is something that necessarily extends beyond language."[16] As he put it in a 1967 letter to Daniel Defert, again appealing to "les analystes anglais," "they allow me indeed to see how one can do nonlinguistic analyses of statements. Treat statements in their functioning."[17] This nonlinguistic level of the analysis of discourse is in fact the level of strategic intelligibility.

This model of analysis is developed further in Foucault's 1974 lectures at the Catholic Pontifical University of Rio de Janeiro, "La Vérité et les formes juridiques," where Foucault urges us to consider the facts of discourse as strategic games.[18] And in 1976, in a brilliant single-page text, "Le Discours ne doit pas être pris comme...," a text that appears in *Dits et écrits* just before the course summary of *"Society Must Be Defended,"* Foucault describes this level of analysis as the political analysis of discourse in which "it is a matter of exhibiting discourse as a strategic field."[19] Here discourse is characterized as a battle, a struggle, a place and an instrument of confrontation, "a weapon of power, of control, of subjection, of qualification and of disqualification."[20] Discourse does not simply express or reproduce already constituted social relations:

> Discourse battle and not discourse reflection... Discourse—the mere fact of speaking, of employing words, of using the words of others (even if it means returning them), words that the others understand and accept (and, possibly, return from their side)—this fact is in itself a force. Discourse is, with respect to the relation of forces, not merely a surface of inscription, but something that brings about effects.[21]

The strategic model of intelligibility, with a vocabulary one of whose primary sources is the schema of war, applies to the forces of discourse as well as to nondiscursive force-relations.[22] In *La Volonté de savoir,* this form of analysis of discourse is employed in part 4, chapter 2, when Foucault discusses the "rule of the tactical polyvalence of discourse," insisting that discourses should be examined at the two levels of their tactical productivity and of their strategic integration.[23] Indeed, speaking of the perspectival character of knowledge in a discussion of Nietzsche, Foucault recurs to this same terminology in order to articulate the Nietzschean claim that "knowledge is always a certain strategic relation in which man finds himself placed":

> The perspectival character of knowledge does not derive from human nature, but always from the polemical and strategic character of knowledge. One can speak of the perspectival character of knowledge because there is a battle and knowledge is the effect of this battle.[24]

And in his course and his summary of *"Society Must Be Defended"* Foucault describes the historico-political discourse of war as putting forward a truth that "functions as a weapon," as speaking of a "perspectival and strategic truth." Discourse, knowledge, and truth, as well as relations of power, can be understood from within the strategic model. Hence the importance of seeing how this model functions at all of its levels of application.

Finally, I want to indicate that this course can be read within the framework of what Foucault called his "circular" project, a project that involves two endeavors that refer back to each other.[25] On the one hand, Foucault wanted to rid us of a juridical representation of power, conceived of in terms of law, prohibition, and sovereignty, a clearing away that raises the question of how we are to analyze what has taken place in history without the use of this system of representation. On the other hand, Foucault wanted to carry out a more meticulous historical examination in order to show that in modern societies power has not in fact functioned in the form of law and sovereignty, a historical analysis that forces one to find another form of representation that does not depend on the juridical system.

> Therefore, one must, at one and the same time, while giving oneself another theory of power, form another grid of historical decipherment, and, while looking more closely at an entire historical material, advance little by little toward another conception of power.[26]

"Society Must Be Defended" participates fully in this historico-theoretical project; it reminds us once again of Foucault's unrivaled conjunction of philosophical and historical analysis. And these lectures, as in the courses to follow, show us the unfolding of Foucault's thought in all of its vivacity, intensity, clarity, and precision.

⚜

I am deeply indebted to Daniel Defert for his help and encouragement, to Michael Denneny and Christina Prestia, who initiated this project at St. Martin's Press, and to Tim Bent and Julia Pastore, who have followed it through.

1. Claude Lévi-Strauss, *Paroles données* (Paris: Plon, 1984), p. 9.

2. Ibid., p. 10.

3. Michel Foucault, "Radioscopie de Michel Foucault," in *Dits et écrits* (Paris: Gallimard, 1994), vol. 2, p. 786.

4. Ibid.

5. Ibid.

6. Ibid.

7. Gilles Deleuze, "Qu'est-ce qu'un dispositif?" in *Michel Foucault, philosophe* (Paris: Éditions du Seuil, 1989), p. 191.

8. Ibid, pp. 192-93.

9. Michel Foucault, *Histoire de la sexualité*, vol. 1, *La Volonté de savoir* (Paris: Gallimard, 1976), p. 117.

10. Michel Foucault, "Les Mailles du pouvoir," in *Dits et écrits*, vol. 4, p. 186.

11. Michel Foucault, "L'Oeil du pouvoir," in *Dits et écrits*, vol. 3, p. 206.

12. Michel Foucault, "La Politique est la continuation de la guerre par d'autres moyens," in *Dits et écrits*, vol. 2, p. 704.

13. Michel Foucault, *La Volonté de savoir*, p. 123.

14. See, for example, Michel Foucault, "Nietzsche, la généalogie, l'histoire," in *Dits et écrits*, vol. 2. A complete study of this issue must await the publication of Foucault's 1971 course at the Collège de France, also entitled "La Volonté de savoir." The course summary can be found in *Dits et écrits*, vol. 2. See also Daniel Defert, "Le 'dispositif de guerre' comme analyseur des rapports de pouvoir," in *Lectures de Michel Foucault: A propos de "Il faut défendre la société*," ed. Jean-Claude Zancarini (Lyon: ENS Éditions, n.d.).

15. See, among other texts, Michel Foucault, "Des Supplices aux cellules," in *Dits et écrits*, vol. 3, pp. 426-27.

16. A tape recording of this lecture can be found in the Centre Michel Foucault.

17. Cited in the "Chronologie." *Dits et écrits*, vol. 1, p. 31. For further discussion see my essay, "Structures and Strategies of Discourse: Remarks Towards a History of Foucault's Philosophy of Language," in *Foucault and His Interlocutors*, ed. Arnold I. Davidson (Chicago: University of Chicago Press, 1997).

18. Michel Foucault, "La Vérité et les formes juridiques," in *Dits et écrits*, vol. 2, p. 539.

19. Michel Foucault, "Le Discours ne doit pas être pris comme . . . ," in *Dits et écrits*, vol. 3, p. 123.

20. Ibid.

21. Ibid., p. 124.

22. See also Michel Foucault, "Dialogue sur le pouvoir," in *Dits et écrits*, vol. 3, p. 465.

23. Michel Foucault, *La Volonté de savoir*, pp. 132-35.

24. Michel Foucault, "La Vérité et les formes juridiques," in *Dits et écrits*, vol. 2, p. 551.

25. Michel Foucault, *La Volonté de savoir*, pp. 119-20.

26. Ibid., p. 120.

"Society Must Be Defended"

one

7 JANUARY 1976

What is a lecture? ~ Subjugated knowledges. ~ Historical knowledge of struggles, genealogies, and scientific discourse. ~ Power, or what is at stake in genealogies. ~ Juridical and economic conceptions of power. ~ Power as repression and power as war. ~ Clausewitz's aphorism inverted.

I WOULD LIKE US to be a bit clearer about what is going on here, in these lectures. You know that the institution where you are, and where I am, is not exactly a teaching institution. Well, whatever meaning it was intended to have when it was founded long ago, the Collège de France now functions essentially as a sort of research institute: we are paid to do research. And I believe that, ultimately, the activity of teaching would be meaningless unless we gave it, or at least lent it, this meaning, or at least the meaning I suggest: Given that we are paid to do research, what is there to monitor the research we are doing? How can we keep informed people who might be interested in it, or who might have some reason for taking this research as a starting point? How can we keep them informed on a fairly regular basis about the work we are doing, except by teaching, or in other words by making a public statement? So I do not regard our Wednesday meetings as a teaching activity, but rather as public reports on the work I am, in other respects, left to get on with more or less as I see fit. To that extent, I actually consider myself to be under an absolute obligation to tell you roughly what I am doing, what point

I've reached, in what direction [...] the work is going; and to that extent, I think that you are completely free to do what you like with what I am saying. These are suggestions for research, ideas, schemata, outlines, instruments; do what you like with them. Ultimately, what you do with them both concerns me and is none of my business. It is none of my business to the extent that it is not up to me to lay down the law about the use you make of it. And it does concern me to the extent that, one way or another, what you do with it is connected, related to what I am doing.

Having said that, you know what has happened over the last few years. As a result of a sort of inflation that is hard to understand, we've reached the point where, I think, something has just about come to a standstill. You've been having to get here at half past four [...] and I've been finding myself faced with an audience made up of people with whom I had strictly no contact because part of the audience, if not half of it, had to go into another room and listen to what I was saying over a mike. It was turning into something that wasn't even a spectacle, because we couldn't see each other. But there was another reason why it's come to a standstill. The problem for me was—I'll be quite blunt about it—the fact that I had to go through this sort of circus every Wednesday was really—how can I put it?— torture is putting it too strongly, boredom is putting it too mildly, so I suppose it was somewhere between the two. The result was that I was really preparing these lectures, putting a lot of care and attention into it, and I was spending a lot less time on research in the real sense of the word if you like, on the interesting but somewhat incoherent things I could have been saying, than on asking myself the question: How, in the space of an hour, an hour and a half, can I put something across in such a way that I don't bore people too much, and that they get some reward for being kind enough to get here so early to hear what I have to say in such a short space of time. It got to the point where I was spending months on it, and I think that the reason for my presence here, and the reason for your presence here, is to do research, to slog away, to blow the dust off certain things, to have ideas, and that all that is the reward for the work that has been done. So I said to myself: It wouldn't be such a bad idea if thirty or forty of us could get together in a room. I could tell you roughly what I've been doing, and at the same time have some contact with you, talk to you, answer your questions and so on, and try to rediscover the possibility of the exchange and contact that are part of the normal practice of research or teaching. So what should I do? In legal terms, I cannot lay down any formal conditions as to who has access to this room. I've therefore adopted the guerrilla method of moving the lecture to nine-thirty in the morning in the belief that, as my correspondent was telling me yesterday, students are no longer capable of getting up at nine-thirty. You might say that it's not a very fair selection criterion: those who get up, and those who don't get up. It's as good as any. In any case, there are always the little mikes there, and the tape machines, and word gets around afterward—sometimes it remains on tape, sometimes it is transcribed, and sometimes it turns up in the bookshops—so I said to myself, word always gets out. So I will try [...] so I'm sorry if I've got you out of bed early, and my apologies to those who can't be with us; it was a way of getting our Wednesday conversations and meetings back into the normal pattern of research, of ongoing work, and that means reporting on it at regular institutional intervals.

So what was I going to say to you this year? That I've just about had enough; in other words, I'd like to bring to a close, to put an end to, up to a point, the series of research projects—well, yes, "research"—we all talk about it, but what does it actually mean?—that we've been working on for four or five years, or practically ever since I've been here, and I realize that there were more and more drawbacks, for both you and me. Lines of research that were very closely interrelated but that never added up to a coherent body of work, that had no continuity. Fragments of research, none of which was completed, and none of which was followed through; bits and pieces of research, and at the same time it was getting very repetitive, always falling into the same rut, the same themes, the same concepts. A few remarks on the history of penal procedure; a few chapters on the evolution, the institutionalization of psychiatry in the nineteenth century; considerations on sophistry or Greek coins; an outline history of sexuality, or at least a history of knowledge about sexuality based upon seventeenth-century confessional practices, or controls on infantile sexuality in the eighteenth and nineteenth centuries; pinpointing the genesis of a theory and knowledge of anomalies, and of all the related techniques. We are making no progress, and it's all leading nowhere. It's all repetitive, and it doesn't add up. Basically, we keep saying the same thing, and there again, perhaps we're not saying anything at all. It's all getting into something of an inextricable tangle, and it's getting us nowhere, as they say.

I could tell you that these things were trails to be followed, that it didn't matter where they led, or even that the one thing that did matter was that they didn't lead anywhere, or at least not in some predetermined direction. I could say they were like an outline for something. It's up to you to go on with them or to go off on a tangent; and it's up to me to pursue them or give them a different configuration. And then, we—you or I—could see what could be done with these fragments. I felt a bit like a sperm whale that breaks the surface of the water, makes a little splash, and lets you believe, makes you believe, or want to believe, that down there where it can't be seen, down there where it is neither seen nor monitored by anyone, it is following a deep, coherent, and premeditated trajectory.

That is more or less the position we were in, as I see it: I don't know what it looked like from where you are sitting. After all, the fact that the work I described to you looked both fragmented, repetitive, and discontinuous was quite in keeping with what might be called a "feverish laziness." It's a character trait of people who love libraries, documents, references, dusty manuscripts, texts that have never been read, books which, no sooner printed, were closed and then slept on the shelves and were only taken down centuries later. All this quite suits the busy inertia of those who profess useless knowledge, a sort of sumptuary knowledge, the wealth of a parvenu— and, as you well know, its external signs are found at the foot of the page. It should appeal to all those who feel sympathetic to one of those secret societies, no doubt the oldest and the most characteristic in the West, one of those strangely indestructible secret societies that were, I think, unknown in antiquity and which were formed in the early Christian era, probably at the time of the first monasteries, on the fringes of invasions, fires, and forests. I am talking about the great, tender, and warm freemasonry of useless erudition.

Except that it was not just a liking for this freemasonry that led me to do what I've been doing. It seems to me that we could justify the work we've been doing, in a somewhat empirical and haphazard way on both my part and yours, by saying that it was quite in keeping with a certain period; with the very limited period we have been living through for the last ten or fifteen years, twenty at the most. I am talking about a period in which we can observe two phenomena which were, if not really important, rather interesting. On the one hand, this has been a period characterized by what we might call the efficacy of dispersed and discontinuous offensives. I am thinking of many things, of, for instance, the strange efficacy, when it came to jamming the workings of the psychiatric institution, of the discourse, the discourses—and they really were very localized—of antipsychiatry. And you know perfectly well that they were not supported, are not supported, by any overall systematization, no matter what their points of reference were and are. I am thinking of the original reference to existential analysis,[1] and of contemporary references to, broadly speaking, Marxism or Reich's theories.[2] I am also thinking of the strange efficacy of the attacks that have been made on, say, morality and the traditional sexual hierarchy; they too referred in only vague and distant terms to Reich or Marcuse.[3] I am also thinking of the efficacy of the attacks on the judiciary and penal apparatus, some of which were very distantly related to the general—and fairly dubious—notion of "class justice," while others were basically related, albeit almost as distantly, to an anarchist thematic. I am also thinking much more specifically of the efficacy of something—I hesitate to call it a book— like *Anti-Oedipus*,[4] which referred to, which refers to nothing but its own prodigious theoretical creativity—that book, that event, or that

thing that succeeded, at the level of day-to-day practice, in introducing a note of hoarseness into the whisper that had been passing from
couch to armchair without any interruption for such a long time.

So I would say: for the last ten or fifteen years, the immense and
proliferating criticizability of things, institutions, practices, and discourses; a sort of general feeling that the ground was crumbling beneath our feet, especially in places where it seemed most familiar,
most solid, and closest [nearest] to us, to our bodies, to our everyday
gestures. But alongside this crumbling and the astonishing efficacy of
discontinuous, particular, and local critiques, the facts were also revealing something that could not, perhaps, have been foreseen from
the outset: what might be called the inhibiting effect specific to totalitarian theories, or at least—what I mean is—all-encompassing and
global theories. Not that all-encompassing and global theories haven't,
in fairly constant fashion, provided—and don't continue to provide—
tools that can be used at the local level; Marxism and psychoanalysis
are living proof that they can. But they have, I think, provided tools
that can be used at the local level only when, and this is the real
point, the theoretical unity of their discourse is, so to speak, sus-
pended, or at least cut up, ripped up, torn to shreds, turned inside
out, displaced, caricatured, dramatized, theatricalized, and so on. Or
at least that the totalizing approach always has the effect of putting
the brakes on. So that, if you like, is my first point, the first characteristic of what has been happening over the last fifteen years or so:
the local character of the critique; this does not, I think, mean soft
eclecticism, opportunism, or openness to any old theoretical undertaking, nor does it mean a sort of deliberate asceticism that boils down
to losing as much theoretical weight as possible. I think that the
essentially local character of the critique in fact indicates something
resembling a sort of autonomous and noncentralized theoretical production, or in other words a theoretical production that does not need
a visa from some common regime to establish its validity.

This brings us to a second feature of what has been happening for
some time now. The point is this: It is what might be called "returns
of knowledge" that makes this local critique possible. What I mean

by "returns of knowledge" is this: While it is true that in recent years we have often encountered, at least at the superficial level, a whole thematic: "life, not knowledge," "the real, not erudition," "money, not books,"* it appears to me that beneath this whole thematic, through it and even within it, we have seen what might be called the insurrection of subjugated knowledges. When I say "subjugated knowledges," I mean two things. On the one hand, I am referring to historical contents that have been buried or masked in functional coherences or formal systematizations. To put it in concrete terms if you like, it was certainly not a semiology of life in the asylum or a sociology of delinquence that made an effective critique of the asylum or the prison possible; it really was the appearance of historical contents. Quite simply because historical contents alone allow us to see the dividing lines in the confrontations and struggles that functional arrangements or systematic organizations are designed to mask. Subjugated knowledges are, then, blocks of historical knowledges that were present in the functional and systematic ensembles, but which were masked, and the critique was able to reveal their existence by using, obviously enough, the tools of scholarship.

Second, I think subjugated knowledges should be understood as meaning something else and, in a sense, something quite different. When I say "subjugated knowledges" I am also referring to a whole series of knowledges that have been disqualified as nonconceptual knowledges, as insufficiently elaborated knowledges: naive knowledges, hierarchically inferior knowledges, knowledges that are below the required level of erudition or scientificity. And it is thanks to the reappearance of these knowledges from below, of these unqualified or even disqualified knowledges, it is thanks to the reappearance of these knowledges: the knowledge of the psychiatrized, the patient, the nurse, the doctor, that is parallel to, marginal to, medical knowledge, the knowledge of the delinquent, what I would call, if you like, what people know (and this is by no means the same thing as comon knowledge or common sense but, on the contrary, a particular knowl-

---

*In the manuscript, "travel" replaces "money."

edge, a knowledge that is local, regional, or differential, incapable of unanimity and which derives its power solely from the fact that it is different from all the knowledges that surround it), it is the reappearance of what people know at a local level, of these disqualified knowledges, that made the critique possible.

You might object that there is something very paradoxical about grouping together and putting into the same category of "subjugated knowledges," on the one hand, historical, meticulous, precise, technical expertise and, on the other, these singular, local knowledges, the noncommonsensical knowledges that people have, and which have in a way been left to lie fallow, or even kept in the margins. Well, I think it is the coupling together of the buried scholarly knowledge and knowledges that were disqualified by the hierarchy of erudition and sciences that actually gave the discursive critique of the last fifteen years its essential strength. What was at stake in both cases, in both this scholarly knowledge and these disqualified knowledges, in these two forms of knowledge—the buried and the disqualified? A historical knowledge of struggles. Both the specialized domain of scholarship and the disqualified knowledge people have contained the memory of combats, the very memory that had until then been confined to the margins. And so we have the outline of what might be called a genealogy, or of multiple genealogical investigations. We have both a meticulous rediscovery of struggles and the raw memory of fights. These genealogies are a combination of erudite knowledge and what people know. They would not have been possible—they could not even have been attempted—were it not for one thing: the removal of the tyranny of overall discourses, with their hierarchies and all the privileges enjoyed by theoretical vanguards. If you like, we can give the name "genealogy" to this coupling together of scholarly erudition and local memories, which allows us to constitute a historical knowledge of struggles and to make use of that knowledge in contemporary tactics. That can, then, serve as a provisional definition of the genealogies I have been trying to trace with you over the last few years.

You can see that this activity, which we can describe as genealogical, is certainly not a matter of contrasting the abstract unity of theory with the concrete multiplicity of the facts. It is certainly not a matter of some form or other of scientism that disqualifies speculation by contrasting it with the rigor of well-established bodies of knowledge. It is therefore not an empiricism that runs through the genealogical project, nor does it lead to a positivism, in the normal sense of the word. It is a way of playing local, discontinuous, disqualified, or nonlegitimized knowledges off against the unitary theoretical instance that claims to be able to filter them, organize them into a hierarchy, organize them in the name of a true body of knowledge, in the name of the rights of a science that is in the hands of the few. Genealogies are therefore not positivistic returns to a form of science that is more attentive or more accurate. Genealogies are, quite specifically, antisciences. It is not that they demand the lyrical right to be ignorant, and not that they reject knowledge, or invoke or celebrate some immediate experience that has yet to be captured by knowledge. That is not what they are about. They are about the insurrection of knowledges. Not so much against the contents, methods, or concepts of a science; this is above all, primarily, an insurrection against the centralizing power-effects that are bound up with the institutionalization and workings of any scientific discourse organized in a society such as ours. That this institutionalization of scientific discourse is embodied in a university or, in general terms, a pedagogical apparatus, that this institutionalization of scientific discourses is embodied in a theoretico-commercial network such as psychoanalysis, or in a political apparatus—with everything that implies—is largely irrelevant. Genealogy has to fight the power-effects characteristic of any discourse that is regarded as scientific.

To put it in more specific terms, or at least in terms that might mean more to you, let me say this: you know how many people have been asking themselves whether or not Marxism is a science for many years now, probably for more than a century. One might say that the same question has been asked, and is still being asked, of psychoanalysis or, worse still, of the semiology of literary texts. Genealogies' or genealogists' answer to the question "Is it a science or not?" is: "Turning Marxism, or psychoanalysis, or whatever else it is, into a science is precisely what we are criticizing you for. And if there is one objection to be made against Marxism, it's that it might well be a science." To put it in more—if not more sophisticated terms—[at least] milder terms, let me say this: even before we know to what extent something like Marxism or psychoanalysis is analogous to a scientific practice in its day-to-day operations, in its rules of construction, in the concepts it uses, we should be asking the question, asking ourselves about the aspiration to power that is inherent in the claim to being a science. The question or questions that have to be asked are: "What types of knowledge are you trying to disqualify when you say that you are a science? What speaking subject, what discursive subject, what subject of experience and knowledge are you trying to minorize when you begin to say: 'I speak this discourse, I am speaking a scientific discourse, and I am a scientist.' What theoretico-political vanguard are you trying to put on the throne in order to detach it from all the massive, circulating, and discontinuous forms that knowledge can take?" And I would say: "When I see you trying to prove that Marxism is a science, to tell the truth, I do not really see you trying to demonstrate once and for all that Marxism has a rational structure and that its propositions are therefore the products of verification procedures. I see you, first and foremost, doing something different. I see you connecting to Marxist discourse, and I see you assigning to those who speak that discourse the power-effects that the West has, ever since the Middle Ages, ascribed to a science and reserved for those who speak a scientific discourse."

Compared to the attempt to inscribe knowledges in the power-hierarchy typical of science, genealogy is, then, a sort of attempt to desubjugate historical knowledges, to set them free, or in other words to enable them to oppose and struggle against the coercion of a unitary, formal, and scientific theoretical discourse. The project of these disorderly and tattered genealogies is to reactivate local knowledges—Deleuze would no doubt call them "minor"[5]—against the scientific hierarchicalization of knowledge and its intrinsic power-effects. To put it in a nutshell: Archaeology is the method specific to the analysis of local discursivities, and genealogy is the tactic which, once it has described these local discursivities, brings into play the desubjugated knowledges that have been released from them. That just about sums up the overall project.

So you can see that all the fragments of research, all the interconnected and interrupted things I have been repeating so stubbornly for four or five years now, might be regarded as elements of these genealogies, and that I am not the only one to have been doing this over the last fifteen years. Far from it. Question: So why not go on with such a theory of discontinuity, when it is so pretty and probably so hard to verify?[6] Why don't I go on, and why don't I take a quick look at something to do with psychiatry, with the theory of sexuality?

It's true that one could go on—and I will try to go on up to a point—were it not, perhaps, for a certain number of changes, and changes in the conjuncture. What I mean is that compared to the situation we had five, ten, or even fifteen years ago, things have, perhaps, changed; perhaps the battle no longer looks quite the same. Well, are we really still in the same relationship of force, and does it allow us to exploit the knowledges we have dug out of the sand, to exploit them as they stand, without their becoming subjugated once more? What strength do they have in themselves? And after all, once we have excavated our genealogical fragments, once we begin to exploit them and to put in circulation these elements of knowledge that we have been trying to dig out of the sand, isn't there a danger that they will be recoded, recolonized by these unitary discourses which, having first disqualified them and having then ignored them when they reappeared, may now be ready to reannex them and include them in their own discourses and their own power-knowledge effects? And if we try to protect the fragments we have dug up, don't we run the risk of building, with our own hands, a unitary discourse? That is what we are being invited to do, that is the trap that is being set for us by all those who say, "It's all very well, but where does it get us? Where does it lead us? What unity does it give us?" The temptation is, up to a point, to say: Right, let's continue, let's accumulate. After all, there is no danger at the moment that we will be colonized. I was saying a moment ago that these genealogical fragments might be in danger of being recoded, but we could throw down a challenge and say, "Just try it!" We could, for instance, say, Look: ever since the very beginnings of antipsychiatry or of the genealogies of psychiatric institutions—and it has been going on for a good fifteen years now—has a single Marxist, psychoanalyst, or psychiatrist ever attempted to redo it in their own terms or demonstrated that these genealogies were wrong, badly elaborated, badly articulated, or ill-founded? The way things stand, the fragments of genealogy that have been done are in fact still there, surrounded by a wary silence. The only arguments that have been put forward against them are—at the very best—propositions like the one we recently heard from, I think it was M. Juquin:[7] "All this is very well. But the fact remains that Soviet psychiatry is the best in the world." My answer to that is: "Yes, of course, you're right. Soviet psychiatry is the best in the world. That's just what I hold against it." The silence, or rather the caution with which unitary theories avoid the genealogy of knowledges might therefore be one reason for going on. One could at any rate unearth more and more genealogical fragments, like so many traps, questions, challenges, or whatever you want to call them. Given that we are talking about a battle—the battle knowledges are waging against the power-effects of scientific discourse—it is probably overoptimistic to assume that our adversary's silence proves that he is afraid of us. The silence of an adversary—and this is a methodological principle or a tactical principle that must always be kept in mind—could just as easily be a sign that he is not afraid of us at all. And we must, I think, behave as though he really is not frightened of us. And I am not suggesting that we give all these scattered genealogies a continuous, solid theoretical basis—the last thing I want to do is give them, superimpose on them, a sort of theoretical crown that would unify them—but that we should try, in future lectures, probably beginning this year, to specify or identify what is at stake when knowledges begin to challenge, struggle against, and rise up against the instutition and the power- and knowledge-effects of scientific discourse.

As you know, and as I scarcely need point out, what is at stake in all these genealogies is this: What is this power whose irruption, force, impact, and absurdity have become palpably obvious over the last forty years, as a result of both the collapse of Nazism and the retreat of Stalinism? What is power? Or rather—given that the question "What is power?" is obviously a theoretical question that would provide an answer to everything, which is just what I don't want to do—the issue is to determine what are, in their mechanisms, effects, their relations, the various power-apparatuses that operate at various levels of society, in such very different domains and with so many different extensions? Roughly speaking, I think that what is at stake in all this is this: Can the analysis of power, or the analysis of powers, be in one way or another deduced from the economy?

This is why I ask the question, and this is what I mean by it. I certainly do not wish to erase the countless differences or huge differences, but, despite and because of these differences, it seems to me that the juridical conception and, let's say, the liberal conception of political power—which we find in the philosophers of the eighteenth century—do have certain things in common, as does the Marxist conception, or at least a certain contemporary conception that passes for the Marxist conception. Their common feature is what I will call "economism" in the theory of power. What I mean to say is this: In the case of the classic juridical theory of power, power is regarded as a right which can be possessed in the way one possesses a commodity, and which can therefore be transferred or alienated, either completely or partly, through a juridical act or an act that founds a right—it does not matter which, for the moment—thanks to the surrender of something or thanks to a contract. Power is the concrete power that any individual can hold, and which he can surrender, either as a whole or in part, so as to constitute a power or a political sovereignty. In the body of theory to which I am referring, the constitution of political power is therefore constituted by this series, or is modeled on a juridical operation similar to an exchange of contracts. There is therefore an obvious analogy, and it runs through all these theories, between power and commodities, between power and wealth.

In the other case, and I am obviously thinking here of the general Marxist conception of power, there is obviously none of this. In this

Marxist conception, you have something else that might be called the "economic functionality" of power. "Economic functionality" to the extent that the role of power is essentially both to perpetuate the relations of production and to reproduce a class domination that is made possible by the development of the productive forces and the ways they are appropriated. In this case, political power finds its historical raison d'être in the economy. Broadly speaking, we have, if you like, in one case a political power which finds its formal model in the process of exchange, in the economy of the circulation of goods; and in the other case, political power finds its historical raison d'être, the principle of its concrete form and of its actual workings in the economy.

The problem that is at issue in the research I am talking about can, I think, be broken down as follows. First: Is power always secondary to the economy? Are its finality and function always determined by the economy? Is power's raison d'être and purpose essentially to serve the economy? Is it designed to establish, solidify, perpetuate, and reproduce relations that are characteristic of the economy and essential to its workings? Second question: Is power modeled on the commodity? Is power something that can be possessed and acquired, that can be surrendered through a contract or by force, that can be alienated or recuperated, that circulates and fertilizes one region but avoids others? Or if we wish to analyze it, do we have to operate—on the contrary—with different instruments, even if power relations are deeply involved in and with economic relations, even if power relations and economic relations always constitute a sort of network or loop? If that is the case, the indissociability of the economy and politics is not a matter of functional subordination, nor of formal isomorphism. It is of a different order, and it is precisely that order that we have to isolate.

What tools are currently available for a noneconomic analysis of power? I think that we can say that we really do not have a lot. We have, first of all, the assertion that power is not something that is given, exchanged, or taken back, that it is something that is exercised and that it exists only in action. We also have the other assertion, that power is not primarily the perpetuation and renewal of economic relations, but that it is primarily, in itself, a relationship of force. Which raises some questions, or rather two questions. If power is exercised, what is the exercise of power? What does it consist of? What is its mechanism? We have here what I would call an off-the-cuff answer, or at least an immediate response, and it seems to me that this is, ultimately, the answer given by the concrete reality of many contemporary analyses: Power is essentially that which represses. Power is that which represses nature, instincts, a class, or individuals. And when we find contemporary discourse trotting out the definition that power is that which represses, contemporary discourse is not really saying anything new. Hegel was the first to say this, and then Freud and then Reich.[8] In any case, in today's vocabulary, being an organ of repression is almost power's Homeric epithet. So, must the analysis of power be primarily, essentially even, an analysis of the mechanisms of repression?

Second—second off-the-cuff answer, if you like—if power is indeed the implementation and deployment of a relationship of force, rather than analyzing it in terms of surrender, contract, and alienation, or rather than analyzing it in functional terms as the reproduction of the relations of production, shouldn't we be analyzing it first and foremost in terms of conflict, confrontation, and war? That would give us an alternative to the first hypothesis—which is that the mechanism of power is basically or essentially repression—or a second hypothesis: Power is war, the continuation of war by other means. At this point, we can invert Clausewitz's proposition[9] and say that politics is the continuation of war by other means. This would imply three things. First, that power relations, as they function in a society like ours, are essentially anchored in a certain relationship of force that was established in and through war at a given historical moment that can be historically specified. And while it is true that political power puts an end to war and establishes or attempts to establish the reign of peace in civil society, it certainly does not do so in order to suspend the effects of power or to neutralize the disequilibrium revealed by the last battle of the war. According to this hypothesis, the role of political power is perpetually to use a sort of silent war to reinscribe that relationship of force, and to reinscribe it in institutions, economic inequalities, language, and even the bodies of individuals. This is the initial meaning of our inversion of Clausewitz's aphorism—politics is the continuation of war by other means. Politics, in other words, sanctions and reproduces the disequilibrium of forces manifested in war. Inverting the proposition also means something else, namely that within this "civil peace," these political struggles, these clashes over or with power, these modifications of relations of force—the shifting balance, the reversals—in a political system, all these things must be interpreted as a continuation of war. And they are interpreted as so many episodes, fragmentations, and displacements of the war itself. We are always writing the history of the same war, even when we are writing the history of peace and its institutions.

Inverting Clausewitz's aphorism also has a third meaning: The final decision can come only from war, or in other words a trial by strength in which weapons are the final judges. It means that the last battle would put an end to politics, or in other words, that the last battle would at last—and I mean "at last"—suspend the exercise of power as continuous warfare.

So you see, once we try to get away from economistic schemata in our attempt to analyze power, we immediately find ourselves faced with two grand hypotheses; according to one, the mechanism of power is repression—for the sake of convenience, I will call this Reich's hypothesis, if you like—and according to the second, the basis of the power-relationship lies in a warlike clash between forces—for the sake of convenience, I will call this Nietzsche's hypothesis. The two hypotheses are not irreconcilable; on the contrary, there seems to be a fairly logical connection between the two. After all, isn't repression the political outcome of war, just as oppression was, in the classical theory of political right, the result of the abuse of sovereignty within the juridical domain?

We can, then, contrast two great systems for analyzing power. The first, which is the old theory you find in the philosophers of the seventeenth century, is articulated around power as a primal right that is surrendered, and which constitutes sovereignty, with the contract as the matrix of political power. And when the power that has been so constituted oversteps the limit, or oversteps the limits of the contract, there is a danger that it will become oppression. Power-contract, with oppression as the limit, or rather the transgression of the limit. And then we have the other system, which tries to analyze power not in terms of the contract-oppression schema, but in terms of the war-repression schema. At this point, repression is not what oppression was in relation to the contract, namely an abuse, but, on the contrary, simply the effect and the continuation of a relationship of domination. Repression is no more than the implementation, within a pseudopeace that is being undermined by a continuous war, of a perpetual relationship of force. So, two schemata for the analysis of power: the contract-oppression schema, which is, if you like, the juridical schema, and the war-repression or domination-repression schema, in which the pertinent opposition is not, as in the previous schema, that between the legitimate and the illegitimate, but that between struggle and submission.

It is obvious that everything I have said to you in previous years is inscribed within the struggle-repression schema. That is indeed the schema I was trying to apply. Now, as I tried to apply it, I was eventually forced to reconsider it; both because, in many respects, it is still insufficiently elaborated—I would even go so far as to say that it is not elaborated at all—and also because I think that the twin notions of "repression" and "war" have to be considerably modified and ultimately, perhaps, abandoned. At all events, we have to look very closely at these two notions of "repression" and "war"; if you like, we have to look a little more closely at the hypothesis that the mechanisms of power are essentially mechanisms of repression, and at the alternative hypothesis that what is rumbling away and what is at work beneath political power is essentially and above all a warlike relation.

Without wishing to boast, I think that I have in fact long been suspicious of this notion of "repression," and I have attempted to show you, in relation to the genealogies I was talking about just now, in relation to the history of penal law, psychiatric power, controls on infantile sexuality, and so on, that the mechanisms at work in these power formations were something very different from—or at least much more than—repression. I cannot go any further without re-peating some of this analysis of repression, without pulling together everything I have said about it, no doubt in a rambling sort of way. The next lecture, perhaps the next two lectures, will therefore be devoted to a critical reexamination of the notion of "repression," to trying to show how and why what is now the widespread notion of repression cannot provide an adequate description of the mechanisms and effects of power, cannot define them.[10]

Most of the next lecture will, however, be devoted to the other side of the question, or in other words the problem of war. I would like to try to see the extent to which the binary schema of war and struggle, of the clash between forces, can really be identified as the basis of civil society, as both the principle and motor of the exercise of political power. Are we really talking about war when we analyze the workings of power? Are the notions of "tactics," "strategy," and "relations of force" valid? To what extent are they valid? Is power quite simply a continuation of war by means other than weapons and battles? Does what has now become the commonplace theme, though it is a relatively recent theme, that power is responsible for defending civil society imply, yes or no, that the political structure of society is so organized that some can defend themselves against others, or can defend their domination against the rebellion of others, or quite sim-ply defend their victory and perpetuate it by subjugating others?

The outline for this year's course will, then, be as follows: one or two lectures devoted to a reexamination of the notion of repression; then I will begin [to look at]—I may go on in the years to come, I've no idea—this problem of the war in civil society. I will begin by eliminating the very people who are said to be the theorists of the war in civil society, and who are in my view no such thing, namely Machiavelli and Hobbes. Then I will try to look again at the theory that war is the historical principle behind the workings of power, in the context of the race problem, as it was racial binarism that led the

West to see for the first time that it was possible to analyze political power as war. And I will try to trace this down to the moment when race struggle and class struggle became, at the end of the nineteenth century, the two great schemata that were used to identify the phenomenon of war and the relationship of force within political society.

1. Michel Foucault is referring to the psychiatric movement (defined either as "anthropo-phenomenology" or *Daseinanalyse*) which derived new conceptual instruments from the philosophy of Husserl and Heidegger. Foucault examines this in his earliest writings. Cf. chapter 4 of *Maladie mentale et personalité* (Paris: PUF, 1954) ("La Maladie et l'existence"); the introduction to Ludwig Binswanger, *Le Rêve et l'existence* (Paris: Desclée de Brouwer) (reprinted in *Dits et écrits* vol. 1, pp. 65-119; English translation by Forrest Williams, "Dream, Imagination, and Existence," in Michel Foucault and Ludwig Binswanger, *Dream and Existence*, ed. Keith Holler [Atlantic Highlands, N.J.: Humanities Press]; "La Psychologie de 1850 à 1950," in A. Weber and D. Husiman, *Tableau de la philosophie contemporaine* (Paris: Fischbacher, 1954) (reprinted in *Dits et écrits* vol. 1, pp. 120-37); "La Recherche en psychologie," in J. E. Morrère, ed., *Des Chercheurs s'interrogent* (Paris: PUF, 1957) (reprinted in *Dits et écrits* vol. 1, pp. 137-58). Foucault returned to these topics in his last years; cf. *Colloqui con Foucault* (Salerno: 10/17 Cooperativa editrice, 1981) (French translation: "Entretien avec Michel Foucault," *Dits et écrits* vol. 4, pp. 41-95; English translation by James Goldstein and James Cascaito, *Remarks on Marx* [New York: Semiotext(e), 1991]).

2. See Wilhelm Reich, *Die Funktion des Orgasmus; zur Psychopathologie und zur Sociologie des Geschlechtslebens* (Vienna: Internationaler psychanalytischer Verlag, 1927) (French translation: *La Fonction de l'orgasme* [Paris: L'Arche, 1971]; English translation: *The Function of the Orgasm* [New York: Condor Books, 1983]); *Der Einbrach des Sexualmoral* (Berlin: Verlag fur Sexualpolitik, 1932) (French translation: *L'Irruption de la morale sexuelle* [Paris: Payot, 1972]; English translation: *The Invasion of Compulsory Sex Morality* [New York: Farrar, Straus & Giroux, 1971]); *Charakteranalyse* (Vienna: Selbstverlag des Verfassers, 1933) (French translation: *L'Analyse caractérielle* [Paris: Payot, 1971]; English translation: *Character Analysis* [New York: Farrar, Straus & Giroux, 1972]); *Massenpsychologie des Faschismus: zur Sexualönomie der politischen Reaktion und zur proletarischen Sexualpolitik* (Copenhagen, Paris, and Zurich: Verlag fur Sexualpolitik, 1933) (French translation: *La Psychologie de masse du fascisme* [Paris: Payot, 1974]; English translation: *The Mass Psychology of Fascism* [New York: Simon and Schuster, 1970]); *Die Sexualität im Kulturkampf* (Copenhagen: Sexpol Verlag, 1936) (English translation: *The Sexual Revolution* [London: Vision Press, 1972]).

3. Michel Foucault is obviously referring here to Herbert Marcuse, *Eros and Civilization: A Philosophical Inquiry into Freud* (Boston: Beacon Press, 1955) (French translation: *Eros et civilisation* [Paris: Seuil, 1971]) and *One-Dimensional Man: Studies in the Ideology of Advanced Industrial Society* (Boston: Beacon Press, 1966) (French translation: *L'Homme unidimensionnel* [Paris: Seuil, 1970]).

4. Gilles Deleuze and Félix Guattari, *Anti-Oedipe* (Paris: Éditions de Minuit, 1972). It will be recalled that Foucault develops this interpretation of *Anti-Oedipe* as *livre événement* in his preface to the English translation (English translation by Robert Hurley, Mark Seem, and Helen R. Lane, *Anti-Oedipus* [New York: Viking, 1983]). For the French version see *Dits et écrits* vol. 3, pp. 133-36.

5. The concepts of "minor" and "minority"—singular events rather than individual essences, individuation through "ecceity" rather than substantiality—were elaborated by Gilles Deleuze and Félix Guattari in their *Kafka, pour une littérature mineure* (Paris: Éditions de Minuit, 1975) (English translation by Réda Bensmaia, *Kafka: For a Minor Literature* [Minneapolis: University of Minnesota Press, 1986]), reworked by Deleuze in his article "Philosophie et minorité" (*Critique*, February 1978) and then further developed, notably in Gilles Deleuze and Félix Guattari, *Mille Plateaux; capitalisme et schizophrénie* (Paris: Éditions de Minuit, 1980) (English translation by Brian Massumi, *A Thousand Plateaus: Capitalism and Schizophrenia* [Minneapolis: University of Minnesota Press]). "Minority" also relates to the concept of "molecular" elaborated by Félix Guattari in *Psychanalyse et*

transversalité, Essai d'analyse institutionnelle (Paris: Maspero, 1972). Its logic is that of "becoming" and "intensities."

6. Michel Foucault is referring to the debate about the concept of the episteme and the status of discontinuity that was opened up by the publication of *Les Mots et les choses: une archaeologie des sciences humaines* (Paris: Gallimard, 1966) (English translation: *The Order of Things* [London: Tavistock, 1970]). He replied to criticisms in a series of theoretical and methodological *mises au point*. See in particular "Réponse à une question," *Esprit*, May 1968, reprinted in *Dits et écrits* vol. 1, pp. 673-95; "Réponse au Cercle d'épistémologie," *Cahiers pour l'analyse* 9 (1968), pp. 9-40, reprinted in *Dits et écrits* vol. 1, pp. 694-731; English translation: "On the Archaeology of the Science: Response to the Epistemology Circle," *Essential Works* vol. 2, pp. 297-353.

7. At that time, a *député* in the Parti Communiste Français.

8. Cf. G. W. F. Hegel, *Grundlinien der Philosophie des Rechtes* (Berlin, 1821), pp. 182-340 (French translation: *Principes de la philosophie du droit* [Paris: Vrin, 1975]); *Hegel's Philosophy of Right*, translated with notes by T. M. Knox (Oxford: Clarendon Press, 1952); Sigmund Freud, "Das Unbewussten," in *Internationale Zeitschrifte fur ärtzliche Psychoanalyse*, vol. 3 (1915) (English translation: "The Unconscious," in *Pelican Freud Library, Vol. 11: On Metapsychology: The Theory of Psychoanalysis* [Harmondsworth: Penguin, 1984]); and *Die Zukunft einer Illusion* (Leipzig/Vienna/Zurich: Internationaler Psychoanalytischer Verlag, 1927) (French translation: *L'Avenir d'une illusion* [Paris: Denoël, 1932], reprinted Paris: PUF, 1995; English translation: *The Future of an Illusion*, in *The Pelican Freud Library, Vol. 12: Civilization, Society and Religion, Group Psychology, Civilization and Its Discontents and Other Works* [Harmondsworth: Penguin, 1985]); on Reich, cf. note 2 above.

9. Foucault alludes to the well-known formulation of Carl von Clausewitz's principle (*Vom Kriege* book 1, chap. 1, xxiv, in *Hinterlassene Werke*, bd. 1-2-3 [Berlin, 1832]): "War is a mere continuation of policy by other means.... War is not merely a political act, but also a truly political instrument, a continuation of political commerce, a carrying out of the same by other means." *On War*, edited with an introduction by Anatol Rapoport (Harmondsworth: Penguin, 1982) (French translation: *De la guerre* [Paris: Éditions de Minuit, 1955]).

10. This promise was not kept. A lecture on "repression" is, however, intercalated in the manuscript; it was presumably given at a foreign university. Foucault returns to this question in *La Volonté de savoir* (Paris: Gallimard, 1976) (English translation by Robert Hurley: *The History of Sexuality, Volume I: An Introduction* [Harmondsworth: Penguin, 1981]).

two

14 JANUARY 1976

War and power. ~ Philosophy and the limits of power. ~ Law and royal power. ~ Law, domination, and subjugation. ~ Analytics of power: questions of method. ~ Theory of sovereignty. ~ Disciplinary power. ~ Rule and norm.

THIS YEAR, I WOULD like to begin—and to do no more than begin—a series of investigations into whether or not war can possibly provide a principle for the analysis of power relations: can we find in bellicose relations, in the model of war, in the schema of struggle or struggles, a principle that can help us understand and analyze political power, to interpret political power in terms of war, struggles, and confrontations? I would like to begin, obviously, with a contrapuntal analysis of the military institution, of the real, actual, and historical way in which military institutions have functioned in our societies from the seventeenth century until the present day.

Until now, or for roughly the last five years, it has been disciplines; for the next five years, it will be war, struggle, the army. At the same time, I would like to sum up what I have been trying to say in previous years, because doing so will give me more time for my research on war, which has not got very far, and also because doing so might provide a framework of reference for those of you who were not here in previous years. In any case, I'd like to sum up what I have been trying to cover for my own benefit.

What I have been trying to look at since 1970-1971 is the "how" of power. Studying the "how of power," or in other words trying to understand its mechanisms by establishing two markers, or limits; on the one hand, the rules of right that formally delineate power, and on the other hand, at the opposite extreme, the other limit might be the truth-effects that power produces, that this power conducts and which, in their turn, reproduce that power. So we have the triangle: power, right, truth. In schematic terms, let us say that there is a traditional question, which is, I think, that of political philosophy. It can be formulated thus: How does the discourse of truth or, quite simply, philosophy—in the sense that philosophy is the discourse of truth par excellence—establish the limits of power's right? That is the traditional question. Now the question I would like to ask is a question from below, and it is a very factual question compared to that traditional, noble, and philosophical question. My problem is roughly this: What are the rules of right that power implements to produce discourses of truth? Or: What type of power is it that is capable of producing discourses of truth that have, in a society like ours, such powerful effects?

What I mean is this: In a society such as ours—or in any society, come to that—mulitiple relations of power traverse, characterize, and constitute the social body; they are indissociable from a discourse of truth, and they can neither be established nor function unless a true discourse is produced, accumulated, put into circulation, and set to work. Power cannot be exercised unless a certain economy of discourses of truth functions in, on the basis of, and thanks to, that power. This is true of all societies, but I think that in our society, this relationship among power, right, and truth is organized in a very particular way.

In order to characterize not just the mechanism of the relationship between power, right, and truth itself but its intensity and constancy, let us say that we are obliged to produce the truth by the power that demands truth and needs it in order to function: we are forced to tell the truth, we are constrained, we are condemned to admit the truth or to discover it. Power constantly asks questions and questions us; it constantly investigates and records; it institutionalizes the search for the truth, professionalizes it, and rewards it. We have to produce the truth in the same way, really, that we have to produce wealth, and we have to produce the truth in order to be able to produce wealth. In a different sense, we are also subject to the truth in the sense that truth lays down the law: it is the discourse of truth that decides, at least in part; it conveys and propels effects of power. After all, we are judged, condemned, forced to perform tasks, and destined to live and die in certain ways by discourses that are true, and which bring with them specific power-effects. So: rules of right, mechanisms of power, truth-effects. Or: rules of power, and the power of true discourses. That, roughly, is the very general domain I wanted to examine, and which I have been examining to some extent and with, as I am well aware, many digressions.

I would now like to say a few words about this domain. What general principle guided me, and what were the imperative commands, or the methodological precautions that I resolved to take? Where relations between right and power are concerned, the general principle is, it seems to me, that one fact must never be forgotten: In Western societies, the elaboration of juridical thought has essentially centered around royal power ever since the Middle Ages. The juridical edifice of our societies was elaborated at the demand of royal power, as well as for its benefit, and in order to serve as its instrument or its justification. In the West, right is the right of the royal command. Everyone is of course familiar with the famous, celebrated, repeated, and repetitive role played by jurists in the organization of royal power. It must not be forgotten that the reactivation of Roman law in the middle of the Middle Ages—and this was the great phenomenon that made it possible to reconstruct a juridical edifice that had collapsed after the fall of the Roman Empire—was one of the instruments that was used to constitute monarchical, authoritarian, administrative, and, ultimately, absolute power. The juridical edifice was, then, formed around the royal personage, at the demand of royal power, and for the benefit of royal power. When in later centuries this juridical edifice escaped from royal control, when it was turned against royal power, the issue at stake was always, and always would be, the limits of that power, the question of its prerogatives. In other words, I believe that the king was the central character in the entire Western juridical edifice. The general system, or at least the general organization of the Western juridical system, was all about the king: the king, his rights, his power, and the possible limits of his power. That, basically, is what the general system, or at least the general organization, of the Western juridical system is all about. No matter whether the jurists were the king's servants or his adversaries, the great edifices of juridical thought and juridical knowledge were always about royal power.

It was all about royal power in two senses. Either it had to be demonstrated that royal power was invested in a juridical armature, that the monarch was indeed the living body of sovereignty, and that his power, even when absolute, was perfectly in keeping with a basic right; or it had to be demonstrated that the power of the sovereign had to be limited, that it had to submit to certain rules, and that, if that power were to retain its legitimacy, it had to be exercised within certain limits. From the Middle Ages onward, the essential role of the theory of right has been to establish the legitimacy of power; the major or central problem around which the theory of right is organized is the problem of sovereignty. To say that the problem of sovereignty is the central problem of right in Western societies means that the essential function of the technique and discourse of right is to dissolve the element of domination in power and to replace that domination, which has to be reduced or masked, with two things: the legitimate rights of the sovereign on the one hand, and the legal obligation to obey on the other. The system of right is completely centered on the king; it is, in other words, ultimately an elimination of domination and its consequences.

In previous years when we were talking about the various little things I have mentioned, the general project was, basically, to invert the general direction of the analysis that has, I think, been the entire discourse of right ever since the Middle Ages. I have been trying to do the opposite, or in other words to stress the fact of domination in all its brutality and its secrecy, and then to show not only that right is an instrument of that domination—that is self-evident—but also how, to what extent, and in what form right (and when I say right, I am not thinking just of the law, but of all the apparatuses, institutions, and rules that apply it) serves as a vehicle for and implements relations that are not relations of sovereignty, but relations of domination. And by domination I do not mean the brute fact of the domination of the one over the many, or of one group over another, but the multiple forms of domination that can be exercised in society; so, not the king in his central position, but subjects in their reciprocal relations; not sovereignty in its one edifice, but the multiple subjugations that take place and function within the social body.

The system of right and the judiciary field are permanent vehicles for relations of domination, and for polymorphous techniques of subjugation. Right must, I think, be viewed not in terms of a legitimacy that has to be established, but in terms of the procedures of subjugation it implements. As I see it, we have to bypass or get around the problem of sovereignty—which is central to the theory of right—and the obedience of individuals who submit to it, and to reveal the problem of domination and subjugation instead of sovereignty and obedience. Having said that, a certain number of methodological precautions had to be taken in order to follow this line, which was an attempt to bypass or deviate from the general line of the juridical analysis.

Methodological precautions. Our object is not to analyze rule-governed and legitimate forms of power which have a single center, or to look at what their general mechanisms or its overall effects might be. Our object is, on the contrary, to understand power by looking at its extremities, at its outer limits at the point where it becomes capillary; in other words, to understand power in its most regional forms and institutions, and especially at the points where this power transgresses the rules of right that organize and delineate it, oversteps those rules and is invested in institutions, is embodied in techniques and acquires the material means to intervene, sometimes in violent ways. We can take an example if you like: rather than trying to see where and how the power to punish finds its basis in the sovereignty, as described by philosophy, of either monarchical right or democratic right, I tried to look at how the power to punish was embodied in a certain number of local, regional, and material institutions, such as torture or imprisonment, and to look at the simultaneously institutional, physical, regulatory, and violent world of the actual apparatuses of punishment. I tried, in other words, to understand power by looking at its extremities, at where its exercise became less and less juridicial. That was my first precaution.

Second precaution: My goal was not to analyze power at the level of intentions or decisions, not to try to approach it from inside, and not to ask the question (which leads us, I think, into a labyrinth from which there is no way out): So who has power? What is going on in his head? And what is he trying to do, this man who has power? The goal was, on the contrary, to study power at the point where his intentions—if, that is, any intention is involved—are completely invested in real and effective practices; to study power by looking, as it were, at its external face, at the point where it relates directly and immediately to what we might, very provisionally, call its object, its target, its field of application, or, in other words, the places where it implants itself and produces its real effects. So the question is not: Why do some people want to be dominant? What do they want? What is their overall strategy? The question is this: What happens at the moment of, at the level of the procedure of subjugation, or in the continuous and uninterrupted processes that subjugate bodies, direct gestures, and regulate forms of behavior? In other words, rather than asking ourselves what the sovereign looks like from on high, we should be trying to discover how multiple bodies, forces, energies, matters, desires, thoughts, and so on are gradually, progressively, actually and materially constituted as subjects, or as the subject. To grasp the material agency of subjugation insofar as it constitutes subjects would, if you like, be to do precisely the opposite of what Hobbes was trying to do in *Leviathan*.[1] Ultimately, I think that all jurists try to do the same thing, as their problem is to discover how a multiplicity of individuals and wills can be shaped into a single will or even a single body that is supposedly animated by a soul known as sovereignty. Remember the schema of *Leviathan*.[2] In this schema, the Leviathan, being an artificial man, is no more than the coagulation of a certain number of distinct individualities that find themselves united by a certain number of the State's constituent elements. But at the heart, or rather the head, of the State, there is something that constitutes it as such, and that something is sovereignty, which Hobbes specifically describes as the soul of the Leviathan. Well, rather than raising this problem of the central soul, I think we should be trying—and this is what I have been trying to do—to study the multiple peripheral bodies, the bodies that are constituted as subjects by power-effects.

Third methodological precaution: Do not regard power as a phenomenon of mass and homogeneous domination—the domination of one individual over others, of one group over others, or of one class over others; keep it clearly in mind that unless we are looking at it from a great height and from a very great distance, power is not something that is divided between those who have it and hold it exclusively, and those who do not have it and are subject to it. Power must, I think, be analyzed as something that circulates, or rather as something that functions only when it is part of a chain. It is never localized here or there, it is never in the hands of some, and it is never appropriated in the way that wealth or a commodity can be appropriated. Power functions. Power is exercised through networks, and individuals do not simply circulate in those networks; they are in a position to both submit to and exercise this power. They are never the inert or consenting targets of power; they are always its relays. In other words, power passes through individuals. It is not applied to them.

It is therefore, I think, a mistake to think of the individual as a sort of elementary nucleus, a primitive atom or some multiple, inert matter to which power is applied, or which is struck by a power that subordinates or destroys individuals. In actual fact, one of the first effects of power is that it allows bodies, gestures, discourses, and desires to be identified and constituted as something individual. The individual is not, in other words, power's opposite number; the individual is one of power's first effects. The individual is in fact a power-effect, and at the same time, and to the extent that he is a power-effect, the individual is a relay: power passes through the individuals it has constituted.

Fourth implication at the level of methodological precautions: When I say, "Power is exercised, circulates, and forms networks," this might be true up to a certain point. We can also say, "We all have some element of fascism inside our heads," or, at a more basic level still, "We all have some element of power in our bodies." And power does—at least to some extent—pass or migrate through our bodies. We can indeed say all that, but I do not think that we therefore have to conclude that power is the best-distributed thing, the most widely distributed thing, in the world, even though this is, up to a point, the case. Power is not distributed throughout the body in democratic or anarchic fashion. What I mean is this: it seems to me—and this will be our fourth methodological precaution—it is important not to, so to speak, deduce power by beginning at the center and trying to see how far down it goes, or to what extent it is reproduced or renewed in the most atomistic elements of society. I think that, on the contrary—and this is a methodological precaution that has to be taken—we should make an ascending analysis of power, or in other words begin with its infinitesimal mechanisms, which have their own history, their own trajectory, their own techniques and tactics, and then look at how these mechanisms of power, which have their solidity and, in a sense, their own technology, have been and are invested, colonized, used, inflected, transformed, displaced, extended, and so on by increasingly general mechanisms and forms of overall domination. Overall domination is not something that is pluralized and then has repercussions down below. I think we have to analyze the way in which the phenomena, techniques, and procedures of power come into play at the lowest levels; we have to show, obviously, how these procedures are displaced, extended, and modified and, above all, how they are invested or annexed by global phenomena, and how more general powers or economic benefits can slip into the play of these technologies of power, which are at once relatively autonomous and infinitesimal.

To make things clearer, I will take the example of madness. We could say this, we could make the descending analysis we have to distrust. We could say that from the late sixteenth century or the seventeenth century onward, the bourgeoisie became the ruling class. Having said that, how can we deduce that the mad will be confined? You can certainly make that deduction; it is always easy, and that is precisely what I hold against it. It is in fact easy to show how, because the mad are obviously of no use to industrial production, they have to be got rid of. We could, if you like, say the same thing, not about the madman this time, but about infantile sexuality—and a number of people have done so: Wilhelm Reich[3] does so up to a point, and Reimut Reich certainly does so.[4] We could ask how the rule of the bourgeoisie allows us to understand the repression of infantile sexuality. Well, it's quite simple: from the seventeenth or eighteenth century onward, the human body essentially became a productive force, and all forms of expenditure that could not be reduced to these relations, or to the constitution of the productive forces, all forms of expenditure that could be shown to be unproductive, were banished, excluded, and repressed. Such deductions are always possible; they are both true and false. They are essentially too facile, because we can say precisely the opposite. We can deduce from the principle that the bourgeoisie became a ruling class that controlling sexuality, and infantile sexuality, is not absolutely desirable. We can reach the opposite conclusion and say that what is needed is a sexual apprenticeship, sexual training, sexual precocity, to the extent that the goal is to use sexuality to reproduce a labor force, and it is well known that, at least in the early nineteenth century, it was believed that the optimal labor force was an infinite labor force: the greater the labor force, the greater the capitalist system of production's ability to function fully and efficiently.

I think that we can deduce whatever we like from the general phenomenon of the domination of the bourgeois class. It seems to me that we should be doing quite the opposite, or in other words looking in historical terms, and from below, at how control mechanisms could come into play in terms of the exclusion of madness, or the repression and suppression of sexuality; at how these phenomena of repression or exclusion found their instruments and their logic, and met a certain number of needs at the actual level of the family and its immediate entourage, or in the cells or the lowest levels of society. We should be showing what their agents were, and we should be looking for those agents not in the bourgeoisie in general, but in the real agents that exist in the immediate entourage: the family, parents, doctors, the lowest levels of the police, and so on. And we should be looking at how, at a given moment, in a specific conjuncture and subject to a certain number of transformations, these power-mechanisms began to become economically profitable and politically useful. And I think we could easily succeed in demonstrating—and this is, after all, what I have tried to do on a number of occasions in the past—that, basically, what the bourgeoisie needed, and the reason why the system ulti-mately proved to work to its advantage, was not that the mad had to be excluded or that childhood masturbation had to be controlled or forbidden—the bourgeois system can, I repeat, quite easily tolerate the opposite of this. What did prove to be in its interest, and what it did invest, was not the fact that they were excluded, but the tech-nique and procedures of their exclusion. It was the mechanisms of exclusion, the surveillance apparatus, the medicalization of sexuality, madness, and delinquency, it was all that, or in other words the mi-cromechanics of power that came at a certain moment to represent, to constitute the interest of the bourgeoisie. That is what the bour-geoisie was interested in.

To put it another way: to the extent that these notions of "the bourgeoisie" and "the interests of the bourgeoisie" probably have no content, or at least not in terms of the problems we have just raised, what we have to realize is precisely that there was no such thing as a bourgeoisie that thought that madness should be excluded or that infantile sexuality had to be repressed; but there were mechanisms to exclude madness and techniques to keep infantile sexuality under surveillance. At a given moment, and for reasons that have to be studied, they generated a certain economic profit, a certain political utility, and they were therefore colonized and supported by global mechanisms and, finally, by the entire system of the State. If we concentrate on the techniques of power and show the economic profit or political utility that can be derived from them, in a certain context and for certain reasons, then we can understand how these mechanisms actually and eventually became part of the whole. In other words, the bourgeoisie doesn't give a damn about the mad, but from the nineteenth century onward and subject to certain transformations, the procedures used to exclude the mad produced or generated a political profit, or even a certain economic utility. They consolidated the system and helped it to function as a whole. The bourgeoisie is not interested in the mad, but it is interested in power over the mad; the bourgeoisie is not interested in the sexuality of children, but it is interested in the system of power that controls the sexuality of children. The bourgeoisie does not give a damn about delinquents, or about how they are punished or rehabilitated, as that is of no great economic interest. On the other hand, the set of mechanisms whereby delinquents are controlled, kept track of, punished, and reformed does generate a bourgeois interest that functions within the economico-political system as a whole. That is the fourth precaution, the fourth methodological line I wanted to follow.

⑤ Fifth precaution: It is quite possible that ideological production did coexist with the great machineries of power. There was no doubt an ideology of education, an ideology of monarchical power, an ideology of parliamentary democracy, and so on. But I do not think that it is ideologies that are shaped at the base, at the point where the networks of power culminate. It is much less and much more than that. It is the actual instruments that form and accumulate knowledge, the observational methods, the recording techniques, the investigative research procedures, the verification mechanisms. That is, the delicate mechanisms of power cannot function unless knowledge, or rather knowledge apparatuses, are formed, organized, and put into circulation, and those apparatuses are not ideological trimmings or edifices. *What are they then?*

To sum up these five methodological precautions, let me say that rather than orienting our research into power toward the juridical edifice of sovereignty, State apparatuses, and the ideologies that accompany them, I think we should orient our analysis of power toward material operations, forms of subjugation, and the connections among and the uses made of the local systems of subjugation on the one hand, and apparatuses of knowledge on the other.

In short, we have to abandon the model of Leviathan, that model of an artificial man who is at once an automaton, a fabricated man, but also a unitary man who contains all real individuals, whose body is made up of citizens but whose soul is sovereignty. We have to study power outside the model of Leviathan, outside the field delineated by juridical sovereignty and the institution of the State. We have to analyze it by beginning with the techniques and tactics of domination. That, I think, is the methodological line we have to follow, and which I have tried to follow in the different research projects we have undertaken in previous years on psychiatric power, infantile sexuality, the punitive system, and so on.

Now if we look at this domain and take these methodological precautions, I think that one massive historical fact emerges, and that it will help to provide us with an introduction to the problem I wish to talk about from now onward. The massive historical fact is this: The juridico-political theory of sovereignty—the theory we have to get away from if we want to analyze power—dates from the Middle Ages. It dates from the reactivation of Roman law and is constituted around the problem of the monarch and the monarchy. And I believe that, in historical terms, this theory of sovereignty—which is the great trap we are in danger of falling into when we try to analyze power—played four roles.

First, it referred to an actual power mechanism: that of the feudal monarchy. Second, it was used as an instrument to constitute and justify the great monarchical administrations. From the sixteenth and especially the seventeenth century onward, or at the time of the Wars of Religion, the theory of sovereignty then became a weapon that was in circulation on both sides, and it was used both to restrict and to strengthen royal power. You find it in the hands of Catholic monarchists and Protestant antimonarchists; you also find it in the hands of more or less liberal Protestant monarchists; you also find it in the hands of Catholics who advocate regicide or a change of dynasty. You find this theory of sovereignty being brought into play by aristocrats and *parlementaires*,[5] by the representatives of royal power and by the last feudalists. It was, in a word, the great instrument of the political and theoretical struggles that took place around systems of power in the sixteenth and seventeenth centuries. In the eighteenth century, finally, you find the same theory of sovereignty, the same reactivation of Roman law, in the work of Rousseau and his contemporaries, but it now played a fourth and different role; at this point in time, its role was to construct an alternative model to authoritarian or absolute monarchical administration: that of the parliamentary democracies. And it went on playing that role until the time of the Revolution.

It seems to me that if we look at these four roles, we find that, so long as feudal-type societies survived, the problems dealt with by the theory of sovereignty, or to which it referred, were actually coextensive with the general mechanics of power, or the way power was exercised from the highest to the lowest levels. In other words, the relationship of sovereignty, understood in both the broad and the narrow sense, was, in short, coextensive with the entire social body. And the way in which power was exercised could indeed be transcribed, at least in its essentials, in terms of the sovereign/subject relationship.

Now, an important phenomenon occurred in the seventeenth and eighteenth centuries: the appearance—one should say the invention— of a new mechanism of power which had very specific procedures, completely new instruments, and very different equipment. It was, I believe, absolutely incompatible with relations of sovereignty. This new mechanism of power applies primarily to bodies and what they do rather than to the land and what it produces. It was a mechanism of power that made it possible to extract time and labor, rather than commodities and wealth, from bodies. It was a type of power that was exercised through constant surveillance and not in discontinuous fashion through chronologically defined systems of taxation and obligation. It was a type of power that presupposed a closely meshed grid of material coercions rather than the physical existence of a sovereign, and it therefore defined a new economy of power based upon the principle that there had to be an increase both in the subjugated forces and in the force and efficacy of that which subjugated them.

It seems to me that this type of power is the exact, point-for-point opposite of the mechanics of power that the theory of sovereignty described or tried to transcribe. The theory of sovereignty is bound up with a form of power that is exercised over the land and the produce of the land, much more so than over bodies and what they do. [This theory] concerns power's displacement and appropriation not of time and labor, but of goods and wealth. This makes it possible to transcribe, into juridical terms, discontinuous obligations and tax records, but not to code continuous surveillance; it is a theory that makes it possible to found absolute power around and on the basis of the physical existence of the sovereign, but not continuous and permanent systems of surveillance. The theory of sovereignty is, if you like, a theory which can found absolute power on the absolute expenditure of power, but which cannot calculate power with minimum expenditure and maximum efficiency. This new type of power, which can therefore no longer be transcribed in terms of sovereignty, is, I believe, one of bourgeois society's great inventions. It was one of the basic tools for the establishment of industrial capitalism and the corresponding type of society. This nonsovereign power, which is foreign to the form of sovereignty, is "disciplinary" power. This power cannot be described or justified in terms of the theory of sovereignty. It is radically heterogeneous and should logically have led to the complete disappearance of the great juridical edifice of the theory of sovereignty. In fact, the theory of sovereignty not only continued to exist as, if you like, an ideology of right; it also continued to organize the juridical codes that nineteenth-century Europe adopted after the Napoleonic codes.[6] Why did the theory of sovereignty live on in this way

as an ideology and as the organizing principle behind the great juridical codes?

I think there are two reasons. On the one hand, the theory of
sovereignty was, in the seventeenth century and even the nineteenth
century, a permanent critical instrument to be used against the monarchy and all the obstacles that stood in the way of the development
of the disciplinary society. On the other hand, this theory, and the
organization of a juridical code centered upon it, made it possible to
superimpose on the mechanism of discipline a system of right that
concealed its mechanisms and erased the element of domination and
the techniques of domination involved in discipline, and which, finally, guaranteed that everyone could exercise his or her own sovereign rights thanks to the sovereignty of the State. In other words,
juridical systems, no matter whether they were theories or codes,
allowed the democratization of sovereignty, and the establishment of
a public right articulated with collective sovereignty, at the very time
when, to the extent that, and because the democratization of sovereignty was heavily ballasted by the mechanisms of disciplinary coercion. To put it in more condensed terms, one might say that once
disciplinary constraints had to both function as mechanisms of domination and be concealed to the extent that they were the mode in
which power was actually exercised, the theory of sovereignty had to
find expression in the juridical apparatus and had to be reactivated
or complemented by judicial codes.

From the nineteenth century until the present day, we have then
in modern societies, on the one hand, a legislation, a discourse, and
an organization of public right articulated around the principle of the
sovereignty of the social body and the delegation of individual sovereignty to the State; and we also have a tight grid of disciplinary
coercions that actually guarantees the cohesion of that social body.
Now that grid cannot in any way be transcribed in right, even though
the two necessarily go together. A right of sovereignty and a mechanics of discipline. It is, I think, between these two limits that
power is exercised. The two limits are, however, of such a kind and
so heterogeneous that we can never reduce one to the other. In mod-

ern societies, power is exercised through, on the basis of, and in the very play of the heterogeneity between a public right of sovereignty and a polymorphous mechanics of discipline. This is not to say that you have, on the one hand, a garrulous and explicit system of right, and on the other hand, obscure silent disciplines that operate down below, in the shadows, and which constitute the silent basement of the great mechanics of power. Disciplines in fact have their own discourse. They do, for the reasons I was telling you about a moment ago, create apparatuses of knowledge, knowledges and multiple fields of expertise. They are extraordinarily inventive when it comes to creating apparatuses to shape knowledge and expertise, and they do support a discourse, but it is a discourse that cannot be the discourse of right or a juridical discourse. The discourse of discipline is alien to that of the law; it is alien to the discourse that makes rules a product of the will of the sovereign. The discourse of disciplines is about a rule: not a juridical rule derived from sovereignty, but a discourse about a natural rule, or in other words a norm. Disciplines will define not a code of law, but a code of normalization, and they will necessarily refer to a theoretical horizon that is not the edifice of law, but the field of the human sciences. And the jurisprudence of these disciplines will be that of a clinical knowledge.

In short, what I have been trying to show over the last few years is certainly not how, as the front of the exact sciences advances, the uncertain, difficult, and confused domain of human behavior is gradually annexed by science: the gradual constitution of the human sciences is not the result of an increased rationality on the part of the exact sciences. I think that the process that has made possible the discourse of the human sciences is the juxtaposition of, the confrontation between, two mechanisms and two types of discourse that are absolutely heterogeneous: on the one hand, the organization of right around sovereignty, and on the other, the mechanics of the coercions exercised by disciplines. In our day, it is the fact that power is exercised through both right and disciplines, that the techniques of discipline and discourses born of discipline are invading right, and that normalizing procedures are increasingly colonizing the procedures of the law, that might explain the overall workings of what I would call a "normalizing society."

To be more specific, what I mean is this: I think that normalization, that disciplinary normalizations, are increasingly in conflict with the juridical system of sovereignty; the incompatibility of the two is increasingly apparent; there is a greater and greater need for a sort of arbitrating discourse, for a sort of power and knowledge that has been rendered neutral because its scientificity has become sacred. And it is precisely in the expansion of medicine that we are seeing—I wouldn't call it a combination of, a reduction of—but a perpetual exchange or confrontation between the mechanics of discipline and the principle of right. The development of medicine, the general medicalization of behavior, modes of conduct, discourses, desires, and so on, is taking place on the front where the heterogeneous layers of discipline and sovereignty meet.

That is why we now find ourselves in a situation where the only existing and apparently solid recourse we have against the usurpations of disciplinary mechanics and against the rise of a power that is bound up with scientific knowledge is precisely a recourse or a return to a right that is organized around sovereignty, or that is articulated on that old principle. Which means in concrete terms that when we want to make some objection against disciplines and all the knowledge-effects and power-effects that are bound up with them, what do we do in concrete terms? What do we do in real life? What do the Syndicat de la magistrature and other institutions like it do? What do we do? We obviously invoke right, the famous old formal, bourgeois right. And it is in reality the right of sovereignty. And I think that at this point we are in a sort of bottleneck, that we cannot go on working like this forever; having recourse to sovereignty against discipline will not enable us to limit the effects of disciplinary power.

Sovereignty and discipline, legislation, the right of sovereignty and disciplinary mechanics are in fact the two things that constitute—in an absolute sense—the general mechanisms of power in our society. Truth to tell, if we are to struggle against disciplines, or rather against disciplinary power, in our search for a nondisciplinary power, we should not be turning to the old right of sovereignty; we should be looking for a new right that is both antidisciplinary and emancipated from the principle of sovereignty.

At this point we come back to the notion of "repression." I may talk to you about that next time, unless I have had enough of repeating things that have already been said, and move on immediately to other things to do with war. If I feel like it and if I can be bothered to, I will talk to you about the notion of "repression," which has, I think, the twofold disadvantage, in the use that is made of it, of making obscure reference to a certain theory of sovereignty—the theory of the sovereign rights of the individual—and of bringing into play, when it is used, a whole set of psychological references borrowed from the human sciences, or in other words from discourses and practices that relate to the disciplinary domain. I think that the notion of "repression" is still, whatever critical use we try to make of it, a juridico-disciplinary notion; and to that extent the critical use of the notion of "repression" is tainted, spoiled, and rotten from the outset because it implies both a juridical reference to sovereignty and a disciplinary reference to normalization. Next time, I will either talk to you about repression or move on to the problem of war.

---

1. Thomas Hobbes, *Leviathan, or the Matter, Forme and Power of a Common-Wealth Ecclesiasticall and Civill* (London, 1651). The Latin translation of the text, which was in fact a new version, was published in Amsterdam in 1668.
2. Foucault is alluding to the famous frontispiece to the "Head" edition of *Leviathan* published by Andrew Crooke. It depicts the body of a state constituted by its subjects, with the head representing the sovereign, who holds a sword in one hand and a crosier in the other. The basic attributes of civil and ecclesiastical power are depicted below it.
3. Wilhelm Reich, *Der Einbruch der Sexualmoral*.
4. Reimut Reich, *Sexualität und Klassenkampf: zur Abwehr repressiver Ensublimierung* (Frankfurt am Main: Verlag Neue Kritik, 1968) (French translation: *Sexualité et lutte de classe* [Paris: Maspero, 1969]).
5. The thirteen *parlements* of the Ancien Régime were high courts of appeal and had no legislative powers, though the parlement de Paris did attempt to usurp such powers. [Trans.]
6. The reference is to the "Napoleonic codes," or in other words the Code civil of 1804, the Code d'instruction criminelle of 1808, and the Code pénal of 1810.

three

21 JANUARY 1976

[
*Theory of sovereignty and operators of domination. ~ War as
analyzer of power relations. ~ The binary structure of
society. ~ Historico-political discourse, the discourse of perpetual
war. ~ The dialectic and its codifications. ~ The discourse of race
struggle and its transcriptions.*
]

LAST TIME, WE SAID a sort of farewell to the theory of sovereignty insofar as it could—and can—be described as a method for analyzing power relations. I would like to show you that the juridical model of sovereignty was not, I believe, able to provide a concrete analysis of the multiplicity of power relations. In fact, it seems to me—to sum it all up in a few words, in three words to be precise—that the theory of sovereignty necessarily tries to establish what I would call a cycle—the subject-to-subject cycle—and to show how a subject—understood as meaning an individual who is naturally endowed (or endowed by nature) with rights, capabilities, and so on—can and must become a subject, this time in the sense of an element that is subjectified in a power relationship. Sovereignty is the theory that goes from subject to subject, that establishes the political relationship between subject and subject. Second, it seems to me that the theory of sovereignty assumes from the outset the existence of a multiplicity of powers that are not powers in the political sense of the term; they are capacities, possibilities, potentials, and it can constitute them as powers in the political sense of the term only if it has in the meantime established a moment of fundamental and foundational unity between possibilities and powers, namely the unity of power. Whether this unity of power takes on the face of the monarch or the form of the State is irrelevant; the various forms, aspects, mechanisms, and institutions of power will be derived from this unitary power. The multiplicity of powers, in the sense of political powers, can be established and can function only on the basis of this unitary power, which is founded by the theory of sovereignty. Third and finally, it seems to me that the theory of sovereignty shows, or attempts to show, how a power can be constituted, not exactly in accordance with the law, but in accordance with a certain basic legitimacy that is more basic than any law and that allows laws to function as such. The theory of sovereignty is, in other words, the subject-to-subject cycle, the cycle of power and powers, and the cycle of legitimacy and law. So we can say that in one way or another—and depending, obviously, upon the different theoretical schemata in which it is deployed—the theory of sovereignty presupposes the subject; its goal is to establish the essential unity of power, and it is always deployed within the preexisting element of the law. It therefore assumes the existence of three "primitive" elements: a subject who has to be subjectified, the unity of the power that has to be founded, and the legitimacy that has to be respected. Subject, unitary power, and law: the theory of sovereignty comes into play, I think, among these elements, and it both takes them as given and tries to found them. My project—which I immediately abandoned— was to show you how the instrument that politico-psychological analysis acquired almost three or four hundred years ago, or in other words the notion of repression—which does look, rather, as though it was borrowed from Freudianism or Freudo-Marxism—was in fact inscribed in an interpretation of power as sovereignty. To do that would, however, take us back over things that have already been said, so I will move on, though I may come back to this at the end of the year if we have enough time left.

The general project, both in previous years and this year, is to try to release or emancipate this analysis of power from three assumptions—of subject, unity, and law—and to bring out, rather than these basic elements of sovereignty, what I would call relations or operators of domination. Rather than deriving powers from sovereignty, we should be extracting operators of domination from relations of power, both historically and empirically. A theory of domination, of dominations, rather than a theory of sovereignty: this means that rather than starting with the subject (or even subjects) and elements that exist prior to the relationship and that can be localized, we begin with the power relationship itself, with the actual or effective relationship of domination, and see how that relationship itself determines the elements to which it is applied. We should not, therefore, be asking subjects how, why, and by what right they can agree to being subjugated, but showing how actual relations of subjugation manufacture subjects. Our second task should be to reveal relations of domination, and to allow them to assert themselves in their multiplicity, their differences, their specificity, or their reversibility; we should not be looking for a sort of sovereignty from which powers spring, but showing how the various operators of domination support one another, relate to one another, at how they converge and reinforce one another in some cases, and negate or strive to annul one another in other cases. I am obviously not saying that great apparatuses of power do not exist, or that we can neither get at them nor describe them. But I do think that they always function on the basis of these apparatuses of domination. To put it in more concrete terms, we can obviously describe a given society's school apparatus or its set of educational apparatuses, but I think that we can analyze them effectively only if we do not see them as an overall unity, only if we do not try to derive them from something like the Statist unity of sovereignty. We can analyze them only if we try to see how they interact, how they support one another, and how this apparatus defines a certain number of global strategies on the basis of multiple subjugations (of child to adult, progeny to parents, ignorance to knowledge, apprentice to master, family to administration, and so on). All these mechanisms and operators of domination are the actual plinth of the global apparatus that is the school apparatus. So, if you like, we have to see the structures of power as global strategies that traverse and use local tactics of domination.

Third and finally, revealing relations of domination rather than the source of sovereignty means this: We do not try to trace their origins back to that which gives them their basic legitimacy. We have to try, on the contrary, to identify the technical instruments that guarantee that they function. So to sum up and to, if not settle the issue for the moment, at least clarify it somewhat: Rather than looking at the three prerequisites of law, unity, and subject—which make sovereignty both the source of power and the basis of institutions—I think that we have to adopt the threefold point of view of the techniques, the heterogeneity of techniques, and the subjugation-effects that make technologies of domination the real fabric of both power relations and the great apparatuses of power. The manufacture of subjects rather than the genesis of the sovereign: that is our general theme. But while it is quite clear that relations of domination provide the access road that leads to the analysis of power, how can we analyze these relations of domination? While it is true that we should be studying domination and not sovereignty, or rather that we should be studying dominations and operators of domination, how can we pursue our analysis of relations of domination? To what extent can a relationship of domination boil down to or be reduced to the notion of a relationship of force? To what extent and how can the relationship of force be reduced to a relationship of war?

That is, so to speak, the preliminary question I would like to look at a bit this year: Can war really provide a valid analysis of power relations, and can it act as a matrix for techniques of domination? You might say to me that we cannot, from the outset, confuse power relations with relations of war. Of course not. I am simply taking an extreme [case] to the extent that war can be regarded as the point of maximum tension, or as force-relations laid bare. Is the power relationship basically a relationship of confrontation, a struggle to the death, or a war? If we look beneath peace, order, wealth, and authority, beneath the calm order of subordinations, beneath the State and State apparatuses, beneath the laws, and so on, will we hear and discover a sort of primitive and permanent war? I would like to begin by asking this question, not forgetting that we will also have to raise a whole series of other questions. I will try to deal with them in years to come. As a first approximation, we can simply say that they include the following questions. Can the phenomenon of war be regarded as primary with respect to other relations (relations of inequality, dissymmetries, divisions of labor, relations of exploitation, et cetera)? Must it be regarded as primary? Can we and must we group together in the general mechanism, the general form, known as war, phenomena such as antagonism, rivalry, confrontation, and struggles between individuals, groups, or classes? We might also ask whether notions derived from what was known in the eighteenth century and even the nineteenth century as the art of war (strategy, tactics, et cetera) constitute in themselves a valid and adequate instrument for the analysis of power relations. We could, and must, also ask ourselves if military institutions, and the practices that surround them—and in more general terms all the techniques that are used to fight a war— are, whichever way we look at them, directly or indirectly, the nucleus of political institutions. And finally, the first question I would like to study this year is this: How, when, and why was it noticed or imagined that what is going on beneath and in power relations is a war? When, how, and why did someone come up with the idea that it is a sort of uninterrupted battle that shapes peace, and that the civil order—its basis, its essence, its essential mechanisms—is basically an order of battle? Who came up with the idea that the civil order is an order of battle? [...] Who saw war just beneath the surface of peace; who sought in the noise and confusion of war, in the mud of battles, the principle that allows us to understand order, the State, its institutions, and its history?

That, then, is the question I am going to pursue a bit in coming lectures, and perhaps for the rest of the year. Basically, the question can be put very simply, and that is how I began to put it myself: Who, basically, had the idea of inverting Clausewitz's principle, and who thought of saying: "It is quite possible that war is the continuation of politics by other means, but isn't politics itself a continuation of war by other means?" Now I think that the problem is not so much who inverted Clausewitz's principle as it is the question of the principle Clausewitz inverted, or rather of who formulated the principle Clausewitz inverted when he said: "But, after all, war is no more than a continuation of politics." I in fact think—and will attempt to prove—that the principle that politics is a continuation of war by other means was a principle that existed long before Clausewitz, who simply inverted a sort of thesis that had been in circulation since the seventeenth and eighteenth centuries and which was both diffuse and specific.

So: Politics is the continuation of war by other means. This thesis—and the very existence of this thesis, which predates Clausewitz—contains a sort of historical paradox. We can indeed say, schematically and somewhat crudely, that with the growth and development of States throughout the Middle Ages and up to the threshold of the modern era, we see the practices and institutions of war undergoing a marked, very visible change, which can be characterized thus: The practices and institutions of war were initially concentrated in the hand of a central power; it gradually transpired that in both de facto and de jure terms, only State powers could wage wars and manipulate the instruments of war. The State acquired a monopoly on war. The immediate effect of this State monopoly was that what might be called day-to-day warfare, and what was actually called "private warfare," was eradicated from the social body, and from relations among men and relations among groups. Increasingly, wars, the practices of war, and the institutions of war tended to exist, so to speak, only on the frontiers, on the outer limits of the great State units, and only as a violent relationship—that actually existed or threatened to exist—between States. But gradually, the entire social body was cleansed of the bellicose relations that had permeated it through and through during the Middle Ages.

So, thanks to the establishment of this State monopoly and to the fact that war was now, so to speak, a practice that functioned only at the outer limits of the State, it tended to become the technical and professional prerogative of a carefully defined and controlled military apparatus. This led, broadly speaking, to the emergence of something that did not exist as such in the Middle Ages: the army as institution. It is only at the end of the Middle Ages that we see the emergence of a State endowed with military institutions that replace both the day-to-day and generalized practice of warfare, and a society that was perpetually traversed by relations of war. We will have to come back to this development, but I think we can accept it as at least a first historical hypothesis.

So where is the paradox? The paradox arises at the very moment when this transformation occurs (or perhaps immediately afterward). When war was expelled to the limits of the State, or was both centralized in practice and confined to the frontier, a certain discourse appeared. A new discourse, a strange discourse. It was new, first, because it was, I think, the first historico-political discourse on society, and it was very different from the philosophico-juridical discourse that had been habitually spoken until then. And the historico-political discourse that appeared at this moment was also a discourse on war, which was understood to be a permanent social relationship, the ineradicable basis of all relations and institutions of power. And what is the date of birth of this historico-political discourse that makes war the basis of social relations? Symptomatically, it seems, I think—and I will try to prove this to you—to be after the end of the civil and religious wars of the sixteenth century. The appearance of this discourse is, then, by no means the product of a history or an analysis of the civil wars of the sixteenth century. On the contrary, it was already, if not constituted, at least clearly formulated at the beginning of the great political struggles of seventeenth-century England, at the time of the English bourgeois revolution. We then see it reappear in France at the end of the seventeenth century, at the end of the reign of Louis XIV, and in other political struggles—let us say, the rearguard struggle waged by the French aristocracy against the establishment of the great absolute-administrative monarchy. So you see, the discourse was immediately ambiguous. In England it was one of the instruments used in bourgeois, petit bourgeois—and sometimes popular—struggles and polemics against the absolute monarchy, and it was a tool for political organization. It was also an aristocratic discourse directed against that same monarchy. Those who spoke this discourse often bore names that were at once obscure and heterogeneous. In England we find people such as Edward Coke[1] or John Lilburne,[2] who represented popular movements; in France, too, we find names such as those of Boulainvilliers,[3] Freret,[4] and a gentleman from the Massif Central called the Comte d'Estaing.[5] The same discourse was then taken up by Sieyès,[6] but also by Buonarroti,[7] Augustin Thierry,[8] and Courtet.[9] And, finally, you will find it in the racist biologists and eugenicists of the late nineteenth century. It is a sophisticated discourse, a scientific discourse, an erudite discourse spoken by people with dust in their eyes and dust on their fingers, but it is also—as you will see—a discourse that certainly had an immense number of popular and anonymous speakers. What is this discourse saying? Well, I think it is saying this: No matter what philosophico-juridical theory may say, political power does not begin when the war ends. The organization and juridical structure of power, of States, monarchies, and societies, does not emerge when the clash of arms ceases. War has not been averted. War obviously presided over the birth of States: right, peace, and laws were born in the blood and mud of battles. This should not be taken to mean the ideal battles and rivalries dreamed up by philosophers or jurists: we are not talking about some theoretical savagery. The law is not born of nature, and it was not born near the fountains that the first shepherds frequented: the law is born of real battles, victories, massacres, and conquests which can be dated and which have their horrific heroes; the law was born in burning towns and ravaged fields. It was born together with the famous innocents who died at break of day.

This does not, however, mean that society, the law, and the State are like armistices that put an end to wars, or that they are the products of definitive victories. Law is not pacification, for beneath the law, war continues to rage in all the mechanisms of power, even in the most regular. War is the motor behind institutions and order. In the smallest of its cogs, peace is waging a secret war. To put it another way, we have to interpret the war that is going on beneath peace; peace itself is a coded war. We are therefore at war with one another; a battlefront runs through the whole of society, continuously and permanently, and it is this battlefront that puts us all on one side or the other. There is no such thing as a neutral subject. We are all inevitably someone's adversary.

A binary structure runs through society. And here you see the emergence of something I will try to come back to, as it is very important. The great pyramidal description that the Middle Ages or philosophico-political theories gave of the social body, the great image of the organism or the human body painted by Hobbes, or even the ternary organization (the three orders) that prevailed in France (and to a certain extent a number of other countries in Europe) and which continued to articulate a certain number of discourses, or in any case most institutions, is being challenged by a binary conception of society. This had happened before, but this is the first time the binary conception has been articulated with a specific history. There are two groups, two categories of individuals, or two armies, and they are opposed to each other. And beneath the lapses of memory, the illusions, and the lies that would have us believe that there is a ternary order, a pyramid of subordinations, beneath the lies that would have us believe that the social body is governed by either natural necessities or functional demands, we must rediscover the war that is still going on, war with all its accidents and incidents. Why do we have to rediscover war? Well, because this ancient war is a [...] permanent war. We really do have to become experts on battles, because the war has not ended, because preparations are still being made for the decisive battles, and because we have to win the decisive battle. In other words, the enemies who face us still pose a threat to us, and it is not some reconciliation or pacification that will allow us to bring the war to an end. It will end only to the extent that we really are the victors.

That is a first, and obviously very vague, characterization of this type of discourse. I think that, even on this basis, we can began to understand why it is important. It is, I think, important because it is the first discourse in postmedieval Western society that can be strictly described as being historico-political. First because the subject who speaks in this discourse, who says "I" or "we," cannot, and is in fact not trying to, occupy the position of the jurist or the philosopher, or in other words the position of a universal, totalizing, or neutral subject. In the general struggle he is talking about, the person who is speaking, telling the truth, recounting the story, rediscovering memories and trying not to forget anything, well, that person is inevitably on one side or the other: he is involved in the battle, has adversaries, and is working toward a particular victory. Of course, he speaks the discourse of right, asserts a right and demands a right. But what he is demanding and asserting is "his" rights—he says: "We have a right." These are singular rights, and they are strongly marked by a relationship of property, conquest, victory, or nature. It might be the right of his family or race, the right of superiority or seniority, the right of triumphal invasions, or the right of recent or ancient occupations. In all cases, it is a right that is both grounded in history and decentered from a juridical universality. And if this subject who speaks of right (or rather, rights) is speaking the truth, that truth is no longer the universal truth of the philosopher. It is true that this discourse about the general war, this discourse that tries to interpret the war beneath peace, is indeed an attempt to describe the battle as a whole and to reconstruct the general course of the war. But that does not make it a totalizing or neutral discourse; it is always a perspectival discourse. It is interested in the totality only to the extent that it can see it in one-sided terms, distort it and see it from its own point of view. The truth is, in other words, a truth that can be deployed only from its combat position, from the perspective of the sought-for victory and ultimately, so to speak, of the survival of the speaking subject himself.

This discourse established a basic link between relations of force and relations of truth. This also means that the identification of truth with peace or neutrality, or with the median position which, as Jean-Pierre Vernant has clearly demonstrated, was, at least from a certain point onward, a constituent element of Greek philosophy, is being dissolved.[10] In a discourse such as this, being on one side and not the other means that you are in a better position to speak the truth. It is the fact of being on one side—the decentered position—that makes it possible to interpret the truth, to denounce the illusions and errors that are being used—by your adversaries—to make you believe we are living in a world in which order and peace have been restored. "The more I decenter myself, the better I can see the truth; the more I accentuate the relationship of force, and the harder I fight, the more effectively I can deploy the truth ahead of me and use it to fight, survive, and win." And conversely, if the relationship of force sets truth free, the truth in its turn will come into play—and will, ultimately, be sought—only insofar as it can indeed become a weapon within the relationship of force. Either the truth makes you stronger, or the truth shifts the balance, accentuates the dissymmetries, and finally gives the victory to one side rather than the other. Truth is an additional force, and it can be deployed only on the basis of a relationship of force. The fact that the truth is essentially part of a relationship of force, of dissymmetry, decentering, combat, and war, is inscribed in this type of discourse. Ever since Greek philosophy, philosophico-juridical discourse has always worked with the assumption of a pacified universality, but it is now being seriously called into question or, quite simply, cynically ignored.

We have a historical and political discourse—and it is in that sense that it is historically anchored and politically decentered—that lays a claim to truth and legitimate right on the basis of a relationship of force, and in order to develop that very relationship of force by therefore excluding the speaking subject—the subject who speaks of right and seeks the truth—from juridico-philosophical universality. The role of the person who is speaking is therefore not the role of the legislator or the philosopher who belongs to neither side, a figure of peace and armistices who occupies the position dreamed of by Solon and that Kant was still dreaming of.[11] Establishing oneself between the adversaries, in the center and above them, imposing one general law on all and founding a reconciliatory order: that is precisely what this is not about. It is, rather, about establishing a right marked by dissymmetry, establishing a truth bound up with a relationship of force, a truth-weapon and a singular right. The subject who is speaking is—I wouldn't even say a polemical subject—a subject who is fighting a war. This is one of the first points that makes a discourse of this type important, and it certainly introduced a rift into the discourse of truth and law that had been spoken for thousands of years, for over a thousand years.

Second, this is a discourse that inverts the values, the equilibrium, and the traditional polarities of intelligibility, and which posits, demands, an explanation from below. But in this explanation, the "below" is not necessarily what is clearest and simplest. Explaining things from below also means explaining them in terms of what is most confused, most obscure, most disorderly and most subject to chance, because what is being put forward as a principle for the interpretation of society and its visible order is the confusion of violence, passions, hatreds, rages, resentments, and bitterness; and it is the obscurity of contingencies and all the minor incidents that bring about defeats and ensure victories. This discourse is essentially asking the elliptical god of battles to explain the long days of order, labor, peace, and justice. Fury is being asked to explain calm and order.

So what is the principle that explains history?* First, a series of brute facts, which might already be described as physico-biological facts: physical strength, force, energy, the proliferation of one race, the weakness of the other, and so on. A series of accidents, or at least contingencies: defeats, victories, the failure or success of rebellions, the failure or success of conspiracies or alliances; and finally, a bundle of psychological and moral elements (courage, fear, scorn, hatred, forgetfulness, et cetera). Intertwining bodies, passions, and accidents: according to this discourse, that is what constitutes the permanent web of history and societies. And something fragile and superficial will be built on top of this web of bodies, accidents, and passions, this seething mass which is sometimes murky and sometimes bloody: a growing rationality. The rationality of calculations, strategies, and

---

*The manuscript has "and right."

ruses; the rationality of technical procedures that are used to perpetuate the victory, to silence, or so it would seem, the war, and to preserve or invert the relationship of force. This is, then, a rationality which, as we move upward and as it develops, will basically be more and more abstract, more and more bound up with fragility and illusions, and also more closely bound up with the cunning and wickedness of those who have won a temporary victory. And given that the relationship of domination works to their advantage, it is certainly not in their interest to call any of this into question.

In this schema, we have, then, an ascending axis which is, I believe, very different, in terms of the values it distributes, from the traditional axis. We have an axis based upon a fundamental and permanent irrationality, a crude and naked irrationality, but which proclaims the truth; and, higher up, we have a fragile rationality, a transitory rationality which is always compromised and bound up with illusion and wickedness. Reason is on the side of wild dreams, cunning, and the wicked. At the opposite end of the axis, you have an elementary brutality: a collection of deeds, acts, and passions, and cynical rage in all its nudity. Truth is therefore on the side of unreason and brutality; reason, on the other hand, is on the side of wild dreams and wickedness. Quite the opposite, then, of the discourse that had until now been used to explain right and history. That discourse's attempts at explanation consisted in extracting from all these superficial and violent accidents, which are linked to error, a basic and permanent rationality which is, by its very essence, bound up with fairness and the good. The explanatory axis of the law and history has, I believe, been inverted.

The third reason why the type of discourse I would like to analyze a bit this year is important is, you see, that it is a discourse that develops completely within the historical dimension. It is deployed within a history that has no boundaries, no end, and no limits. In a discourse like this, the drabness of history cannot be regarded as a superficial given that has to be reordered about a few basic, stable principles. It is not interested in passing judgment on unjust governments, or on crimes and acts of violence, by referring them to a certain ideal schema (that of natural law, the will of God, basic principles, and so on). On the contrary, it is interested in defining and discovering, beneath the forms of justice that have been instituted, the order that has been imposed, the forgotten past of real struggles, actual victories, and defeats which may have been disguised but which remain profoundly inscribed. It is interested in rediscovering the blood that has dried in the codes, and not, therefore, the absolute right that lies beneath the transience of history; it is interested not in referring the relativity of history to the absolute of the law, but in discovering, beneath the stability of the law or the truth, the indefiniteness of history. It is interested in the battle cries that can be heard beneath the formulas of right, in the dissymmetry of forces that lies beneath the equilibrium of justice. Within a historical field that cannot even be said to be a relative field, as it does not relate to any absolute, it is an infinity of history that is in a sense being "irrelativized," the infinity of the eternal dissolution into the mechanisms and events known as force, power, and war.

You might think—and this is, I think, another reason why this discourse is important—that this must be a sad, gloomy discourse, a discourse for nostalgic aristocrats or scholars in a library. It is in fact a discourse which has, ever since it began and until very late in the nineteenth century, and even the twentieth, also been supported by very traditional mythical forms, and it is often invested in those forms. This discourse twins subtle knowledge and myths that are—I wouldn't say crude, but they are basic, clumsy, and overloaded. We can, after all, easily see how a discourse of this type can be articulated (and, as you will see, was actually articulated) with a whole mythology: [the lost age of great ancestors, the imminence of new times and a millenary revenge, the coming of the new kingdom that will wipe out the defeats of old].[12] This mythology tells of how the victories of giants have gradually been forgotten and buried, of the twilight of the gods, of how heroes were wounded or died, and of how kings fell asleep in inaccessible caves. We also have the theme of the rights and privileges of the earliest race, which were flouted by cunning invaders, the theme of the war that is still going on in secret, of the plot that has to be revived so as to rekindle that war and to drive out the invaders or enemies; the theme of the famous battle that will take place tomorrow, that will at last invert the relationship of force, and transform the vanquished into victors who will know and show no mercy. Throughout the whole of the Middle Ages, and even later, the theme of perpetual war will be related to the great, undying hope that the day of revenge is at hand, to the expectation of the emperor of the last years, the *dux novus*, the new leader, the new guide, the new Führer; the idea of the fifth monarchy, the third empire or the Third Reich, the man who will be both the beast of the Apocalypse and the savior of the poor. It's the return of Alexander, who got lost in India; the return, expected for so long in England, of Edward the Confessor; it's the two Fredericks—Barbarossa and Frederick II— waiting in their caves for their people and their empires to reawaken; it's Charlemagne sleeping in his tomb, and who will wake up to revive the just war; it's the king of Portugal, lost in the sands of Africa, returning for a new battle and a new war which, this time, will lead to a final, definitive victory.

This discourse of perpetual war is therefore not just the sad brain- child of a few intellectuals who were indeed marginalized long ago. It seems to me that, because it bypasses the great philosophico- juridical systems, this discourse is in fact tied up with a knowledge which is sometimes in the possession of a declining aristocracy, with great mythical impulses, and with the ardor of the revenge of the people. In short, this may well be the first exclusively historico- political discourse—as opposed to a philosophico-juridical discourse— to emerge in the West; it is a discourse in which truth functions exclusively as a weapon that is used to win an exclusively partisan victory. It is a somber, critical discourse, but it is also an intensely mythical discourse; it is a discourse of bitterness [...] but also of the most insane hopes. For philosophers and jurists, it is obviously an external, foreign discourse. It is not even the discourse of their adversary, as they are not in dialogue with it. It is a discourse that is inevitably disqualified, that can and must be kept in the margins, precisely because its negation is the precondition for a true and just discourse that can at last begin to function—in the middle, between the adversaries, above their heads—as a law. The discourse I am talking about, this partisan discourse, this discourse of war and history, can therefore perhaps take the form of the cunning sophist of the Greek era. Whatever form it takes, it will be denounced as the discourse of a biased and naive historian, a bitter politician, a dispossessed aristocracy, or as an uncouth discourse that puts forward inarticulate demands.

Now this discourse, which was basically or structurally kept in the margins by that of the philosophers and jurists, began its career—or perhaps its new career in the West—in very specific conditions between the end of the sixteenth and the beginning of the seventeenth centuries and represented a twofold—aristocratic and popular—challenge to royal power. From this point onward, I think, it proliferated considerably, and its surface of extension extended rapidly and considerably until the end of the nineteenth century and the beginning of the twentieth. It would, however, be a mistake to think that the dialectic can function as the great reconversion of this discourse, or that it can finally convert it into philosophy. The dialectic may at first sight seem to be the discourse of the universal and historical movement of contradiction and war, but I think that it does not in fact validate this discourse in philosophical terms. On the contrary, it seems to me that it had the effect of taking it over and displacing it into the old form of philosophico-juridical discourse. Basically, the dialectic codifies struggle, war, and confrontations into a logic, or so-called logic, of contradiction; it turns them into the twofold process of the totalization and revelation of a rationality that is at once final but also basic, and in any case irreversible. The dialectic, finally, ensures the historical constitution of a universal subject, a reconciled truth, and a right in which all particularities have their ordained place. The Hegelian dialectic and all those that came after it must, I think and as I will try to demonstrate to you, be understood as philosophy and right's colonization and authoritarian colonization of a historico-political discourse that was both a statement of fact, a proclamation, and a practice of social warfare. The dialectic colonized a historico-political discourse which, sometimes conspicuously and often in the shadows, sometimes in scholarship and sometimes in blood, had been gaining ground for centuries in Europe. The dialectic is the philosophical order's, and perhaps the political order's, way of colonizing this bitter and partisan discourse of basic warfare. There you have the general frame within which I would like to try this year to retrace the history of this discourse.

I would now like to tell you how we should study this, and what our starting point should be. First of all, we have to get rid of a number of false paternities that are usually mentioned in connection with this historico-political discourse. As soon as we begin to think about the power/war relationship or about power/relations of force, two names immediately spring to mind: we think of Machiavelli and we think of Hobbes. I would like to show that they have nothing to do with it, that this historico-political discourse is not, and cannot be, that of the Prince's politics[13] or, obviously, that of absolute power. It is in fact a discourse that inevitably regards the Prince as an illusion, an instrument, or, at best, an enemy. This is, basically, a discourse that cuts off the king's head, or which at least does without a sovereign and denounces him. Having eliminated these false paternities, I would then like to show you this discourse's point of emergence. And it seems to me that we have to try to situate it in the seventeenth century, which has a number of important characteristics. First, this discourse was born twice. On the one hand, we see it emerging roughly in the 1630s, and in the context of the popular or petit bourgeois demands that were being put forward in prerevolutionary and revolutionary England. It is the discourse of the Puritans, the discourse of the Levellers. And then fifty years later, in France at the end of the reign of Louis XIV, you find it on the opposite side, but it is still the discourse of a struggle against the king, a discourse of aristocratic bitterness. And then, and this is the important point, we find even at this early stage, or in other words from the seventeenth century onward, that the idea that war is the uninterrupted frame of history takes a specific form: The war that is going on beneath order and peace, the war that undermines our society and divides it in a binary mode is, basically, a race war. At a very early stage, we find the basic elements that make the war possible, and then ensure its continuation, pursuit, and development: ethnic differences, differences between languages, different degrees of force, vigor, energy, and violence; the differences between savagery and barbarism; the conquest and subjugation of one race by another. The social body is basically articulated around two races. It is this idea that this clash between two races runs through society from top to bottom which we see being formulated as early as the seventeenth century. And it forms the matrix for all the forms beneath which we can find the face and mechanisms of social warfare.

I would like to trace the history of this theory of races, or rather of race war, during the French Revolution and especially in the early nineteenth century with Augustin and Amédée Thierry,[14] and to show how it underwent two transcriptions. On the one hand, there was an openly biological transcription, which occurred long before Darwin and which borrowed its discourse, together with all its elements, concepts, and vocabulary, from a materialist anatomo-physiology. It also has the support of philology, and thus gives birth to the theory of races in the historico-biological sense of the term. Once again and almost as in the seventeenth century, this is a very ambiguous theory, and it is articulated with, on the one hand, nationalist movements in Europe and with nationalities' struggles against the great State apparatuses (essentially the Russian and the Austrian); you will then see it articulated with European policies of colonization. That is the first—biological—transcription of the theory of permanent struggle and race struggle. And then you find a second transcription based upon the great theme and theory of social war, which emerges in the very first years of the nineteenth century, and which tends to erase every trace of racial conflict in order to define itself as class struggle. We have, then, a sort of major parting of the ways, which I will try to reconstruct. It corresponds to a recasting of the theme of the analysis of these struggles in the form of the dialectic, and to a recasting of the theme of racial confrontations in terms of the theory of evolutionism and the struggle for existence. Having established this, and placing special emphasis on the latter argument—the biological transcription—I will try to trace the full development of a biologico-social racism. By this, I mean the idea—which is absolutely new and which will make the discourse function very differently—that the other race is basically not the race that came from elsewhere or that was, for a time, triumphant and dominant, but that it is a race that is permanently, ceaselessly infiltrating the social body, or which is, rather, constantly being re-created in and by the social fabric. In other words, what we see as a polarity, as a binary rift within society, is not a clash between two distinct races. It is the splitting of a single race into a superrace and a subrace. To put it a different way, it is the reappearance, within a single race, of the past of that race. In a word, the obverse and the underside of the race reappears within it.

This has one fundamental implication: The discourse of race struggle—which, when it first appeared and began to function in the seventeenth century, was essentially an instrument used in the struggles waged by decentered camps—will be recentered and will become the discourse of power itself. It will become the discourse of a centered, centralized, and centralizing power. It will become the discourse of a battle that has to be waged not between races, but by a race that is portrayed as the one true race, the race that holds power and is entitled to define the norm, and against those who deviate from that norm, against those who pose a threat to the biological heritage. At this point, we have all those biological-racist discourses of degeneracy, but also all those institutions within the social body which make the discourse of race struggle function as a principle of exclusion and segregation and, ultimately, as a way of normalizing society. At this point, the discourse whose history I would like to trace abandons the initial basic formulation, which was "We have to defend ourselves against our enemies because the State apparatuses, the law, and the power structures not only do not defend us against our enemies; they are the instruments our enemies are using to pursue and subjugate us." That discourse now disappears. It is no longer: "We have to defend ourselves against society," but "We have to defend society against all the biological threats posed by the other race, the subrace,

the counterrace that we are, despite ourselves, bringing into existence." At this point, the racist thematic is no longer a moment in
the struggle between one social group and another; it will promote
the global strategy of social conservatisms. At this point—and this is
a paradox, given the goals and the first form of the discourse I have
been talking about—we see the appearance of a State racism: a racism
that society will direct against itself, against its own elements and its
own products. This is the internal racism of permanent purification,
and it will become one of the basic dimensions of social normalization.
This year, I would like to look a little at the history of this discourse
of race struggle and war from the seventeenth century to the emergence of State racism in the early nineteenth century.

---

1. Edward Coke's most important works are *A Book of Entries* (London, 1614); *Commentaries on Littleton* (London, 1628); *A Treatise of Bail and Mainprize* (London, 1635); *Institutes of the Laws of England* (London, vol. 1, 1628; vol. 2, 1642; vols. 3-4, 1644); *Reports* (London, vols. 1-11, 1600-1615; vol. 12, 1656; vol. 13, 1659). On Coke, see the lecture of 4 February in the present volume.

2. On Lilburne, see the lecture of 4 February in the present volume.

3. On H. de Boulainvilliers, see the lectures of 11 February, 18 February, and 25 February in the present volume.

4. Most of Freret's works were first published in the *Mémoires de l'Académie des Sciences.* They were subsequently collected in his *Oeuvres complètes*, 20 vols. (Paris, 1796-1799). See, inter alia, *De l'origine des Français et de leur établissement dans la Gaule* (vol. 5), *Recherches historiques sur les moeurs et le gouvernement des Français, dans les divers temps de la monarchie* (vol. 6), *Réflexions sur l'étude des anciennes histoires et sur le degré de certitude de leurs preuves* (vol. 7), *Vues générales sur l'origine et le mélange des anciennes nations et sur la manière d'en étudier l'histoire* (vol. 18), and *Observations sur les Mérovingiens* (vol. 20). On Freret, see the lecture of 18 February in the present volume.

5. Joachim, comte d'Estaing, *Dissertation sur la noblesse d'extraction et sur les origines des fiefs, des surnoms et des armoiries* (Paris, 1690).

6. Foucault's lecture on 10 March, and now in the present volume, is based mainly on E.-J. Sieyès, *Qu'est-ce que le Tiers État?* (1789). (Cf. the reprinted editions, Paris: PUF, 1982 and Paris: Flammarion, 1988.)

7. Cf. F. Buonarroti, *Conspiration pour l'égalité, dite de Babeuf, suivie du procès auquel elle donna lieu et les pièces justicatives*, 2 vols. (Brussels, 1828).

8. The historical works by Augustin Thierry referred to by Foucault, particularly in his lecture of 10 March, are as follows: *Vues des révolutions d'Angleterre* (Paris, 1917); *Histoire de la conquête de l'Angleterre par les Normands, de ses causes et de ces suites jusqu'à nos jours* (Paris, 1825); *Lettres sur l'histoire de France pour servir d'introduction à l'étude de cette histoire* (Paris, 1827); *Dix ans d'études historiques* (Paris, 1834); *Récits des temps mérovingiens, précédés de considérations sur l'histoire de France* (Paris, 1834); *Essais sur l'histoire de la formation et des progrès du Tiers-Etat* (Paris, 1853).

9. See in particular A. V. Courtet de l'Isle, *La Science politique fondée sur la science de l'homme* (Paris, 1837),

10. Cf. J.-P. Vernant, *Les Origines de la pensée grecque* (Paris: PUF, 1965), especially chapters 7 and 8; *Mythe et pensée chez les Grecs: Études de psychologie historique* (Paris: La Découverte, 1965), especially chapters 3, 4, and 7; *Mythe et société en Grèce ancienne* (Paris: Seuil, 1974); J.-P. Vernant and P. Vidal-Naquet, *Mythe et tragédie en Grèce ancienne* (Paris: La Découverte, 1972), particularly chapter 3. English translations: *The Origins of Greek Thought* (London: Methuen, 1982); *Myth and Thought among the Greeks* (London: Routledge and Kegan Paul, 1982); *Myth and Tragedy in Ancient Greece*, tr. Janet Lloyd (New York: Zone Books, 1990).

11. For Solon (see in particular fragment 16 in the Diehl edition), the reader is referred to the analysis of *"mesure"* made by Michel Foucault in his lectures at the Collège de France in 1970-1971 on *The Will to Knowledge*. On Kant, the reader is simply referred to "What Is Enlightenment?" trans. Catherine Porter, in Paul Rabinow, ed., *The Foucault Reader* (Harmondsworth: Penguin, 1986), pp. 32-50, reprinted with emendations in *Ethics: The Essential Works*, vol. 1, pp. 303-20 (French original, *Dits et écrits* vol. 4, pp. 562-84); "Qu'est-ce que les Lumières?" *Dits et écrits* vol. 4, pp. 679-88 (English translation by Colin Gordon, "Kant on Enlightenment and Revolution," *Economy and Society*, vol. 15, no. 1 [February 1986], pp. 88-96); and the lecture given to the Société Française de Philosophie on 27 May 1978 on "Qu'est-ce que la critique," *Bulletin de la Société Française de Philosophie*, April-June 1990, pp. 35-67; see also I. Kant, *Zum weigen Frieden: ein philoso-*

phischer Enwurf (Königsberg, 1795; see in particular the second edition of 1796) in *Werke in zwölf Bänden* (Frankfurt am Main: Insel Verlag, 1968), vol. 11, pp. 191-251; *Der Sreti der Fakultäten in drei abschnitten* (Königsberg, 1798), ibid., pp. 261-393. (English translation: *Perpetual Peace: A Philosophical Sketch* and "The Conflict of Faculties," in *Political Writings*, ed. Hanns Reiss, trans. H. B. Nisbet [Cambridge: Cambridge University Press, 1970].) Foucault owned the complete works of Kant in Ernst Cassirer's 12-volume edition (Berlin: Bruno Cassirer, 1912-1922), and Ernst Cassirer's *Kants Leben un Lehre* (Berlin, 1921) (English translation by Haden James, *Kant's Life and Work* [New Haven: Yale University Press, 1983]).

12. The interpolation is based upon the course summary for the year 1975-1976, in *Dits et écrits*, vol 3, no. 187, pp. 124-130.

13. On Machiavelli, see the lecture of 1 February 1978 ("Governmentality") in the course of lectures given at the Collège de France on "Sécurité territoire et population en 1977-1978" (English translation: "Governmentality," in Graham Burchell, Colin Gordon, and Peter Miller, eds., *The Foucault Effect: Studies in Governmentality* [Hemel Hempstead: Harvester Wheatsheaf, 1991]); "Omnes et Singulatim: Towards a Critique of Political Reason" (1981), in *The Tanner Lectures on Human Values*, ed. Sterling M. McMurrin, vol. 2 (Salt Lake City: University of Utah Press and Cambridge: Cambridge University Press, 1981); "The Political Technology of Individuals" (1982), *Dits et écrits* vol. 3, no. 239, and vol. 4, no. 219, no. 364, in Luther H. Martin, Huck Gutman, and Patrick H. Hucton, eds., *Technologies of the Self: A Seminar with Michel Foucault* (London: Tavistock, 1988).

14. On Augustin Thierry, see note 8 above. For Amédée Thierry, see his *Histoires des Gaulois, depuis les temps les plus reculés jusqu'à l'entière soumission de la Gaule à la domination romaine* (Paris, 1828); *Histoire de la Gaule sous l'administration romaine* (Paris, 1840-1847).

four

28 JANUARY 1976

[
*Historical discourse and its supporters. ~ The counterhistory of
race struggle. ~ Roman history and biblical
history. ~ Revolutionary discourse. ~ Birth and transformations of
racism. ~ Race purity and State racism: the Nazi transformation
and the Soviet transformation.*
]

YOU MIGHT HAVE THOUGHT, last time, that I was trying to both
trace the history of racist discourse and praise it. And you would not
have been entirely wrong, except in one respect. It was not exactly
racist discourse whose history I was tracing and that I was praising:
it was the discourse of race war or race struggle. I think we should
reserve the expression "racism" or "racist discourse" for something
that was basically no more than a particular and localized episode in
the great discourse of race war or race struggle. Racist discourse was
really no more than an episode, a phase, the reversal, or at least the
reworking, at the end of the nineteenth century, of the discourse of
race war. It was a reworking of that old discourse, which at that point
was already hundreds of years old, in sociobiological terms, and it
was reworked for purposes of social conservatism and, at least in a
certain number of cases, colonial domination. Having said that to
situate both the link and the difference between racist discourse and
the discourse of race war, I was indeed praising the discourse of race
war. I was praising it in the sense that I wanted to show you how—at
least for a time, or in other words up to the end of the nineteenth

century, at which point it turned into a racist discourse—this discourse of race war functioned as a counterhistory. And today I would like to say something about its counterhistorical function.

It seems to me that we can say—perhaps somewhat hastily or schematically, but we would still be essentially correct—that historical discourse, the discourse of historians, or this practice of recounting history, was for a long time what it had no doubt been in antiquity and what it still was in the Middle Ages: for a long time, it remained related to the rituals of power. It seems to me that we can understand the discourse of the historian to be a sort of ceremony, oral or written, that must in reality produce both a justification of power and a reinforcement of that power. It also seems to me that the traditional function of history, from the first Roman annalists[1] until the late Middle Ages, and perhaps the seventeenth century or even later, was to speak the right of power and to intensify the luster of power. It had two roles. The point of recounting history, the history of kings, the mighty sovereigns and their victories (and, if need be, their temporary defeats) was to use the continuity of the law to establish a juridical link between those men and power, because power and its workings were a demonstration of the continuity of the law itself. History's other role was to use the almost unbearable intensity of the glory of power, its examples and its exploits, to fascinate men. The yoke of the law and the luster of glory appear to me to be the two things historical discourse strives to use to reinforce power. Like rituals, coronations, funerals, ceremonies, and legendary stories, history is an operator of power, an intensifier of power.

It seems to me that in the Middle Ages, the twofold function of historical discourse can be found on its three traditional axes. The genealogical axis spoke of the antiquity of kingdoms, brought great ancestors back to life, and rediscovered the heroes who founded empires and dynasties. The goal of this "genealogical" task was to ensure that the greatness of the events or men of the past could guarantee the value of the present, and transform its pettiness and mundanity into something equally heroic and equally legitimate. This genealogical axis of history—which we find mainly in forms of historical narratives

about ancient kingdoms and great ancestors—must proclaim right to
be something ancient; it must demonstrate the uninterrupted nature
of the right of the sovereign and, therefore, the ineradicable force that
he still possesses in the present day. Genealogy must, finally, also
magnify the name of kings and princes with all the fame that went
before them. Great kings found, then, the right of the sovereigns who
succeed them, and they transmit their luster to the pettiness of their
successors. We might call this the genealogical function of historical
narratives.

Then there is the memorialization function, which we find not in
stories of antiquity or in the resurrection of ancient kings and heroes,
but in the annals and chronicles that were kept day by day and year
by year throughout history itself. The annalists' practice of permanently recording history also serves to reinforce power. It too is a sort
of ritual of power; it shows that what sovereigns and kings do is never
pointless, futile, or petty, and never unworthy of being narrated.
Everything they do can be, and deserves to be, spoken of and must
be remembered in perpetuity, which means that the slightest deed or
action of a king can and must be turned into a dazzling action and
an exploit. At the same time, each of his decisions is inscribed in a
sort of law for his subjects and an obligation for his successors. History, then, makes things memorable and, by making them memorable,
inscribes deeds in a discourse that constrains and immobilizes minor
actions in monuments that will turn them to stone and render them,
so to speak, present forever. The third function of a history that intensifies power is to put examples into circulation. An example is a
living law or a resuscitated law; it makes it possible to judge the
present, and to make it submit to a stronger law. An example is, so
to speak, glory made law; it is the law functioning in the luster of a
name. It is because it associates the law and the luster with a name
that an example has the force of—and functions as—a sort of punctual
element that helps to reinforce power.

Binding and dazzling, subjugating, subjugating by imposing obligations and intensifying the luster of force: it seems to me that these
are, very schematically, the two functions that we find in the various

forms of history, as practiced both in Roman civilization and in the societies of the Middle Ages. Now, these two functions correspond very closely to two aspects of power, as represented in religions, rituals, and Roman legends, and more generally in Indo-European legends. In the Indo-European system of representing power,[2] power always has two aspects or two faces, and they are perpetually conjugated. On the one hand, the juridical aspect: power uses obligations, oaths, commitments, and the law to bind; on the other, power has a magical function, role, and efficacy: power dazzles, and power petrifies. Jupiter, that eminently divine representative of power, the preeminent god of the first function and the first order in the Indo-European tripartite system, is both the god who binds and the god who hurls thunderbolts. Well, I believe that history, as it still functioned in the Middle Ages, with its antiquarian research, its day-to-day chronicles, and its circulating collections of examples, was still this same representation of power. It is not simply an image of power, but also a way of reinvigorating it. History is the discourse of power, the discourse of the obligations power uses to subjugate; it is also the dazzling discourse that power uses to fascinate, terrorize, and immobilize. In a word, power both binds and immobilizes, and is both the founder and guarantor of order; and history is precisely the discourse that intensifies and makes more efficacious the twin functions that guarantee order. In general terms, we can therefore say that until a very late stage in our society, history was the history of sovereignty, or a history that was deployed in the dimension and function of sovereignty. It is a "Jupiterian" history. In that sense, there was still a direct continuity between the historical practice of the Middle Ages and the history of the Romans, history as recounted by the Romans, Livy's history[3] or that of the early annalists. This means that medieval historians never saw any difference, discontinuity, or break between Roman history and their own history, the history they were recounting. The continuity between the historical practice of the Middle Ages and that of Roman society runs deeper still to the extent that the historical narratives of the Romans, like those of the Middle Ages, had a certain political function. History was a ritual that reinforced sovereignty.

Although this is no more than a crude sketch, it does, I think, provide a starting point for our attempt to reconstruct and characterize what is specific about the new form of discourse that appeared precisely at the very end of the Middle Ages or, really, in the sixteenth and early seventeenth centuries. Historical discourse was no longer the discourse of sovereignty, or even race, but a discourse about races, about a confrontation between races, about the race struggle that goes on within nations and within laws. To that extent it is, I think, a history that is the complete antithesis of the history of sovereignty, as constituted up to that time. This is the first non-Roman or anti-Roman history that the West had ever known. Why is it anti-Roman and why is it a counterhistory, compared to the ritual of sovereignty I was telling you about a moment ago? For a number of reasons which we can easily identify. First, because in this history of races and of the permanent confrontation that goes on between races, beneath and through laws, we see the appearance, or rather the disappearance, of the implicit identification of people with monarch, and nation with sovereign, that the history of sovereignty—and sovereigns—had made apparent. Henceforth, in this new type of discourse and historical practice, sovereignty no longer binds everything together into a unity—which is of course the unity of the city, the nation, or the State. Sovereignty has a specific function. It does not bind; it enslaves. The postulate that the history of great men contains, a fortiori, the history of lesser men, or that the history of the strong is also the history of the weak, is replaced by a principle of heterogeneity: The history of some is not the history of others. It will be discovered, or at least asserted, that the history of the Saxons after their defeat at the Battle of Hastings is not the same as the history of the Normans who were the victors in that same battle. It will be learned that one man's victory is another man's defeat. The victory of the Franks and Clovis must also be read, conversely, as the defeat, enserfment, and enslavement of the Gallo-Romans. What looks like

right, law, or obligation from the point of view of power looks like
the abuse of power, violence, and exaction when it is seen from the
viewpoint of the new discourse, just as it does when we go over to
the other side. After all, the fact that the land is in the possession of
great feudal lords, and the fact that they are demanding all these taxes,
will look to the defeated populations like acts of violence, confiscations, pillage, and war taxes that are being levied through violence.
As a result, the great form of the general obligation, whose form was
intensified by a history that magnified the glory of the sovereign, is
undone, and the law comes to be seen as a Janus-faced reality: the
triumph of some means the submission of others.

In that sense, the history that appears at this point, or the history
of the race struggle, is a counterhistory. But I think it is also a counterhistory in a different and more important sense. Not only does this
counterhistory break up the unity of the sovereign law that imposes
obligations; it also breaks the continuity of glory, into the bargain. It
reveals that the light—the famous dazzling effect of power—is not
something that petrifies, solidifies, and immobilizes the entire social
body, and thus keeps it in order; it is in fact a divisive light that
illuminates one side of the social body but leaves the other side in
shadow or casts it into the darkness. And the history or counterhistory that is born of the story of the race struggle will of course speak
from the side that is in darkness, from within the shadows. It will be
the discourse of those who have no glory, or of those who have lost
it and who now find themselves, perhaps for a time—but probably
for a long time—in darkness and silence. Which means that this discourse—unlike the uninterrupted ode in which power perpetuated
itself, and grew stronger by displaying its antiquity and its genealogy—will be a disruptive speech, an appeal: "We do not have any
continuity behind us; we do not have behind us the great and glorious
genealogy in which the law and power flaunt themselves in their
power and their glory. We came out of the shadows, we had no glory
and we had no rights, and that is why we are beginning to speak and
to tell of our history." This way of speaking related this type of discourse not so much to the search for the great uninterrupted juris-

prudence of a long-established power, as to a sort of prophetic rupture. This also means that this new discourse is similar to a certain number of epic, religious, or mythical forms which, rather than telling of the untarnished and uneclipsed glory of the sovereign, endeavor to formulate the misfortune of ancestors, exiles, and servitude. It will enumerate not so much victories, as the defeats to which we have to submit during our long wait for the promised land and the fulfillment of the old promises that will of course reestablish both the rights of old and the glory that has been lost.

With this new discourse of race struggle, we see the emergence of something that, basically, is much closer to the mythico-religious discourse of the Jews than to the politico-legendary history of the Romans. We are much closer to the Bible than to Livy, in a Hebraic-biblical form much more than in the form of the annalist who records, day by day, the history and the uninterrupted glory of power. I think that, in general terms, it must not be forgotten that, at least from the second half of the Middle Ages onward, the Bible was the great form for the articulation of religious, moral, and political protests against the power of kings and the despotism of the church. Like the reference to biblical texts itself, this form functioned, in most cases, as a protest, a critique, and an oppositional discourse. In the Middle Ages, Jerusalem was always a protest against all the Babylons that had come back to life; it was a protest against eternal Rome, against the Rome of the Caesars, against the Rome that shed the blood of the innocent in the circus. The Bible was the weapon of poverty and insurrection; it was the word that made men rise up against the law and against glory, against the unjust law of kings and the beautiful glory of the Church. To that extent, it is not surprising that we see, at the end of the Middle Ages, in the sixteenth century, in the period of the Reformation, and at the time of the English Revolution, the appearance of a form of history that is a direct challenge to the history of sovereignty and kings—to Roman history—and that we see a new history that is articulated around the great biblical form of prophecy and promise.

The historical discourse that appears at this point can therefore be regarded as a counterhistory that challenges Roman history for this reason: in this new historical discourse, the function of memory acquires a whole new meaning. In Roman-style history, the function of memory was essentially to ensure that nothing was forgotten—or in other words, to preserve the law and perpetually to enhance the luster of power for so long as it endured. The new history that now emerges, in contrast, has to disinter something that has been hidden, and which has been hidden not only because it has been neglected, but because it has been carefully, deliberately, and wickedly misrepresented. Basically, what the new history is trying to show is that power, the mighty, the kings, and the laws have concealed the fact that they were born of the contingency and injustice of battles. After all, William the Conqueror did not want to be called "the conqueror," for he wanted to conceal the fact that the rights he exercised, or the violence he was inflicting on England, were the rights of conquest. He wanted to be seen as the legitimate dynastic successor and therefore hid the name of "conqueror," just as Clovis, after all, wandered around with a parchment in his hand to make people believe that he owed his royalty to the fact that he had been recognized as king by some Roman Caesar or other. These unjust and biased kings tried to make it look as though they were acting on behalf of all and in the name of all; they certainly wanted people to talk of their victories, but they did not want it to be known that their victories were someone else's defeats: "It was our defeat." The role of history will, then, be to show that laws deceive, that kings wear masks, that power creates illusions, and that historians tell lies. This will not, then, be a history of continuity, but a history of the deciphering, the detection of the secret, of the outwitting of the ruse, and of the reappropriation of a knowledge that has been distorted or buried. It will decipher a truth that has been sealed.

I think, finally, that this history of the race struggle that appears in the sixteenth and seventeenth centuries is a counterhistory in a different sense too. It is a counterhistory in a simpler or more elementary sense, but also in a stronger sense. The point is that, far from being a ritual inherent in the exercise, deployment, and reinforcement

Counterhistory

of power, it is not only a critique of power, but also an attack on it and a demand. Power is unjust not because it has forfeited its noblest examples, but quite simply because it does not belong to us. In one sense, it can be said that this new history, like the old, is indeed an attempt to speak of a right that survives the vicissitudes of time. But its goal is not to establish the great, long jurisprudence of a power that has always retained its rights, or to demonstrate that power is where it is, and that it has always been where it is now. It is to demand rights that have not been recognized, or in other words, to declare war by declaring rights. Historical discourse of the Roman type pacifies society, justifies power, and founds the order—or the order of the three orders—that constitutes the social body. In contrast, the discourse I am telling you about, and which is deployed in the late sixteenth century, and which can be described as a biblical-style historical discourse, tears society apart and speaks of legitimate rights solely in order to declare war on laws.

I would like to sum all this up by advancing a sort of hypothesis. Can we not say that until the end of the Middle Ages and perhaps beyond that point, we had a history—a historical discourse and practice—that was one of the great discursive rituals of sovereignty, of a sovereignty that both revealed and constituted itself through history as a unitary sovereignty that was legitimate, uninterrupted, and dazzling. Another history now begins to challenge it: the counterhistory of dark servitude and forfeiture. This is the counterhistory of prophecy and promise, the counterhistory of the secret knowledge that has to be rediscovered and deciphered. This, finally, is the counterhistory of the twin and simultaneous declaration of war and of rights. Roman-style history was basically profoundly inscribed within the Indo-European system of representing power, and of power's workings; it was certainly bound up with the organization of the three orders, at whose pinnacle stood the order of sovereignty, and it therefore remained bound up with a certain domain of objects and certain types of figures—with legends about heroes and kings—because it was the discourse of a Janus-faced sovereignty that was at once magical and juridical. This history, based on a Roman model and Indo-European

functions, now finds itself being constrained by a biblical, almost He-
braic, history which, ever since the end of the Middle Ages, has been
the discourse of rebellion and prophecy, of knowledge and of the call
for the violent overthrow of the order of things. Unlike the historical
discourse of Indo-European societies, this new discourse is no longer
bound up with a ternary order, but with a binary perception and
division of society and men; them and us, the unjust and the just, the
masters and those who must obey them, the rich and the poor, the
mighty and those who have to work in order to live, those who invade
lands and those who tremble before them, the despots and the groan-
ing people, the men of today's law and those of the homeland of the
future.

It was in the middle of the Middle Ages that Petrarch asked what
I see as a fairly astonishing or at least fundamental question. He asked:
"Is there nothing more to history than the praise of Rome?"[4] I think
that in asking this question, he characterized in a word what had
always been the actual practice of history, not only in Roman society,
but also in the medieval society to which Petrarch himself belonged.
A few centuries after Petrarch, the West saw the appearance or birth
of a history that contained the very opposite of the praise of Rome.
This was, by contrast, a history that sought to unmask Rome as a new
Babylon, and which challenged Rome by demanding the lost rights
of Jerusalem. A very different form of history and a historical discourse with a very different function had come into being. One might
say that this history is the beginning of the end of Indo-European
historicity, by which I mean the end of a certain Indo-European mode
of talking about and perceiving history. Ultimately, we might say that
antiquity ended with the birth of the great historical discourse on
race war—and by antiquity I mean that awareness of being in continuity with antiquity that existed until the late Middle Ages. The
Middle Ages was, obviously, unaware of being the Middle Ages. But
it was also unaware, so to speak, that it was not, or was no longer,
antiquity. Rome was still present, and functioned as a sort of permanent and contemporary historical presence in the Middle Ages.
Rome was perceived as having been divided into a thousand channels

that flowed through Europe, but all these channels led, it was believed, back to Rome. It must not be forgotten that all the national
(or prenational) political histories that were being written at this
time always took as their starting point a certain Trojan myth. All
the nations of Europe claimed to have been born of the fall of Troy.
Being born of the fall of Troy meant that all the nations, all the States,
and all the monarchies of Europe could claim to be Rome's sisters.
The French monarchy, for instance, was supposed to be descended
from Francus, and the English monarchy from a certain Brutus. All
these great dynasties claimed the sons of Priam as their ancestors, and
that guaranteed a link of genealogical kinship with ancient Rome. As
late as the fifteenth century, a sultan of Constantinople could write
to the doge of Venice: "But why should we wage war on one another,
when we are brothers? It is well known that the Turks were born
of, or emerged from, the burning of Troy, and that they too are descended from Priam." It was, he said, well known that the Turks were
descended from Turcus, who, like Aeneas and Francus, was the son
of Priam. Rome is, then, present within the historical consciousness
of the Middle Ages, and there is no break between Rome and the
countless kingdoms that we see appearing from the fifth and sixth
centuries onward.

Now what the discourse of race struggle will reveal is precisely the
kind of break that will relegate to a different world something that
will come to look like an antiquity: we have a new awareness of a
break that had not previously been recognized. The European consciousness begins to notice events that had previously been no more
than minor incidents which had basically not damaged the great unity,
the great strength, the great legitimacy, and the great, dazzling
strength of Rome. It begins to notice the events which will [then]
constitute Europe's real beginnings, its bloody beginnings. It began
with conquest, with the Frankish invasion and the Norman invasion.
Something that will be specifically individualized as "the Middle
Ages" begins to appear [and it will be only in the early eighteenth
century that historical consciousness will isolate this phenomenon and
call it feudalism]. New characters appear: the Franks, the Gauls, and

the Celts; more general characters such as the peoples of the North and the peoples of the South also begin to appear; rulers and subordinates, the victors and the vanquished begin to appear. It is they who now enter the theater of historical discourse and who now constitute its primary reference. Europe becomes populated by memories and ancestors whose genealogy it had never before written. A very different historical consciousness emerges and is formulated through this discourse on the race struggle and the call for its revival. To that extent, we can identify the appearance of discourses on race war with a very different organization of time in Europe's consciousness, practice, and even its politics. Having established that, I would to make a certain number of comments.

First, I would like to stress the fact that it would be a mistake to regard this discourse on race struggle as belonging, rightfully and completely, to the oppressed, or to say that it was, at least originally, the discourse of the enslaved, the discourse of the people, or a history that was claimed and spoken by the people. It should in fact be immediately obvious that it is a discourse that has a great ability to circulate, a great aptitude for metamorphosis, or a sort of strategic polyvalence. It is true that we see it taking shape, at least initially perhaps, in the eschatological themes or myths that developed together with the popular movements of the second half of the Middle Ages. But it has to be noted that we very quickly—immediately—find it in the form of historical scholarship, popular fiction, and cosmobiological speculations. For a long time it was an oppositional discourse; circulating very quickly from one oppositional group to another, it was a critical instrument to be used in the struggle against a form of power, but it was shared by different enemies or different forms of opposition to that power. We see it being used, in various forms, by radical English thought at the time of the seventeenth-century revolution. A few years later, we see the French aristocratic reaction using it against the power of Louis XIV, and it has scarcely been transformed at all. In the early nineteenth century, it was obviously bound up with the postrevolutionary project of at last writing a history whose real subject is the people.[5] But a few years later, we can see it being used to disqualify colonized subraces. This is, then, a mobile discourse, a polyvalent discourse. Although its origins lie in the Middle Ages, it is not so marked by them that it can have only one political meaning.

Second comment: Although this discourse speaks of races, and although the term "race" appears at a very early stage, it is quite obvious that the word "race" itself is not pinned to a stable biological meaning. And yet the word is not completely free-floating. Ultimately, it designates a certain historico-political divide. It is no doubt wide, but it is relatively stable. One might say—and this discourse does say—that two races exist whenever one writes the history of two groups which do not, at least to begin with, have the same language or, in many cases, the same religion. The two groups form a unity and a single polity only as a result of wars, invasions, victories, and defeats, or in other words, acts of violence. The only link between them is the link established by the violence of war. And finally, we can say that two races exist when there are two groups which, although they coexist, have not become mixed because of the differences, dissymmetries, and barriers created by privileges, customs and rights, the distribution of wealth, or the way in which power is exercised.

Third comment: We can, therefore, recognize that historical discourse has two great morphologies, two main centers, and two political functions. On the one hand, the Roman history of sovereignty; on the other, the biblical history of servitude and exiles. I do not think that the difference between these two histories is precisely the same as the difference between an official discourse and, let us say, a rustic* discourse, or a discourse that is so conditioned by political imperatives that it is incapable of producing a knowledge. This history, which set itself the task of deciphering power's secrets and demystifying it, did in fact produce at least as much knowledge as the history that tried to reconstruct the great uninterrupted jurisprudence of power. I think that we might even go so far as to say that it

---

*The manuscript has "scholarly" and "naive."

removed a lot of obstacles, and that the fertile moments in the constitution of historical knowledge in Europe can, roughly, be situated at the moment when the history of sovereignty suddenly intruded upon the history of the race war. In the early seventeenth century in England, for instance, the discourse that told of invasions and of the great injustices done to the Saxons by the Normans intruded upon all the historical work that the monarchist jurists were undertaking in order to recount the uninterrupted history of the power of the kings of England. It was the intersection between these two historical practices that led to the explosion of a whole field of knowledge. Similarly, when at the end of the seventeenth century and the beginning of the eighteenth, the French nobility began to write its genealogy not in the form of a continuity but in the form of the privileges it once enjoyed, which it then lost and which it wanted to win back, all the historical research that was being done on that axis intruded upon the historiography of the French monarchy instituted by Louis XIV, and there was once more a considerable expansion of historical knowledge. For similar reasons, there was another fertile moment at the beginning of the nineteenth century, when the history of the people, of its servitude and its enslavement, the history of the Gauls and the Franks, of the peasants and the Third Estate, intruded upon the juridical history of regimes. So the clash between the history of sovereignty and the history of the race war leads to a perpetual interaction, and to the production of fields of knowledge and of knowledge-contents.

Final remark: As a result of—or despite—this interaction, the revolutionary discourse of seventeenth-century England, and that of nineteenth-century France and Europe, was on the side of—I almost said biblical history—on the side of history-as-demand, of history-as-insurrection. The idea of revolution, which runs through the entire political workings of the West and the entire history of the West for more than two hundred years, and whose origins and content are still, as it happens, very enigmatic, cannot, in my view, be dissociated from the emergence and existence of this practice of counterhistory. After all, what could the revolutionary project and the revolutionary idea possibly mean without this preliminary interpretation of the dissymmetries, the disequilibriums, the injustice, and the violence that function despite the order of laws, beneath the order of laws, and through and because of the order of laws? Where would the revolutionary project, the revolutionary idea, or revolutionary practice be without the will to rekindle the real war that once went on and which is still going on, even though the function of the silent order of power is to mask and smother it, and even though it is in its interest to do so? Where would revolutionary practice, revolutionary discourse, and the revolutionary project be without the will to reactivate that war thanks to a specific historical knowledge? What would they become, if that knowledge were not used as an instrument in the war—that war—as a tactical element in the real war that is being waged? What would the revolutionary project and revolutionary discourse mean if the goal were not a certain, a final, inversion of relations of power and a decisive displacement within the exercise of power?

The interpretation of dissymmetries, the rekindling of a war, the reactivation of the war—there is more than this to the revolutionary discourse that has constantly undermined Europe since at least the end of the nineteenth century, but it is still an important strand within it, and it was shaped, defined, established, and organized in the great counterhistory that began to speak of the race struggle at the end of the Middle Ages. After all, it should not be forgotten that toward the end of his life, Marx told Engels in a letter written in 1882 that "You know very well where we found our idea of class struggle; we found it in the work of the French historians who talked about the race struggle."[6] The history of the revolutionary project and of revolutionary practice is, I think, indissociable from the counterhistory that broke with the Indo-European form of historical practices, which were bound up with the exercise of sovereignty; it is indissociable from the appearance of the counterhistory of races and of the role played in the West by clashes between races. We might, in a word, say that at the end of the Middle Ages, in the sixteenth and seventeenth centuries, we left, or began to leave, a society whose historical consciousness was still of the Roman type, or which was still centered on the rituals of sovereignty and its myths, and that we then entered a society of—let's say it is of the modern type (given that there is no other word for it and that the word "modern" is devoid of meaning)—a society whose historical consciousness centers not on sovereignty and the problem of its foundation, but on revolution, its promises, and its prophecies of future emancipation.

I think this provides us with a starting point for understanding how and why historical discourse could become a new issue in the mid-nineteenth century. At the time when this discourse [...] was being displaced, translated, or converted into a revolutionary discourse, at the time when the notion of race struggle was about to be replaced by that of class struggle—and in fact, when I say "the mid-nineteenth century," that's too late; it was in the first half of the nineteenth century, as it was [Thiers][7] who transformed race struggle into class struggle—at the time when this conversion was going on, it was in fact only natural that attempts should be made by one side to recode the old counterhistory not in terms of class, but in terms of races—races in the biological and medical sense of that term. And it was at the moment when a counterhistory of the revolutionary type was taking shape that another counterhistory began to take shape—but it will be a counterhistory in the sense that it adopts a biologico-medical perspective and crushes the historical dimension that was present in this discourse. You thus see the appearance of what will become actual racism. This racism takes over and reconverts the form and function of the discourse on race struggle, but it distorts them, and it will be characterized by the fact that the theme of historical war—with its battles, its invasions, its looting, its victories, and its defeats—will be replaced by the postevolutionist theme of the struggle for existence. It is no longer a battle in the sense that a warrior would understand the term, but a struggle in the biological sense: the differentiation of species, natural selection, and the survival of the fittest species. Similarly, the theme of the binary society which is divided into two races or two groups with different languages, laws, and so on will be replaced by that of a society that is, in contrast, biologically monist. Its only problem is this: it is threatened by a certain number of heterogeneous elements which are not essential to it, which do not divide the social body, or the living body of society, into two parts, and which are in a sense accidental. Hence the idea that foreigners have infiltrated this society, the theme of the deviants who are this society's by-products. The theme of the counterhistory of races was, finally, that the State was necessarily unjust. It is now inverted into its opposite: the State is no longer an instrument that one race uses against another: the State is, and must be, the protector of the integrity, the superiority, and the purity of the race. The idea of racial purity, with all its monistic, Statist, and biological implications: that is what replaces the idea of race struggle.

I think that racism is born at the point when the theme of racial purity replaces that of race struggle, and when counterhistory begins to be converted into a biological racism. The connection between racism and antirevolutionary discourse and politics in the West is not, then, accidental; it is not simply an additional ideological edifice that appears at a given moment in a sort of grand antirevolutionary project. At the moment when the discourse of race struggle was being transformed into revolutionary discourse, racism was revolutionary thought. Although they had their roots in the discourse of race struggle, the revolutionary project and revolutionary propheticism now began to take a very different direction. Racism is, quite literally, revolutionary discourse in an inverted form. Alternatively, we could put it this way: Whereas the discourse of races, of the struggle between races, was a weapon to be used against the historico-political discourse of Roman sovereignty, the discourse of race (in the singular) was a way of turning that weapon against those who had forged it, of using it to preserve the sovereignty of the State, a sovereignty whose luster and vigor were no longer guaranteed by magico-juridical rituals, but by medico-normalizing techniques. Thanks to the shift from law to norm, from races in the plural to race in the singular, from the emancipatory project to a concern with purity, sovereignty was able to invest or take over the discourse of race struggle and reutilize it for its own strategy. State sovereignty thus becomes the imperative to protect the race. It becomes both an alternative to and a way of blocking the call for revolution that derived from the old discourse of struggles, interpretations, demands, and promises.

I would like, finally, to make one more point. The racism that came into being as a transformation of and an alternative to revolutionary discourse, or the old discourse of race struggle, underwent two further transformations in the twentieth century. At the end of the nineteenth century, we see the appearance of what might be called a State racism, of a biological and centralized racism. And it was this theme that was, if not profoundly modified, at least transformed and utilized in strategies specific to the twentieth century. On the one hand, we have the Nazi transformation, which takes up the theme, established at the end of the nineteenth century, of a State racism that is responsible for the biological protection of the race. This theme is, however, reworked and converted, in a sort of regressive mode, in such a way that it is implanted in and functions within the very prophetic discourse from which the theme of race struggle once emerged. Nazism was thus able to reuse a whole popular, almost medieval, mythology that allowed State racism to function within an ideologico-mythical landscape similar to that of the popular struggles which, at a given moment, could support and make it possible to formulate the theme of race struggle. In the Nazi period, State racism would be accompanied by a whole set of elements and connotations such as, for example, the struggle of a Germanic race which had, temporarily, been enslaved by the European powers, the Slavs, the Treaty of Versailles, and so on—which Germany had always regarded as its provisional victors. It was also accompanied by the theme of the return of the hero, or heroes (the reawakening of Frederick, and of all the nation's other guides and Führers; the theme of the revival of an ancestral war; that of the advent of a new *Reich*, of the empire of the last days which will ensure the millenarian victory of the race, but which also means that the inevitable apocalypse and the inevitable last days are nigh. We have then a Nazi reinscription or reinsertion of State racism in the legend of warring races.

In contrast to the Nazi transformation, you have a Soviet-style transformation which consists in doing, so to speak, just the opposite. This is not a dramatic or theatrical transformation, but a surreptitious transformation. It does not use the dramaturgy of legends, and it is diffusely "scientific." It consists in reworking the revolutionary discourse of social struggles—the very discourse that derived so many of its elements from the old discourse of the race struggle—and articulating it with the management and the policing that ensure the hygiene of an orderly society. In Soviet State racism, what revolutionary discourse designated as the class enemy becomes a sort of biological threat. So, who is the class enemy now? Well, it's the sick, the deviant, the madman. As a result, the weapon that was once used in the struggle against the class enemy (the weapon of war, or possibly the dialectic and conviction) is now wielded by a medical police which eliminates class enemies as though they were racial enemies. We have then, on the one hand, the Nazi reinscription of State racism in the old legend of warring classes, and on the other, the Soviet reinscription of the class struggle within the silent mechanisms of a State racism. And the hoarse songs of the races that clashed in battles over the lies of laws and kings, and which were after all the earliest form of revolutionary discourse, become the administrative prose of a State that defends itself in the name of a social heritage that has to be kept pure.

So, the glory and the infamy of the discourse of races in struggle. What I have been trying to show you is that this is discourse that definitively detached us from a historico-juridical consciousness centered on sovereignty, and introduced us into a form of history, a form of time that can be both dreamed of and known, both dreamed of and understood, and in which the question of power can no longer be dissociated from that of servitude, liberation, and emancipation. Petrarch asked if there was anything more to history than the praise of Rome. And we ask—and this is no doubt typical of our historical consciousness and is no doubt bound up with the appearance of this counterhistory: "Is there anything more to history than the call for revolution, and the fear of revolution?" And let me simply add this question: "And what if Rome once more conquered the revolution?"

So after these digressions, I will try, beginning next time, to take another look at certain aspects of the history of the discourse on races from the seventeenth century to the early nineteenth and then the twentieth centuries.

1. For Roman writers before Livy, the word "annals" referred to the ancient histories they consulted. Annals are a primitive form of history in which events are related year by year. The *Annales Maximi* drawn up by the Great Pontiff were published in eighty books at the beginning of the second century B.C.

2. Foucault is obviously referring to the work of Georges Dumézil, and particularly to *Mitra-Varuna: Essai sur deux représentations indo-européennes de la souveraineté* (Paris: Gallimard, 1940) (English translation by Derek Coleman: *Mirta-Varuna: An Essay on Two Indo-European Representations of Sovereignty* [New York: Zone Books, 1988]); *Mythe et Épopée* (Paris: Gallimard), vol. 1: *L'Idéologie des trois fonctions dans les épopées des peuples indo-européens*, 1968; vol. 2 : *Types épiques indo-européens: un héros, un sorcier, un roi*, 1971; vol. 3: *Histoires romaines*, 1973.

3. Titus Livius, *Ab Urbe condita libri* (books 1-9, 21-45, and half of the fifth decade have survived).

4. "Quid est enim aliud omnis historia quam romana laus" ("History was nothing but the praise of Rome"). Petrarch, *Invectiva contra eum qui aledixit Italia* (1373). It should be pointed out that Petrarch's words are cited by Erwin Panofsky in his *Renaissance and Renascences in Western Art* (London: Paladin, 1970), p. 10 (first edition, Stockholm: Almqvist & Wiksell, 1960; French translation: *La Renaissance et ses avant-coureurs dans l'art d'Occident* [Paris: Flammarion, 1976], p. 26).

5. From Mignet and the authors Foucault mentions in subsequent lectures to Michelet.

6. The actual reference should in fact be to the letter on 5 March 1852, in which Marx writes to J. Weydemeyer: "Finally, in your place I should in general remark to the democratic gentlemen that they would do better first to acquaint themselves with bourgeois literature before they presume to yap at the opponents of it. For instance, these gentlemen should study the historical works of Thierry, Guizot, John Wade, and others in order to enlighten themselves as to the past 'history of classes.'" In Karl Marx and Friedrich Engels, *Selected Correspondence*, 2d ed. (Moscow: Progress Publishers, 1965), p. 68 (German original: *Karl Marx-Friedrich Engels Gesamtausgabe, Dritte abteilung, Briefwechsel* [Berlin: Diez, 1987], bd. 5, p. 75; French translation: K. Marx and F. Engels, *Correspondance* [Paris: Éditions sociales, 1959], vol. 3, p. 79). Cf. Marx's letter of 27 July 1854 to Engels, where Thierry is defined as "the father of the 'class struggle,'" *Selected Correspondence*, p. 87 (*Gesuamtausgabe*, bd. 7, 1989, p. 130; *Correspondance*, vol. 4, 1975, pp. 148-52). In the manuscript and obviously quoting from memory, M. Foucault writes: "In 1882, Marx again said to Engels: 'The history of the revolutionary project and of revolutionary practice is indissociable from this counterhistory of races, and the role it played in political struggles in the West.'"

7. See in particular A. Thiers, *Histoire de la Révolution française*, 10 vols. (Paris, 1823-1827); *Histoire du Consulat et de l'Empire*, 20 vols. (Paris, 1845-1862).

five

4 FEBRUARY 1976

[*Answer to a question on anti-Semitism. ~ Hobbes on war and*
sovereignty. ~ The discourse on the Conquest in England:
royalists, parliamentarians, and Levellers. ~ The binary schema
and political historicism. ~ What Hobbes wanted to eliminate.]

OVER THE LAST WEEK or two, a certain number of questions and
objections, some written and some oral, have been addressed to me.
I would be quite happy to discuss these with you, but it is difficult
in this space and this climate. In any case, you can come and see me
in my office after the lecture if you have questions to ask me. But
there is one question I would like to try to answer, first because I
have been asked it several times and second because I thought I had
already answered it in advance, but I have to conclude that my ex-
planations were not sufficiently clear. I have been asked: "What does
it mean to say that racism takes off in the sixteenth or seventeenth
century, and to relate racism solely to the problems of the State and
sovereignty, when it is well known that, after all, religious racism
(and religious anti-Semitism in particular) had been in existence
since the Middle Ages?" I would therefore like to go over something
I obviously did not explain adequately or clearly.

I was certainly not trying for one moment to trace the history of
racism in the general and traditional sense of the term. I do not want

to trace the history of what it might have meant, in the West, to have an awareness of belonging to a race, or of the history of the rites and mechanisms that were used to try to exclude, disqualify, or physically destroy a race. I was—and in my own view, I am—trying to look at the emergence in the West of a certain analysis (a critical, historical, and political analysis) of the State, its institutions and its power mechanisms. This analysis was made in binary terms: The social body is not made up of a pyramid of orders or of a hierarchy, and it does not constitute a coherent and unitary organism. It is composed of two groups, and they are not only quite distinct, but also in conflict. And the conflictual relationship that exists between the two groups that constitute the social body and shapes the State is in fact one of war, of permanent warfare. The State is nothing more than the way that the war between the two groups in question continues to be waged in apparently peaceful forms. Having established that, I would like to show how an analysis of this type is obviously articulated with revolutionary hopes, an urgent call for rebellion, and also a politics of rebellion or revolution. That, and not racism, is my basic problem.

It seems to me that there are reasonable historical grounds for saying that this way of making a political analysis of power relations (which are seen as relations of war between two races that coexist within a single society) does not, or at least not in the first instance, have anything to do with the religious problem. You will find that this analysis was actually formulated, or was being formulated, at the end of the sixteenth century and the beginning of the seventeenth. In other words, the divide, the perception of the war between races predates the notions of social struggle or class struggle, but it certainly cannot be identified with a racism of, if you like, the religious type. It is true that I haven't talked about anti-Semitism. I intended to say a bit about it last time, when I was discussing this theme of the race struggle in very general terms, but I did not have time. What I think we can say—but I will come back to this later—is this: Insofar as it is a religious and racial attitude, anti-Semitism had so little influence on the history I was trying to trace for you that it does not have to be taken into account until we reach the nineteenth century. The old religious-type anti-Semitism was reutilized by State racism only in the nineteenth century, or at the point when the State had to look like, function, and present itself as the guarantor of the integrity and purity of the race, and had to defend it against the race or races that were infiltrating it, introducing harmful elements into its body, and which therefore had to be driven out for both political and biological reasons. It is at this point that anti-Semitism develops, picking up, using, and taking from the old form of anti-Semitism all the energy—and a whole mythology—which had until then been devoted solely to the political analysis of the internal war, or the social war. At this point the Jews came to be seen as—and were described as—a race that was present within all races, and whose biologically dangerous character necessitated a certain number of mechanisms of rejection and exclusion on the part of the State. It is therefore, I think, the reutilization within State racism of an anti-Semitism which had developed for other reasons that generated the nineteenth-century phenomena of superimposing the old mechanisms of anti-Semitism on this critical and political analysis of the struggle between races within a single society. That is why I did not raise either the problem of religious racism or the problem of anti-Semitism in the Middle Ages. I will, on the other hand, try to talk about them when I come to the nineteenth century. As I have already said, I am ready to answer more specific questions.

Today I would like to try to look at how war began to emerge as an analyzer of power relations at the end of the sixteenth and the beginning of the seventeenth century. There is, of course, one name that we immediately encounter: it is that of Hobbes, who does, at first glance, appear to be the man who said that war is both the basis of power relations and the principle that explains them. According to Hobbes, it is not just *a* war that we find behind order, behind peace, and beneath the law. It is not *a* war that presides over the birth of the great automaton which constitutes the State, the sovereign, or Leviathan. It is the most general of all wars, and it goes on at all times and in every dimension: "the war of every man against every man."[1] Hobbes does not simply claim that this war of every man against every man gives birth to the State on the morning—which is both real and fictional—on which Leviathan is born. It goes on even when the State has been constituted, and Hobbes sees it as a threat that wells up in the State's interstices, at its limits and on its frontiers. You will recall the three examples of permanent warfare that he cites. He says first that when, even in a civil state, a man takes a journey, he locks his doors, because he knows that thieves are permanently at war with those they rob.[2] He then gives another example: in the forests of America, there are still savage people who live in a condition of war against one another.[3] And even in our States of Europe, what are relations between States, if not those of two men "having their weapons pointed, and their eyes fixed on one another"?[4] So even when the State has been established, the threat of war is there: there is a war in any case. Hence the problem: First, what is this war that exists before the State, and which the State is, in theory, destined to end? What is this war that the State has pushed back into prehistory, into savagery, into its mysterious frontiers, but which is still going on? And second, how does this war give birth to the State? What effect does the fact that it was born of war have on the constitution of the State? What stigmata does war leave on the body of the State once it has been established? These are the two questions I would like [to consider] briefly.

What, then, is this war, the war that Hobbes describes both as going on before the State is established and as leading to its consti-tution? Is it a war that is being waged by the strong against the weak, by the violent against the timorous, by the brave against cowards, by the great against the common people, or by arrogant savages against timorous shepherds? Is it a war that is articulated around unmediated and natural differences? You know that this is not at all the case in Hobbes. The primitive war, the war of every man against every man, is born of equality and takes place in the element of that equality. War is the immediate effect of nondifferences, or at least of insufficient differences. Hobbes in fact says that if there were great differences, if there really were obvious visible disparities between men, it is quite obvious that the war would immediately come to an end. If there were marked, visible, or great natural differences, then one of two things would happen; either there really would be a clash between the strong and the weak—and that clash or that real war would immediately end with the victory of the strong over the weak, and their victory would be definitive precisely because of the strength of the strong; or there would be no real clash because, being aware of, seeing and noting their own weakness, the weak would surrender even before the confrontation began. If, says Hobbes, marked natural differences did exist, there would therefore be no war because either the relationship of force would be established from the outset by an initial war that precluded the possibility of its continuation; or that relationship of force would remain virtual, precisely because the weak are timorous. If, then, there were a difference, there would be no war. Differences lead to peace.[5] And what happens in a state of nondifference or insufficient difference—in a state in which we can say that differences do exist, but that they are creeping, ephemeral, minute, unstable, without order, and without distinction? What happens in this anarchy of minor differences that characterizes the state of nature? Even a man who is a little weaker than other men, than the other man, is sufficiently similar to the strongest man to realize that he is strong enough not to have to surrender. So the weak man never gives up. As for the strong man, he is never strong enough not to be worried and, therefore, not to be constantly on his guard. The absence of natural differences therefore creates uncertainties, risks, hazards, and, therefore, the will to fight on both sides; it is the aleatory element in the primal relationship of force that creates the state of war.

But what exactly is this state of war? Even the weak man knows—or at least thinks—that he is not far from being as strong as his neighbor. And so he does not abandon all thought of war. But the stronger man—or at least the man who is a little stronger than the others—knows, despite it all, that he may be weaker than the other, especially if the other uses wiles, surprise, or an alliance. So the weak man will not abandon all thought of war, and the other—the stronger man—will, despite his strength, try to avoid it. Now a man who wishes to avoid war can do so on only one condition: he must show that he is ready to wage war, and is not prepared to abandon all thought of war. And how can he demonstrate that he is not ready to abandon all thought of war? Well, [by acting] in such a way that the other, who is on the point of waging war, begins to doubt his own strength and therefore abandons the idea; and the other man will abandon all thought of war only to the extent that he knows that the first man is not prepared to abandon the idea. So in the type of relations that are set in motion by these minute differences and these aleatory confrontations where the outcome is uncertain, what does the relationship of force consist of? Three series of elements are in play from the outset. First, calculated presentations: my presentation of the strength, of the other, my presentation of the other's presentation of my strength, and so on. Second, emphatic and pronounced expressions of will: you make it obvious that you want war, you demonstrate that you will not abandon the idea of war. Third, you use mutually intimidatory tactics: I am so afraid of waging war that I will feel safe only if you are at least as afraid of war as I—and, insofar as that is possible, more afraid of it than I. Which means, all in all, that the state Hobbes is describing is not at all a brutish state of nature in which forces clash directly with one another. In Hobbes's state of primitive war, the encounter, the confrontation, the clash, is not one between weapons or fists, or between savage forces that have been unleashed. There are no battles in Hobbes's primitive war, there is no blood and there are no corpses. There are presentations, manifestations, signs, emphatic expressions, wiles, and deceitful expressions; there are traps, intentions disguised as their opposite, and worries disguised as certainties. We are in a theater where presentations are exchanged, in a relationship of fear in which there are no time limits; we are not really involved in a war. Which means, ultimately, that the state of bestial savagery in which living individuals devour one another can in no way be the primary characteristic of Hobbes's state of war. What does characterize the state of war is a sort of unending diplomacy between rivals who are naturally equal. We are not at war; we are in what Hobbes specifically calls a state of war. There is a text in which he states: "Warre consisteth not in Battel onely, or in the act of fighting; but in a tract of time, wherein the Will to contend by Battel is sufficiently known."[6] The tract of time designates, then, the state and not the battle, and what is at stake is not the forces themselves, but the will, a will that is sufficiently known, or in other words [endowed with] a system of representations and manifestations that is effective within this field of primal diplomacy.

We can therefore see how and why this state—and it is not a battle or a direct clash of forces, but a certain state of the interplay of representations—is not a stage that man will abandon forever once the State is born; it is in fact a sort of permanent backdrop which cannot not function, with its elaborate wiles and its complex calculations, once there is nothing to provide security, to establish differences, and finally to give the strength to one side and not the other. So, for Hobbes, it does not all begin with war.

But how does this state, which is not a state of war but a play of presentations that allows us, precisely, to avoid war, give birth to the State—with a capital S—to Leviathan and to sovereignty? Hobbes answers this second question by making a distinction between two categories of sovereignty: sovereignty by institution and sovereignty by acquisition.[7] A great deal has been said about sovereignty by institution, and Hobbes's analysis of sovereignty is usually reduced to that. Things are in fact more complicated than that. You have a commonwealth by institution and a commonwealth by acquisition, and two forms of sovereignty within the latter. In all, we therefore have States by institution, States by acquisition, and the three types or forms of sovereignty that shape those forms of power. Let us first look at commonwealths by institution, which are the most familiar; it won't take long. What is it that [happens] in the state of war that puts an end to that state of war in which, I repeat, it is not war but the representation and threat of war that are in play? Well, men make decisions. But what decisions? Not simply to transfer part of their rights or their powers to someone—or to several people. They do not even decide, basically, to transfer their rights. On the contrary, they decide to grant someone—or an assembly made up of several people— the right to represent them, fully and completely. This is not a relationship in which something belonging to individuals is surrendered or delegated; it is a representation of those individuals that is surrendered or delegated. The sovereign who is so constituted will therefore be equivalent to all those individuals. He will not simply have part of their rights; he will actually take their place, and the whole of their power. As Hobbes puts it, they appoint him "to beare their person."[8] And provided that this displacement does take place, the individuals who are presented in this way are present in their representatives; and whatever their representative—or in other words, the sovereign—does, they must do. Insofar as he represents individuals, the sovereign is an exact model of those very individuals. The sovereign is therefore an artificial individuality, but also a real individuality. The fact that this sovereign is a naturally individual monarch does not alter the fact that he is an artificial sovereign; and when an assembly is involved, the sovereign remains an individuality, even though a group of individuals is involved. So much for commonwealths by institution. As you can see, this mechanism consists solely of the interplay between a will, a covenant, and representation.

Let us now look at the other way in which commonwealths can be established, at what else can happen to this or that commonwealth. Let's look at the mechanism of acquisition.[9] This is apparently something very different, even the very opposite. In the case of commonwealths by acquisition, it seems that we are dealing with a commonwealth that is founded on relations of force that are at once real, historical, and immediate. If we are to understand this mechanism we have to postulate the existence of not a primitive state of war, but a real battle. Take a State that has already been constituted in accordance with the model I have just described, the model of institution. Let us suppose that this State is attacked by another in a war, with real battles and decisions that are taken by force of arms. Let us suppose that one of the States that has been constituted in this way is defeated by the other: its army is defeated and scattered, and its sovereignty is destroyed; the enemy occupies its land. We are now involved in what we were looking for from the start, or in other words, a real war, with a real battle and a real relationship of force.

There are winners and losers, and the losers are at the mercy of
the winners, at their disposal. Let us now look at what happens: the
vanquished are at the disposal of the victors. In other words, the
victors can kill them. If they kill them, the problem obviously goes
away: the sovereignty of the State disappears simply because the individuals who make up that State are dead. But what happens if the
victors spare the lives of the vanquished? If they spare their lives, or
if the defeated are granted the temporary privilege of life, one of two
things may happen. Either they will rebel against the victors, or in
other words begin a new war and try to overthrow the relation of
forces, which takes us back to the real war that their defeat had, at
least for a time, interrupted; either they risk their lives, or do not
begin a new war and agree to work for and obey the others, to surrender their land to the victors, to pay them taxes. Here we obviously
have a relationship of domination based entirely upon war and the
prolongation, during peacetime, of the effects of war. Domination, you
say, and not sovereignty. But Hobbes does not say that: he says we
are still in a relationship of sovereignty. Why? Because once the defeated have shown a preference for life and obedience, they make their
victors their representatives and restore a sovereign to replace the one
who was killed in the war. It is therefore not the defeat that leads to
the brutal and illegal establishment of a society based upon domination, slavery, and servitude; it is what happens during the defeat,
or even after the battle, even after the defeat, and in a way, independently of it. It is fear, the renunciation of fear, and the renunciation
of the risk of death. It is this that introduces us into the order of
sovereignty and into a juridical regime: that of absolute power. The
will to prefer life to death: that is what founds sovereignty, and it is
as juridical and legitimate as the sovereignty that was established
through the mode of institution and mutual agreement.

Strangely enough, Hobbes adds a third form of sovereignty to these
forms—by acquisition and institution—and states that it is very similar to the institution by acquisition that appears after the end of the
war, and after the defeat. This type of sovereignty is, he says, the type
that binds a child to its parents or, more specifically, its mother.[10]

Take, he says, a newborn child. Its parents (its father in a civil society, or its mother in the state of nature) could simply allow it to die, or quite simply have it put to death. It cannot, in any case, live without its parents, without its mother. And for years the child will, quite spontaneously and without having to express its will other than through manifestations of its needs, its cries, its fear, and so on, obey its parents, and do exactly what it is told to do because its life depends upon her and her alone. She will enjoy sovereignty over it. Now Hobbes says that there is no essential difference between the way a child consents to its mother's sovereignty in order to preserve its own life (which does not even involve an express consent or a contract) and the way the defeated give their consent when the battle is over. What Hobbes is trying to demonstrate is that the decisive factor in the establishment of sovereignty is not the quality of the will, or even its form or level of expression. Basically, it does not matter if we have a knife to our throats, or if what we want is explicitly formulated or not. For sovereignty to exist, there must be— and this is all there must be—a certain radical will that makes us want to live, even though we cannot do so unless the other is willing to let us live.

Sovereignty is, therefore, constituted on the basis of a radical form of will, but it counts for little. That will is bound up with fear, and sovereignty is never shaped from above, or in other words, on the basis of a decision taken by the strong, the victor or the parents. Sovereignty is always shaped from below, and by those who are afraid. Despite the apparent differences between the two great forms of commonwealth (a commonwealth of institution born of mutual agreement, and a commonwealth of acquisition born of a battle), the mechanisms at work are at bottom identical. No matter whether we are talking about a covenant, a battle, or relations between parents and children, we always find the same series: will, fear, and sovereignty. It is irrelevant whether the series is triggered by an implicit calculation, a relationship of violence, or a fact of nature; it is irrelevant whether it is fear—the knife at our throats, the weeping of a child—that gives rise to a never-ending diplomacy. Sovereignty will be constituted in any case. Basically, it is as though, far from being the theorist of the relationship between war and political power, Hobbes wanted to eliminate the historical reality of war, as though he wanted to eliminate the genesis of sovereignty. A large part of the discourse of *Leviathan* consists in saying: It doesn't matter whether you fought or did not fight, whether you were beaten or not; in any case, the mechanism that applies to you who have been defeated is the same mechanism that we find in the state of nature, in the constitution of a State, and that we also find, quite naturally, in the most tender and natural relationship of all: that between parents and children. Hobbes turns war, the fact of war and the relationship of force that is actually manifested in the battle, into something that has nothing to do with the constitution of sovereignty. The establishment of sovereignty has nothing to do with war. Basically, Hobbes's discourse is a certain "no" to war. It is not really war that gives birth to States, and it is not really war that is transcribed in relations of sovereignty or that reproduces within the civil power—and its inequalities—the earlier dissymmetries in the relationship of force that were revealed by the very fact of the battle itself.

Hence the problem: To whom, to what, is this elimination of war addressed, given that no previous theory of power had given war the role that Hobbes so stubbornly denies it? Basically, what adversary is Hobbes addressing when, in whole sections—in a whole stratum, a whole line of it—of his discourse he obstinately repeats: But in any case, it does not matter whether there was a war or not; the constitution of sovereignties has nothing to do with war. I think that what Hobbes's discourse is addressing is not, if you like, a specific or determinate theory, or something that could be defined as his adversary, his partner in polemic; nor is it something that could be defined as the unspoken, unavoidable problem in Hobbes's discourse, which Hobbes is doing all he can to try to avoid. At the time when Hobbes was writing, there was in fact something that could be described not as his partner in polemic, but as his strategic opposite number. In other words, not so much a certain discursive content that had to be refuted, as a certain theoretical and political strategy that Hobbes specifically wanted to eliminate and render impossible. What Hobbes is trying, then, not to refute, but to eliminate and render impossible—his strategic opposite number—is a certain way of making historical knowledge work within the political struggle. To be more specific, Leviathan's strategic opposite number is, I think, the political use that was being made in political struggles of a certain historical knowledge pertaining to wars, invasions, pillage, dispossessions, confiscations, robbery, exaction, and the effects of all that, the effects of all these acts of war, all these feats of battle, and the real struggles that go on in the laws and institutions that apparently regulate power.

In a word, what Hobbes wants to eliminate is the Conquest, and also the use that was being made, in both historical discourse and political practice, of the problem of the Conquest. Leviathan's invisible adversary is the Conquest. That enormous artificial man who made all the right-thinking men of the law and philosophers tremble so, that enormous silhouette in the frontispiece to *Leviathan*, which represents the king with his sword raised and with crosier in his other hand, was basically a right-thinking man. And that is basically why even the philosophers who were so critical of him really loved him, and why even the most timorous are enchanted by his cynicism. Although it seems to be proclaiming that war is everywhere from start to finish, Hobbes's discourse is in fact saying quite the opposite. It is saying, war or no war, defeat or no defeat, Conquest or covenant, it all comes down to the same thing: "It's what you wanted, it is you, the subjects, who constituted the sovereignty that represents you." The problem of the Conquest is therefore resolved. At one level, it is resolved by the notion of the war of every man against every man; at another, it is resolved by the wishes—the legally valid will—expressed by the frightened losers when the battle was over. I think, then, that Hobbes may well seem to shock, but he is in fact being reassuring: he always speaks the discourse of contracts and sovereignty, or in other words, the discourse of the State. After all, philosophy and right, or philosophico-juridical discourse, would rather give the State too much power than not enough power, and while they do criticize

Hobbes for giving the State too much power, they are secretly grateful
to him for having warded off a certain insidious and barbarous enemy.

The enemy—or rather the enemy discourse Hobbes is addressing—
is the discourse that could be heard in the civil struggles that were
tearing the State apart in England at this time. It was a discourse that
spoke with two voices. One was saying: "We are the conquerors and
you are the vanquished. We may well be foreigners, but you are servants." To which the other voice replied: "We may well have been
conquered, but we will not remain conquered. This is our land, and
you will leave it." It is this discourse of struggle and permanent civil
war that Hobbes wards off by making all wars and conquests depend
upon a contract, and by thus rescuing the theory of the State. And
that is of course why the philosophy of right subsequently rewarded
Hobbes with the senatorial title of "the father of political philosophy."
When the State capitol was in danger, a goose woke up the sleeping
philosophers. It was Hobbes.

Hobbes devotes whole sections of *Leviathan* to attacking a discourse
(or rather a practice) which seems to me to have appeared—if not
for the first time, at least with its essential dimensions and its political
virulence—in England. This is presumably the result of a combination
of two phenomena. First, of course, the precocity of the bourgeoisie's
political struggle against the absolute monarchy on the one hand and
the aristocracy on the other. And then there is another phenomenon:
the sharp awareness—even among the broad popular masses—that the
Conquest had produced a long-standing division, and that it was a
historical fact.

The presence of William's Norman Conquest, which began at Hastings in 1066, had manifested itself and continued to do so in many
different ways, in both institutions and the historical experience of
political subjects in England. It manifested itself quite explicitly in
the rituals of power as, until Henry VII, or in other words, until the
early sixteenth century, royal acts specifically stated that the king of
England exercised his sovereignty by right of conquest. They described him as an heir to to the Normans' right of conquest. That

formula died with Henry VII. The presence of the Conquest also manifested itself in the practice of the law, as procedures and proceedings took place in French, as did disputes between the lower courts and the royal courts. Formulated from on high and in a foreign language, the law was the stigmata of the foreign presence, the mark of another nation. In legal practice, right was formulated in a foreign language, and what I would call the "linguistic sufferings" of those who could not legally defend themselves in their own language were compounded by the fact that the law looked foreign. The practice of the law was inaccessible in two senses. Hence the demand that appears so early in medieval England: "We want a law of our own, a law that is formulated in our language, that is united from below, on the basis of common law, as opposed to royal statutes." The Conquest also manifested itself in—I am taking things somewhat at random—the presence of, the superimposition of, and the conflict between two heterogeneous sets of legends. On the one hand, we have a set of Saxon stories, which were basically popular tales, mythical beliefs (the return of King Harold), the cult of saintly kings (like King Edward), and popular tales of the Robin Hood type (and you know that Walter Scott—one of the great inspirations behind Marx[11]—drew on this mythology for *Ivanhoe*[12] and a number of other novels which were of great historical importance for the historical consciousness of the nineteenth century). In addition to this mythological-popular set, we also find a set of aristocratic and quasi-monarchical legends that grew up around the Normans and which were reactivated in the sixteenth century, or at the time when Tudor absolutism was developing. They are mainly about the legend of the Arthurian cycle.[13] This is obviously not exactly a Norman legend, but it is a non-Saxon legend. The Normans reactivated the old Celtic legends that lay beneath the Saxon stratum of the population. These Celtic legends could be quite naturally reactivated by the Normans and used to the advantage of the Norman aristocracy and monarchy because of the multiple relations that existed between the Normans and the Bretons in their country of origin—and in Brittany. So we have two powerful mythological sets that allowed England to dream of its past and its history in two completely different ways.

What is much more important than all this is that, in England, a whole historical memory of rebellions, each of which had specific political effects, signaled the presence and the effects of the Conquest. Certain of these rebellions, such as Monmouth's Rebellion, which was the first, were no doubt racial in nature.[14] Others (like the rebellion that ended with the signing of the Magna Carta) placed checks on royal power and introduced specific measures to expel foreigners (most of whom were, as it happens, Poitevins and Angevins rather than Normans). What was at stake was the right of the English people, and that right was bound up with the need to expel foreigners. There was, then, a whole series of elements that allowed major social oppositions to be coded in the historical form of one race's conquest and domination of the other. This coding, or at least the elements that made it possible, was very old. Even in the Middle Ages, we find phrases like this in the chronicles: "The nobles of this country are descended from the Normans; men of lowly condition are the sons of Saxons."[15] Because of the elements I have just enumerated, conflicts— political, economic, and juridical—could, in other words, easily be articulated, coded, and transformed into a discourse, into discourses, about different races. And when at the end of the sixteenth century and the beginning of the seventeenth, there appeared new political forms of struggle between the bourgeoisie on the one hand and the aristocracy and the monarchy on the other, it was, logically enough, the vocabulary of race struggle that was used to describe [these con- flicts]. This type of coding, or at least the elements that were available for this coding, came into play quite naturally. I say "coding" because the theory of races did not function as a particular thesis about one group versus another. The racial divide and the systematic opposition between races were in fact a sort of instrument, both discursive and political, that allowed both sides to formulate their own theses. In seventeenth-century England, juridico-political discussions of the rights of the people and the rights of the sovereign used the kind of

vocabulary [generated] by the event of the Conquest, or the relationship that gave one race dominion over the other, and of the vanquished's rebellion—or the permanent threat of rebellion—against the
victors. And so you will find the theory of races, or the theme of
races, in the positions of both royal absolutism and the parliamentarians or parliamentarists, and in the more extreme positions of the
Levellers and the Diggers.

An effective formulation of the primacy of conquest and domination can be found in what I would call, in a word, "the discourse of
the king." When James I told the Star Chamber that kings sat on the
throne of God,[16] he was obviously referring to the theologico-political
theory of divine right. But in his view, his divine election—which
effectively meant that he owned England—had been prophesied and
guaranteed by the Norman victory. And when he was still only king
of Scotland, James I said that because the Normans had taken possession of England, the laws of the kingdom were established by
them.[17] This had two implications. First, it implied that England had
been taken into possession, and that all English lands belonged to the
Normans and the leader of the Normans, or in other words, the king.
It was insofar as he was the leader of the Normans that the king was
effectively the owner or proprietor of the land of England. Second, it
implied that the different populations over which sovereignty was
exercised did not enjoy the same right; right was the very mark of
Norman sovereignty. It was established by the Normans and, of
course, for their benefit. And with a cunning that caused his adversaries considerable embarrassment, the king, or at least those who
spoke the discourse of the king, used a very strange but very important analogy. I think it was Blackwood who first formulated it in
1581, in a text entitled *Apologia pro regibus*. What he says is very curious. "The situation of England at the time of the Norman Conquest
must in fact be understood in the same way that we now understand
America's situation vis-a-vis what had yet to be called the colonial
powers. The Normans acted in England as people from Europe are
now acting in America." Blackwood drew a parallel between William
the Conqueror and Charles V. He said of Charles V: "He subdued a

part of the West Indies by force, he left the defeated to hold their property not by emancipation, but in usufruct and subject to certain obligations. Well, what Charles V did in America—and we regard it as perfectly legitimate as we are doing the same thing—is what the Normans are doing in England, make no mistake about it. The Normans are in England by the same right that we are in America, that is, by the right of colonization."[18]

At the end of the sixteenth century we have, then, if not the first, at least an early example of the sort of boomerang effect colonial practice can have on the juridico-political structures of the West. It should never be forgotten that while colonization, with its techniques and its political and juridical weapons, obviously transported European models to other continents, it also had a considerable boomerang effect on the mechanisms of power in the West, and on the apparatuses, institutions, and techniques of power. A whole series of colonial models was brought back to the West, and the result was that the West could practice something resembling colonization, or an internal colonialism, on itself.

That is how the theme of race conflict functioned in the discourse of the king. And the same theme of the Norman Conquest articulates the answer the parliamentarians gave when they challenged the discourse of the king. The way in which the parliamentarians refuted the claims of royal absolutism was also articulated around this racial dualism and the fact of the Conquest. The analysis put forward by the parliamentarians and parliamentalists begins, paradoxically, by disavowing the Conquest, or rather by wrapping the Conquest up in a eulogy to William the Conqueror and his legitimacy. They said: Make no mistake about it—and here you can see how close we are to Hobbes—Hastings, the battle, the war itself, none of that is important. Basically, William was indeed the legitimate king. And he was the legitimate king quite simply because (and at this point they exhumed a number of historical facts, some true and some false) Harold—even before the death of Edward the Confessor, who had indeed designated William as his successor—had sworn that he would not become king of England, but would surrender the throne or agree to let William ascend the throne of England. That could not have happened in any case: given that Harold died at the Battle of Hastings, there was no legitimate successor—assuming Harold to have been legitimate—and the crown therefore naturally reverted to William. And so it transpired that William was not the conqueror of England. He inherited rights, not rights of conquest, but the rights of the existing kingdom of England. He was heir to a kingdom that was bound by a certain number of laws—and also heir to a sovereignty that was restricted by the laws of the Saxon regime. Which means, according to this analysis, that the very things that made William's monarchy legitimate also restricted its power.

Besides, add the parliamentarians, if the Conquest had taken place and if the Battle of Hastings had established a relation of pure domination between Normans and Saxons, the Conquest could not have lasted. How do you expect—they say—a few tens of thousands of wretched Normans, lost in the lands of England, to have survived, and to have established and actually maintained a permanent power? They would simply have been murdered in their beds the night after the battle. Now, at least in the early stages, there were no major rebellions, which basically proves that the vanquished did not really regard themselves as having been vanquished and occupied by the victors; they effectively recognized the Normans as people who could exercise power. And that recognition, those nonmassacres of the Normans and this nonrebellion, validated William's monarchy. William, for his part, had sworn an oath and had been crowned by the archbishop of York: he had been given the crown, and in the course of that ceremony he had sworn to respect the laws which the chroniclers described as good and ancient laws that were accepted and approved. William made himself part of the system of the Saxon monarchy that existed before him.

In a text entitled *Argumentum anti-Normannicum*, which is representative of this thesis, we find a frontispiece that provides a parallel with the frontispiece to *Leviathan*.[19] It depicts in strip format a battle, two bodies of armed men (obviously the Normans and the Saxons at Hastings) and, between the two, the corpse of King Harold: so the legitimate monarchy of Saxons is indeed a thing of the past. Above this, a scene, in larger format, depicts William being crowned. But the coronation is staged in this way: A statue called Britannia is handing William a piece of paper on which we can read "The excellent and most famous Laws of St Edward." King William is receiving his crown from the archbishop of York while another ecclesiastic is handing him a paper on which we see the words "Coronation Oath."[20] This is a way of showing that William is not really the conqueror he claimed to be, but the legitimate heir, an heir whose sovereignty is restricted by the laws of England, the recognition given him by the church, and the oath he has sworn. Winston Churchill—the seventeenth-century one—wrote in 1675 that William did not conquer England: it was the English who conquered William.[21] And it was, according to the parliamentarians, only after the transfer of Saxon power to the Norman king—a perfectly legitimate transfer—that the Conquest really began, or in other words, that all the dispossessions, exactions, and abuses of the law began. The Conquest was the long process of usurpation that began after the coming of the Normans, and it took the organized form of what was at this very time known as "Normanism" or the "Norman yoke,"[22] or in other words, a political regime that was systematically dissymmetric and systematically in favor of the Norman monarchy and aristocracy. And all the rebellions of the Middle Ages were directed against Normanism, not against William. When the lower courts insisted on enforcing the "common law" in the face of royal statutes, they were enforcing the rights of Parliament, which was the true heir to the Saxon tradition, and resisting the abuses of power committed by the Norman monarchy and the "Normanism" that had developed after Hastings and the coming of William. The contemporary struggle, that of the seventeenth century, was also an ongoing struggle against Normanism.

Now what was this old Saxon right, which as we have seen was accepted, both de jure and de facto, by William and which, as we have also seen, the Normans attempted to smother or pervert in the years following the Conquest? The Magna Carta, the establishment of Parliament, and the revolution of the seventeenth century were all attempts to reestablish Saxon right. What was it? Well, it was a set of Saxon laws. The major influence here was a jurist called Coke, who claimed to have discovered—and who actually had discovered—a thirteenth-century manuscript that he claimed was a treatise on the old Saxon laws.[23] It was in reality entitled *The Mirrors of Justice*, and it was an account of a certain number of practices of jurisprudence, and of public and private law in the Middle Ages.[24] Coke made it function as a treatise on Saxon right. Saxon right was described as being both the primal and the historically authentic—hence the importance of the manuscript—right of the Saxon people, who elected their leaders, had their own judges,* and recognized the power of the king only in time of war; he was recognized as a wartime leader, and not as a king who exercised an absolute and unchecked sovereignty over the social body. Saxon right was, then, a historical figure, and attempts were made—through research into the ancient history of right—to establish it in a historically accurate form. But at the same time, this Saxon right appeared to be, and was described as, the very expression of human reason in a state of nature. Jurists such as Selden, for example, pointed out that it was a wonderful right and very close to human reason because in civil terms it was more or less similar to that of Athens, and in military terms, more or less similar to that of Sparta.[25] As for the content of its religious and moral laws, the Saxon State was said to have been similar to the laws of Moses, Athens, and Sparta, but the Saxon State was of course the perfect State. In a text published in 1647, we read that "Thus the Saxons became somewhat like the Jewes, divers from all other people; their laws honourable for the King, easie for the subject; and their government above all other likest unto that of Christ's Kingdome, whose yoke is easie, and burthen light."[26] As you can see, the historicism that was being used to challenge the absolutism of the Stuarts tips over into a foundational utopia in which the theory of natural rights merged into a positive historical model and the dream of a sort of kingdom of God. And this utopia of Saxon right, which had supposedly been

---

*The manuscript has "were their own judges."

recognized by the Norman monarchy, was meant to provide the juridical basis for the new republic that the parliamentarians wished to establish.

You will encounter the fact of the Conquest for a third time, this time in the radical position of those who were most opposed not only to the monarchy but even to the parliamentarians, or in other words, in the more petit bourgeois—or more popular, if you like—discourse of the Levellers, the Diggers, and so on. But this time it is only in extreme cases that historicism tips over into the sort of utopia of natural rights I was talking about a moment ago. With the Levellers we find an almost literal version of the very thesis of royal absolutism itself. What the Levellers will say is this: "The monarchy is perfectly right to say that the invasion, defeat, and Conquest did take place. It's true, the Conquest did take place, and that has to be our starting point. But the absolute monarchy interprets the fact that the Conquest took place as providing a legitimate basis for its right. We, on the other hand, interpret the fact that the Conquest did take place, and that the Saxons really were defeated by the Normans, as meaning that the defeat marked, not the beginnings of right—absolute right— but of a state of nonright that invalidates all the laws and social differences that distinguish the aristocracy, the property regime, and so on." All the laws that function in England must be regarded as tricks, traps, and wickedness—this is John Warr's text *The Corruption and Deficiency of the Laws of England*.[27] The laws are traps: they do nothing at all to restrict power. They are the instruments of power. They are not means of guaranteeing the reign of justice, but ways of promoting vested interests. The first objective of the revolution must therefore be the suppression of all post-Norman laws to the extent that, either directly or indirectly, they impose the "Norman yoke." Laws, said Lilburne, are made by conquerors.[28] The entire legal apparatus must therefore be done away with.

Second, we must also do away with all the differences that set the aristocracy—and not just the aristocracy, but the aristocracy and the king, who is a member of the aristocracy—apart from the rest of the people, because the relationship between the nobles and the king, and the people, is not one of protection, but simply one of plunder and theft. Lilburne said that William and his successors "made Dukes, Earles, Barrons and Lords of their fellow Robbers, Rogues and Thieves."[29] It follows that today's property regime is still the wartime regime of occupation, confiscation, and pillage. All property relations—like the entire legal system—must therefore be looked at again, from top to bottom. Property relations are completely invalidated by the fact of the Conquest.

Third, we have—say the Diggers—proof that the government, the laws, and property statutes are, basically, no more than a continuation of the war, the invasion, and the defeat, because the people have always seen governments, laws, and property relations as effects of the Conquest. The people have in a sense never ceased to denounce property as pillage, laws as exactions, and governments as domination. The proof is that they have never stopped rebelling—and for the Diggers, rebellion is nothing but the obverse of the permanent war. Laws, power, and government are the obverse of war. Laws, power, and government are the obverse of the war they are waging against us. Rebellion is therefore not the destruction of a peaceful system of laws for some reason. Rebellion is a response to a war that the government never stops waging. Government means their war against us; rebellion is our war against them. Previous rebellions have, of course, been unsuccessful—not only because the Normans won, but because the rich benefited from the Norman system and treacherously supported "Normanism." The rich became traitors, and the church became a traitor. And even those elements that the parliamentarians claimed would restrict Norman right—even the Magna Carta, Parliament, and the practice of the courts—are all basically part of the Norman system of exactions. The only difference is that part of the population now helps to run it: the most privileged and rich section of the population has betrayed the Saxon cause and gone over to the Norman side. The apparent concessions were in fact no more than acts of treachery and ruses of war. Far from agreeing with the parliamentarians that laws should be established to prevent royal absolutism from prevailing against the law, the Diggers therefore say that a war declared in response to that war must free us from all laws. The civil war against Norman power has to be fought to the end.

From this point onward, the discourse of the Levellers will develop along several very different lines, few of which were very sophisticated. One was the truly theological-radical line which said, rather like the parliamentarians: Bring back the Saxon laws: they are our laws, and they are fair because they are also the laws of nature. And then we see the emergence of another form of discourse, which is rarely spelled out in so many words, and which says: The Norman regime is a regime of pillage and exaction, and it is the outcome of a war, and what do we find beneath that regime? In historical terms, we find Saxon laws. But weren't the Saxon laws themselves the outcome of a war, a form of pillage and exaction? Ultimately, wasn't the Saxon regime itself a regime of domination, just like the Norman regime? And shouldn't we therefore go further still—this is the argument we find in certain Digger tracts[30]—and say that any form of power leads to domination, or in other words, that there are no historical forms of power, whatever they may be, that cannot be analyzed in terms of the dominion of some over others? This formulation obviously remains implicit. We find it being used as a final argument, and it never really gives rise to either a historical analysis or a coherent political practice. Yet the fact remains that you see here the first formulation of the idea that any law, whatever it may be, every form of sovereignty, whatever it may be, and any type of power, whatever it may be, has to be analyzed not in terms of natural right and the establishment of sovereignty, but in terms of the unending movement—which has no historical end—of the shifting relations that make some dominant over others.

The reason I have dwelt so long on this English discourse about the race war is that I think we see here a binary schema, a certain binary schema; and for the first time, it functions in both a political and a historical mode, both as a program for political action and as a search for historical knowledge. A schematic dichotomy between rich and poor no doubt already existed, and it divided perceptions of society in the Middle Ages, just as it did in the Greek polis. But this is the first time a binary schema became something more than a way of articulating a grievance or a demand, or of signaling a danger. This was the first time that the binary schema that divided society into two was articulated with national phemonema such as language, country of origin, ancestral customs, the density of a common past, the existence of an archaic right, and the rediscovery of old laws. This was a binary schema that also made it possible to interpret a whole number of institutions, and their evolution over a long period of history. It also made it possible to analyze contemporary institutions in terms of confrontation and in terms of a race war which was being waged both knowingly and hypocritically, but also violently. This is, finally, a binary schema which justifies rebellion not simply on the ground that the situation of the most wretched has become intolerable and that they have to rebel because they cannot make their voices heard (which was, if you like, the discourse of medieval rebellion). Here, now, we have a call for rebellion being formulated as a sort of absolute right: we have a right to rebel not because we have not been able to make our voices heard, or because the prevailing order has to be destroyed if we wish to establish a fairer system of justice. The justification for rebellion now becomes a sort of historical necessity. It is a response to a certain social order. The social order is a war, and rebellion is the last episode that will put an end to it.

The logical and historical need for rebellion is therefore inscribed within a whole historical analysis that reveals war to be a permanent feature of social relations. War is both the web and the secret of institutions and systems of power. And I think that this is Hobbes's great adversary. Whole sections of *Leviathan* are addressed to the opponents of any philosophico-juridical discourse that founds the sovereignty of the State. The reason why he wants so much to eliminate war is that he wanted, in a very specific and meticulous way, to eliminate the terrible problem of the Conquest of England, that painful historical category, that difficult juridical category. He had to get around the problem of the Conquest, which was central to all the political discourses and programs of the first half of the seventeenth century. That is what he had to eliminate. In more general terms, and in the longer term, what had to be eliminated was what I would call "political historicism," or the type of discourse that we see emerging from the discussions I have been talking about, that is being formulated in certain of its most radical phases, and which consists in saying: Once we begin to talk about power relations, we are not talking about right, and we are not talking about sovereignty; we are talking about domination, about an infinitely dense and multiple domination that never comes to an end. There is no escape from domination, and there is therefore no escape from history. Hobbes's philosophico-juridical discourse was a way of blocking this political historicism, which was the discourse and the knowledge that was actually active in the political struggles of the seventeenth century. Hobbes was trying to block it, just as the dialectical materialism of the nineteenth century blocked the discourse of political historicism. Political historicism encountered two obstacles. In the seventeenth century, philosophico-juridical discourse was the obstacle that tried to disqualify it; in the nineteenth century, it was dialectical materialism. Hobbes's operation consisted in exploiting every possibility—even the most extreme philosophico-juridical discourse—to silence the discourse of political historicism. Well, next time I would like to both trace the history of this discourse of political historicism and praise it.

1. "During the time men live without a common Power to keep them all in awe, they are in that condition which is called Warre; and such a warre, as is of every man, against every man." Thomas Hobbes, *Leviathan*, ed. Richard Tuck (Cambridge: Cambridge University Press, 1991), p. 88. On the *bellum omnium contra omnes*, see also Hobbes's *Elementorum philosophiae secto tertia de cive* (Paris, 1642) (French translation: *Le citoyen, ou les fondements de la politique* [Paris: Flammarion, 1982]).

2. Hobbes, *Leviathan*, p. 89.

3. Ibid., pp. 89-90.

4. Ibid., p. 90.

5. Ibid., pp. 89-90.

6. Ibid., p. 88.

7. Throughout the following discussion, Foucault refers to chapters 17-20 of part 2 of *Leviathan* ("Of Common-wealth").

8. Ibid., p. 120.

9. Ibid., chapter 20.

10. Ibid.; cf. *De Cive*, II, ix.

11. On Marx's reading of Scott, see Eleanor Marx-Aveling, "Karl Marx: lose Blutter," in *Osterreichische Arbeiter-Kalander fur das Jahr 1895*, pp. 51-54 (English translation: "Stray Notes on Karl Marx," in *Reminiscences of Marx and Engels* [Moscow: Foreign Languages Publishing House, n.d.]); F. Mehring, *Karl Marx: Geschichte seines Lebens* (Leipzig: Leipziger Buchbdruckerei Actiengesellschaft, 1918), vol. 15 (French translation: *Karl Marx, Histoire de sa vie* [Paris: Éditions sociales, 1983]; English translation: *Karl Marx: The Story of His Life*, tr. Edward Fitzgerald [London: Allen and Unwin, 1936]); I. Berlin, *Karl Marx* (London: Butterworth, 1939), chap. 11.

12. The action of *Ivanhoe* (1819) is set in the England of Richard the Lion-Hearted; the France of Louis XI provides the backdrop for *Quentin Durward* (1823). *Ivanhoe* is known to have influenced A. Thierry and his theory of conquerors and conquered.

13. The reference is to the cycle of legendary traditions and stories centered on the mythical figure of the British sovereign Arthur, who led the Saxon resistance during the first half of the fifth century. These traditions and legends were first collected in the twelfth century by Geoffrey of Monmouth in his *De origine et gestis regum Britanniae libri XII* (Heidelberg, 1687) and then by Robert Wace in *Le Roman de Brut* (1115) and the *Roman de Rou* (1160-1174). This is the so-called Breton material that was reworked by Chrétien de Troyes in *Lancelot* and *Perceval* in the second half of the twelfth century.

14. Geoffrey of Monmouth's account of the history of the British nation begins with the first conqueror, the Trojan Brutus. It traces British history from the Roman conquests to the British resistance against the Saxon invaders and the decline of the Saxon kingdom. This was one of the most popular works of the Middle Ages, and introduced the Arthurian legend into European literature.

15. In the manuscript, Foucault adds "Chronicle of Gloucester."

16. "Monarchae proprie sunt judices, quibus juris dicendi potestam proprie commisit Deus. Nam in throno Dei sedent, unde omnis ea facultas derivata est." James I, *Oratio habita in camera stellata* [1616], in *Opera edita a Jacabo Montacuta* (Francoforti ad Moenum et Lipsiae, 1689), p. 253. "Nihil est in terris quod non sit infra Monarchiae fastigium. Nec enim solum Dei Vicari sunt Reges, deique throno insident: sed ipso Deo Deorum nominea honorantur." *Oratori habita in comitis regni ad omenes ordines in palatio albaulae* [1690], in *Opera edita*, p. 245. On the "Divine Right of Kings," cf. *Basilikon doron, sive De institutione principis*, in *Opera edita*, pp. 63-85.

17. "Et quamquam in aliis regionibus ingentes regii sanguinis factae sint mutationes, sceptri jure ad novos Dominos jure belli translato; eadem tamen illic cernitur in terram et subditos potestatis regiae vis, quae apud nos, qui cominos numquam mutavimus. Quum

spurius ille Normandicus calidissimo cum exercitu in Angliam transiisset, quo, obsecro nisi armorum et belli jure Rex factus est? At ille leges dedit, non accepit, et vetus jus, et consuetudinem regni antiquavit, et avitis possessionibus eversis homines novos et peregrinos imposuit, suae militiae comites; quemadmodum hodie pleraque Angliae nobilitas Normannicam prae se fert originem; et legis Normandicus scriptae idiomatem facilel trastantur auctorem, nihilomonis poesteri ejus sceptrum illud hactenus faciliter tenerunt. Nec hoc soli Normanno licuit: idem jus omnibus fuit, qui ante illum victa Angliae ges dederunt." James I, *Jus liberae Monarchiae, sive De mutuis Regis liberi et populi nascendi conditione illi subditit officiis* [1598], in *Opera edita*, p. 69.

18. "Carolus quintus imperator nostra memoria partem quandam occidentalium insularum, veteribus ignotam, nobis Americae vocabulo non ita pridem auditam, vi subegit, victis sua reliquit, non macipio, sed usu, nec eo quidem perpetuo, nec gratuito, ac immuni (quod Anglis obtigit Wilielmi nothi beneficio) sed in vitae tempus prestationi certa lege locationis obligata." A. Blackwood, *Adversus Georgii Buchanani dialogum, de jure regni apud Scotus, pro regibus apologia, Pictavis, apud Pagaeum* (1581), p. 69.

19. *Argumentum anti-Normannicum, or an Argument proving, from ancient histories and records, that William, Duke of Normandy made no absolute conquest of England by the word, in the sense of our modern writers* (London, 1682). This work had been wrongly attributed to Coke.

20. For the illustration of the frontispiece see "An Explanation of the Frontispiece" in *Argumentum anti-Normannicum*, pp. 4 ff.

21. W. S. Churchill, *Divi Britannici, being a remark upon the lives of all the Kings of this Isle, from the year of the world 2855 unto the year of grace 1660* (London, 1675), fols. 189-190.

22. The theory of the "Norman yoke" (or "Norman bondage") had been popularized in the sixteenth and seventeenth centuries by political writers (Blackwood, et cetera), by the "Elizabethan Chroniclers" (Holinshed, Speed, Daniel, et cetera), by the Society of Antiquarians (Selden, Harrison, and Nowell), and by jurists (Coke, et cetera). Their goal was to "glorify the pre-Norman past" that existed before the invasion and Conquest.

23. "I have a very auntient and learned treatise of the Lawes of this kingdom whereby this Realme was governed about 1100 years past, of the title and subject of which booke the author shal tel you himself in these words. Which summary I have intituled 'The Mirrors of Justice,' according to the vertues and *substances embellies* which I have observed, and which have ben used by holy customs since the time of King Arthur and C. [...] In this booke in effect appeareth the whole frame of the auntient common Lawes of this Realme." E. Coke, *La Neuf me Part des Reports de S. Edva Coke* (London, 1613), "Lectori/To the Reader," fol. 1-32, unpaginated. Cf. *La Huctieme Part de raports de S. Edv. Coke* (London, 1602), preface, fol. 9-17; *La Dix.me Part des Reports de S. Edv. Coke* (London, 1614) preface, fol. 1-48, contains an exposition of "the nationall Lawes of our native country." It should be noted that Coke also refers to *The Mirrors of Justice* in his *Institutes*. See in particular *The Fourth Part of the Institutes of the Laws of England* (London), chaps. 7, 11, 13, 25, but especially *The Second Part of the Institutes of the Laws of England* (London, 1642), pp. 5-78.

24. *The Mirrors of Justice* was originally written in French in the late fourteenth century, probably by Andrew Horn. The English translation of 1646 made the text a basic point of reference for all supporters—both parliamentarians and radical revolutionaries—of "common law."

25. Foucault is probably referring to *An Historical discourse of the Uniformity of Governments of England. The First Part*, 2 vols. (London, 1647), edited by Nathaniel Bacon on the basis of John Selden's manuscripts (see *An Historical and Political Discourse of the Laws and Government of England ... collected from some manuscript notes of John Selden ... by Nathaniel Bacon* [London, 1689]). Selden says of the Saxons that "their judicial were very suitable to the Athenian, but their military more like the Lacedominian" (p. 15; cf. chapters 4-43). See also Selden's *Analecton anglobritannicon libri duo* (Francofurti, 1615) and *Jani Anglorum* in *Opera omnia latina et anglica* (London, 1726), vol. 2.

26. *An Historical Discourse*, pp. 112-13.

27. John Warr, *The Corruption and Deficiency of the Laws of England* (London, 1649), p. 1: "The laws of England are full of tricks, doubts and contrary to themselves; for they were

invented and established by the Normans, which were of all nations the most quarrel-
some and most fallacious in contriving of controversies and suits." Cf. ibid., chaps. 2 and
3. See also *Administration Civil and spiritual in Two Treatises* (London, 1648), I, xxxvii. It
should be noted that Warr's phrase is cited in part in Christopher Hill, *Puritanism and
Revolution* (London: Secker & Warburg, 1958), p. 78.

28. See in particular John Lilburne, *The Just Man's Justification* (London, 1646), pp. 11-13; *A
Discourse betwixt John Lilburne, close prisoner in the tower of London, and Mr. Hugh Peters*
(London, 1649); *England's Birth-right Justified against all arbitrary usurpation* (London, 1645);
Regall tyrannie Discovered (London, 1647); *England's New Chains Discovered* (London, 1648).
Most of the Levellers' tracts are collected in W. Haller and G. Davies, ed., *The Levellers'
Tracts, 1647-1653* (New York: Columbia University Press, 1944).

29. *Regall tyrranie*, p. 86. The attribution of this tract to Lilburne is uncertain; R. Overton
probably collaborated on it.

30. The best known of the Digger texts, to which Foucault may be referring here, are the
anonymous manifesto *Light Shining in Buckinghamshire* (1648) and *More Light Shining in
Buckinghamshire* (1649). Cf. G. Winstanley et al., *To his Excellency the Lord Fairfax and the
Counsell of Warre the brotherly request of thos that are called diggers sheweth* (London, 1650);
G. Winstanley, *Fire in the Bush* (London, 1650); *The Law of Freedom in a Platform, or True
Magistracy Restored* (London, 1652). See also G. H. Sabine, ed., *The Works of Gerrard
Winstanley, with an Appendix of Documents Relating to the Digger Movement* (Ithaca, N.Y.:
Cornell University Press, 1941).

six

11 FEBRUARY 1976

Stories about origins. ~ The Trojan myth. ~ France's heredity. ~ "Franco-Gallia." ~ Invasion, history, and public right. ~ National dualism. ~ The knowledge of the prince. ~ Boulainvilliers's "Etat de la France." ~ The clerk, the intendant, and the knowledge of the aristocracy. ~ A new subject of history. ~ History and constitution.

I AM GOING TO begin with a story that started to circulate in France at the beginning, or almost the beginning, of the Middle Ages and that was still in circulation during the Renaissance. It tells how the French are descended from the Franks, and says that the Franks themselves were Trojans who, having left Troy under the leadership of Priam's son King Francus when the city was set on fire, initially found refuge on the banks of the Danube, then in Germany on the banks of the Rhine, and finally found, or rather founded, their homeland in France. I am not interested in what this story might have meant in the Middle Ages, or in the role that might have been played by the legend of the wanderings of the Trojans and of the founding of the fatherland. I simply want to look at this issue: it is after all astonishing that this story should have been picked up and gone on circulating in an era like the Renaissance.[1] Not because of the fantastic character of the dynasties or historical facts to which it refers, but basically because this legend completely elides both Rome and Gaul. It elides the Gaul that was the enemy of Rome, the Gaul that invaded Italy and laid siege to Rome; it also elides the Roman colony of Gaul, Caesar, and imperial Rome. And as a result, it elides an entire Roman literature, even though it was perfectly well known at this time.

I don't think we can understand why this Trojan story elides Rome unless we stop regarding this tale of origins as a tentative history that is still tangled up with old beliefs. It seems to me that, on the contrary, it is a discourse with a specific function. Its function is not so much to record the past or to speak of origins as to speak of right, to speak of power's right. Basically, the story is a lesson in public right. It circulated, I think, as a lesson in public right. And it is because it is a lesson in public right that there is no mention of Rome. But Rome is also present in a displaced form, like a double outline or a twin: Rome is there, but it is there in the way that an image is there in a mirror. To say that the Franks are, like the Romans, refugees from Troy, and that France and Rome are in some sense two branches that grow from the same trunk, is in effect to say two or three things that are, I believe, important in both political and juridical terms.

To say that the Franks are, like the Romans, fugitives from Troy means first of all that from the day that the Roman State (which was, after all, no more than a brother, or at best an older brother) vanished, the other brothers—the younger brothers—became its heirs by virtue of the right of peoples. Thanks to a sort of natural right that was recognized by all, France was the heir to the empire. And that means two things. It means first of all that the rights and powers the king of France enjoys over his subjects are inherited from those the Roman emperor enjoyed over his subjects; the sovereignty of the king of France is of the same type as the sovereignty of the Roman emperor. The king's right is a Roman right. And the legend of Troy is a way of using pictures to illustrate, a way of illustrating, the principle that was formulated in the Middle Ages, mainly by Boutillier when he said that the king of France was an emperor in his kingdom.[2] This is an important thesis, you know, because it is basically the historico-mythical counterpart to the way that royal power developed throughout the Middle Ages by modeling itself on the Roman imperium and reactivating the imperial rights that were codified in the era of Justinian.

To say that France is the heir to the empire is also to say that because France is Rome's sister or cousin, France has the same rights as Rome itself. It is to say that France is not part of some universal monarchy which, after the empire, dreamed of reviving the Roman Empire. France is just as imperial as all the Roman Empire's other descendants; it is just as imperial as the German Empire, and is in no sense subordinate to any Germanic Caesar. No bond of vassalage can legitimately make it part of the Hapsburg monarchy and therefore subordinate it to the great dreams of a universal monarchy that it was promoting at this time. That is why, in these conditions, Rome has to be elided. But the Roman Gaul of Caesar, the Gaul that was colonized, also had to be elided, as it might suggest that Gaul and the heirs of the Gauls had once been, or might be, subordinate to an empire. The Frankish invasions, which broke from within the continuity with the Roman Empire, also had to be elided. The internal continuity that existed between the Roman imperium and the French monarchy precluded disruptive invasions. But France's nonsubordination to the empire and to the empire's heirs (and especially the universal monarchy of the Hapsburgs) also implied that France's subordination to ancient Rome had to disappear. Roman Gaul therefore had to disappear. France, in other words, had to be an other Rome— "other" in the sense of being independent of Rome while still remaining Rome. The king's absolutism was therefore as valid in France as it had been in Rome. That, broadly speaking, was the function of the lessons in public right that we can find in the reactivation, or the perpetuation, of this Trojan mythology until late in the Renaissance, or in other words during a period which was very familiar with Roman texts about Gaul, about Roman Gaul.

It is sometimes said it was the Wars of Religion that allowed these old mythologies (which were, in my view, a lesson in public right) to be swept away and that first introduced the theme of what Augustin Thierry would later call "national duality,"[3] or the theme, if you like, of the two hostile groups that constitute the permanent substratum of the State. I do not think this is entirely accurate. Those who say that it was the Wars of Religion that made it possible to think in terms of a national duality are referring to François Hotman's text *Franco-Gallia,* which was published in 1573.[4] And the title does seem to indicate that the author was thinking in terms of some sort of national duality. In this text, Hotman in fact takes up the Germanic thesis that was circulating in the Hapsburg Empire at the time and which was, basically, the equivalent to, the counterpart to, or the homologue of the Trojan thesis that was circulating in France. The Gemanic thesis, which had been formulated on a number of occasions, and notably by someone called Beatus Rhenanus, states: "We Germans are not Romans; we are Germanic. But because of the imperial form we have inherited, we are Rome's natural and legal heirs. Now the Franks who invaded Gaul were, like us, Germans. When they invaded Gaul, they certainly left their native Germany, but on the one hand and to the extent that they were German, they remained German. They therefore remained within our imperium; and as, on the other hand, they invaded and occupied Gaul, and defeated the Gauls, they quite naturally exercised imperium or imperial power over the land they had conquered and colonized, and, being German, they were quite entitled to do so. Gaul, or the land of the Gauls that is now France, is therefore a subordinate part of the universal monarchy of the Hapsburgs for two reasons: right of conquest and victory, and the Germanic origins of the Franks."[5]

This, curiously but up to a point naturally, is the thesis that François Hotman picks up and reintroduces into France in 1573. From that point on, and until at least the beginning of the seventeenth century, it was to enjoy considerable popularity. Hotman takes up the German thesis and says: "The Franks who, at some point, did invade Gaul and establish a new monarchy, are not Trojans, but Germans. They defeated the Romans and drove them out." This is an almost literal reproduction of Rhenanus's Germanic thesis. I say "almost" because there is after all a difference, and it is of fundamental importance:

Hotman does not say that the Franks defeated the Gauls; he says that they defeated the Romans.[6]

Hotman's thesis is certainly very important because it introduces, at much the same time that we see it appearing in England, the basic theme of the invasion (which is both the cross the jurists have to bear and the king's nightmare) that results in the death of some States and the birth of others. All the juridico-political debates will revolve around this theme. Henceforth, and given this basic discontinuity, it is obvious that it is no longer possible to recite a lesson in public right whose function is to guarantee the uninterrupted nature of the genealogy of kings and their power. From now on, the great problem in public right will be the problem of what Étienne Pasquier, who was one of Hotman's followers, calls "the other succession,"[7] or in other words: What happens when one State succeeds another? What happens—and what becomes of public right and the power of kings— when States do not succeed one another as [a result of] a sort of continuity that nothing interrupts, but because they are born, go through a phase of might, then fall into decadence, and finally vanish completely? Hotman certainly raises the problem of the two foreign nations that exist within the State*—but I do not think that the problem he raises is any different, or very different, from that of the cyclical nature and precarious existence of States. And besides, in general terms, no author writing at the time of the Wars of Religion accepted the idea that there was a duality—of race, origins, or nations—within the monarchy. It was impossible because, on the one hand, the supporters of a single religion—who obviously believed in the principle of "one faith, one law, one king"—could not at the same time demand religious unity and accept that there was a duality within the nation; on the other hand, the thesis of those who were arguing the case for religious choice or freedom of conscience was acceptable only if they said, "Neither freedom of consciousness, nor the possibility of religious choice, nor even the existence of two re-

---

*The manuscript has "the problem of the two foreign nations that existed in France."

ligions within the body of a nation can in any circumstances compromise the unity of the State." So no matter whether one adopted the thesis of religious unity or supported the possibility of freedom of consciousness, the thesis of the unity of the State was reinforced throughout the Wars of Religion.

When Hotman told his story, he was saying something very different. It was a way of outlining a juridical model of government, as opposed to the Roman absolutism that the French monarchy wanted to reconstruct. The story of the Germanic origins of the invasion is a way of saying: "No, it is not true, the king of France does not have the right to exercise a Roman-style imperium over his people." Hotman's problem is therefore not the disjunction between two heterogeneous elements within the people; it is the problem of how to place internal restrictions on monarchic power.[8] Hence the way he tells the story when he says: "The Gauls and the Germans were in fact originally fraternal peoples. They settled in two neighboring regions, on either side of the Rhine. When the Germans entered Gaul, they were in no sense foreign invaders. They were in fact almost going home, or at least to visit their brothers.[9] What did 'foreigner' mean to the Gauls? The foreigners were the Romans, who imposed, through invasion and war (the war described by Caesar),[10] a political regime: that of absolutism. Those foreigners established something foreign in Gaul: the Roman imperium. The Gauls resisted for centuries, but in ways that brought them little success. In the fourth or fifth century, their Germanic brothers began to wage a war, and it was a war of liberation fought on behalf of their Gaulish brothers. The Germans therefore did not come as invaders, but as a fraternal people which was helping a brother people to free itself from its invaders, and it was the Romans who were the invaders."[11] So the Romans were driven out and the Gauls were set free. They and their Germanic brothers make up a single nation, whose constitution and basic laws—as the jurists of the period were beginning to put it—were the basic laws of Germanic society. This meant that the people who regularly gathered on the Champ de Mars and in the May assemblies was sovereign. It meant the sovereignty of a people which elects its king as it pleases and deposes him when necessary; the sovereignty of a people who is ruled only by magistrates whose functions are temporary and who are always accountable to the council. This was the Germanic constitution that the king subsequently violated in order to construct the absolutism to which the French monarchy of the sixteenth century bore witness.[12] It is true that the story told by Hotman is not designed to establish a duality. On the contrary, it is intended to establish very strong ties of Germanic-French unity, Franco-Gaulish or Franco-Gallic unity, as he puts it. He is attempting to establish a profound unity and at the same time to explain, in the form of a sort of story, how the present reproduces the past. It is clear that the Roman invaders Hotman is talking about are the equivalent, transposed into the past, of the Rome of the pope and his clergy. The fraternal German liberators are obviously the reformed religion from across the Rhine; and the unity of the kingdom and the sovereignty of the people is the political plan for a constitutional monarchy that was supported by many of the Protestant circles of the day.

Hotman's discourse is important because it established what would doubtless become a definitive link between the project of restricting royal absolutism and the rediscovery, in the past, of a certain specific historical model which at some moment established the reciprocal rights of the king and his people, and which was subsequently forgotten and violated. In the sixteenth century a connection began to be established among restricting the right of the monarchy, reconstructing a past model, and reviving a basic but forgotten constitution; these are, I think, the things that are brought together in Hotman's discourse, and not a dualism. The Germanic thesis was originally Protestant in origin. But it soon began to circulate not only in Protestant circles but also in Catholic circles, when (under the reign of Henri III and especially at the time of Henri IV's conquest of power) Catholics suddenly turned against royal absolutism and when it was in their interest to restrict royal power. Although this pro-Germanic thesis is Protestant in origin, you will therefore also find it in the work of Catholic historians such as Jean du Tillet, Jean de Serres, and so on.[13] From the end of the first third of the seventeenth century, this thesis will be the object of an attempt, if not to disqualify it, at least to get around this Germanic origin, the Germanic element, which monarchic power found unacceptable for two reasons. It was unacceptable in terms of the exercise of power and public right, and the European policy of Richelieu and Louis XIV also made it unacceptable.

A number of ways were used to get around the idea that France had been founded by Germans. Two were of particular importance. One was a sort of return to the Trojan myth, which was reactivated in the mid-seventeenth century. More important still was the foundation and introduction of an absolutely new thesis, which was to be of fundamental importance. This is the theme of what I would call radical "Gallo-centrism." The Gauls, whom Hotman had described as important partners in this prehistory of the French monarchy, were in a sense an inert matter or substratum: they were people who had been defeated and occupied, and who had to be liberated by outsiders. But from the seventeenth century onward, these Gauls became the principle or, so to speak, the motor of history. Thanks to a sort of inversion of polarities and values, the Gauls became the first or fundamental element, and the Germans came to be described as a mere extension of the Gauls. The Germans are no more than an episode in the history of the Gauls. This is the thesis that you find in people such as Audigier[14] and Tarault.[15] Audigier, for example, states that the Gauls were the fathers of all the peoples of Europe. A certain king of Gaul called Ambigate found himself with a nation so rich, so wealthy, so plethoric, and with such a surplus population that he had to liquidate part of it. He therefore sent one of his nephews to Italy and another, one Sigovège, to Germany. This was the beginning of a sort of expansion and colonization, and the French nation became the womb of all the other peoples of Europe (and even peoples outside Europe). And so, says Audigier, the French nation had "the same origins as all that was most terrible, most courageous, and most glorious, in other words the Vandals, the Goths, the Burgundians, the English, the Herules, the Silingals, the Huns, the Gepidae, the Alans, the Quadi, the Hurons, the Ruffai, the Thuringians, the Lombards, the Turks, the Tatars, the Persians, and even the Normans."¹⁶

So the Franks who invaded Gaul in the fourth and fifth centuries* were simply the offspring a sort of primitive Gaul; they were simply Gauls who were eager to see their own country once more. For them, liberating a Gaul that had been enslaved or liberating their defeated brothers was not the issue. What was at issue was a deep nostalgia, and also a desire to enjoy a flourishing Gallo-Roman civilization. The cousins, or the prodigal sons, were going home. But when they went home, the certainty did not sweep away the Roman right that had been implanted in Gaul; on the contrary, they reabsorbed it. They reabsorbed Roman Gaul—or allowed themselves to be reabsorbed into it. The conversion of Clovis proves that the ancient Gauls, who had become Germans and Franks, readopted the values and the political and religious system of the Roman Empire. And if, at the time of their return, the Franks did have to fight, it was not against the Gauls or even the Romans (whose values they were absorbing); it was against the Burgundians and the Goths (who, being Aryans, were heretics), or against the Saracen infidels. That is whom they waged war on. And in order to reward the warriors who had fought the Goths, Burgundians, and Saracens, their kings granted them fiefs. The origins of what, at this time, had yet to be called feudalism can thus be traced back to a war.

This fable made it possible to assert the native character of the Gaulish population. It also made it possible to assert that Gaul had natural frontiers—those described by Caesar.¹⁷ Establishing those same frontiers was also the political objective of the foreign policy of Richelieu and Louis XIV. The purpose of this tale was also not only to erase all racial differences, but above all to erase any heterogeneity between Germanic right and Roman right. It had to be demonstrated that the Germans had renounced their own right in order to adopt

---

*The manuscript has "fifth and sixth centuries," which corresponds to the actual date of the conquest.

the juridico-political system of the Romans. And finally, the fiefs and prerogatives of the nobility had to be shown to derive not from the basic or archaic rights of that same nobility, but simply from the will of a king whose power and absolutism predated the organization of feudalism itself. The point of all this was, and this is my last point, to lay a French claim to the universal monarchy. If Gaul was what Tacitus called the *vagina nationum* (he was in fact referring mainly to Germany),[18] and if Gaul was indeed the womb of all nations, then to whom should the universal monarchy revert, if not to the monarch who had inherited the land of France?

There are obviously many variations on this schema, but I will not go into them. The reason why I have told this rather long story is that I wanted to relate it to what was happening in England at the same time. There is at least one point in common, and one basic difference, between what was being said in England about the origins and foundations of the English monarchy, and what was being said in the mid-seventeenth century about the foundations of the French monarchy. The common feature—and I think it is important—is that invasion, with its forms, motifs, and effects, became a historical problem to the extent that it involved an important politico-juridical issue. It is up to the invasion to define the nature, rights, and limits of monarchical power, it is up to the history of the invasion to define the role of royal councils, assemblies, and sovereign courts. It is up to the invasion to define the respective roles of the nobility, the rights of the nobility, royal councils, and the people, as opposed to the king. In short, the invasion is being asked to define the very principles of public right.

At the very time when Grotius, Pufendorf, and Hobbes were trying to ground the rules that constitute the just State in natural law, a wide-ranging contrapuntal historical investigation was getting under way into the origins and validity of the rights that were actually being exercised—and it was looking at a historical event or, if you like, at a slice of history that was, in both juridical and political terms, the most sensitive region in the entire history of France. I refer, roughly speaking, to the period between Merovius and Charlemagne, or be-

tween the fifth and the ninth centuries. It has always been said (ever
since the seventeenth century) that this is the least-known period.
Least known? Perhaps. But definitely the most widely studied. Be
that as it may, new figures, new texts, and new problems now—and,
I think, for the first time—begin to appear on the horizon of the
history of France, whose purpose had until now been to establish the
royal imperium's continuity of power, and which spoke only of Trojans and Franks. The new figures were Merovius, Clovis, Charles Mar-
tel, Charlemagne, and Pipin; the new texts were by Gregory of Tours[19]
and Charlemagne's cartularies. New customs appear: the Champ de
Mars, the May gatherings, the ritual of carrying kings shoulder-high,
and so on. Events occur: the baptism of Clovis, the Battle of Poitiers,
the coronation of Charlemagne; we also have symbolic anecdotes such
as the story of the vase of Soissons, in which we see King Clovis
renouncing his claim, acknowledging the rights of his warriors, and
then taking his revenge later.

All this gives us a new historical landscape, and a new system of
reference which can be understood only to the extent that there is a
very close correlation between this new material and political discussions about public right. History and public right in fact go hand in
hand. There is a strict correlation between the problems posed by
public right and the delineation of the historical field—and "history
and public right" will in fact remain a set phrase until the end of the
eighteenth century. If you look at how history, and the pedagogy of
history, was actually taught until well after the eighteenth century
and even in the twentieth, you will find that it is public right that
you are being told about. I don't know what school textbooks look
like these days, but it is not so long ago that the history of France
began with the history of the Gauls. And the expression "our ancestors the Gauls" (which makes us laugh because it was taught to
Algerians and Africans) had a very specific meaning. To say "our
ancestors the Gauls" was, basically, to formulate a proposition that
meant something in the theory of constitutional law and in the problems raised by public right. Detailed accounts of the Battle of Poitiers
also had a very specific meaning to the extent that it was precisely

not the war between the Franks and the Gauls, but the war between the Franks and the Gauls and invaders of a different race and religion that allowed the origins of feudalism to be traced back to something other than an internal conflict between Franks and Gauls. And the story of the Soissons vase—which, I think, crops up in all the history books and which is still taught today—was certainly studied very seriously throughout the whole of the seventeenth century. The story of the Soissons vase tells the story of a problem in constitutional law: when wealth was first distributed, what were the rights of the king, and what were the rights of his warriors, and possibly of the nobility (in the sense that the nobility were originally warriors)? We thought that we were learning history; but in the nineteenth century, and even the twentieth, history books were in fact textbooks on public right. We were learning about public right and constitutional law by looking at pictures from history.

So, first point: the appearance in France of this new historical field, which is quite similar (in terms of its material) to what was happening in England at the time when the theme of the invasion was being reactivated in discussions of the problem of the monarchy. There is, however, one basic difference between England and France. In England, the Conquest and the Norman/Saxon racial duality was history's essential point of articulation, whereas in France there was, until the end of the seventeenth century, no heterogeneity within the body of the nation. The whole system of a fabled kinship between the Gauls and the Trojans, the Gauls and the Germans, and then the Gauls and the Romans, and so on, made it possible to guarantee both a continuous transmission of power and the unproblematic homogeneity of the body of the nation. Now it is precisely that homogeneity that was shattered at the end of the seventeenth century, not by the supplementary or differential theoretical, or theoretico-mythological, edifice I was talking about just now, but by a discourse which is, I believe, absolutely new in terms of its functions, its objects, and its effects.

The introduction of the theme of national dualism was not a reflection or expression of either the civil or social wars, the religious struggles of the Renaissance, or the conflicts of the Fronde. It was a conflict, an apparently lateral problem or something that has usually— and, I think, wrongly, as you will see—been described as a rearguard action, and it made it possible to conceptualize two things that had not previously been inscribed in either history or public right. One was the problem of whether or not the war between hostile groups really does constitute the substructure of the State; the other was the problem of whether political power can be regarded both as a product of that war and, up to a point, its referee, or whether it is usually a tool, the beneficiary of, and the destabilizing, partisan element in that war. This is a specific and limited problem, but it is, I think, also an essential problem because it leads to the refutation of the implicit thesis that the social body is homogeneous (which was so widely accepted that it did not have to be formulated). How? Well, because it raises what I would call a problem in political pedagogy: What must the prince know, where and from whom must he acquire his knowledge, and who is qualified to constitute the knowledge of the prince? To be more specific, this was quite simply the issue of how the duc de Bourgogne should be educated. As you know, this raised innumerable problems for a whole host of reasons (I am thinking not just of his elementary education, as he was already an adult at the time of the events I will be talking about). What was at stake was the body of information about the State, the government, and the country needed by the man who would, in a few years or after the death of Louis XIV, be called upon to lead that State, that government, and that country. We are therefore not talking about *Télé-maque*,[20] but about the enormous report on the state of France that Louis XIV ordered his administration and his intendants or stewards to produce for his heir and grandson, the duc de Bourgogne. It was a survey of France (a general study of the situation of the economy, institutions, and customs of France), and it was intended to constitute the knowledge of the king, or the knowledge that would allow him to rule.

So Louis XIV asked his intendants for these reports. Within a few months, they were assembled and ready. The duc de Bourgogne's entourage—an entourage made up of the very kernel of the nobiliary opposition, or of nobles who were critical of Louis XIV's regime because it had eroded their economic might and political power—received this report and appointed someone called Boulainvilliers to present it to the duc de Bourgogne. Because it was so enormous, they commissioned him to abridge it, and to explain or interpret it: to recode it, if you like. Boulainvilliers filleted or abridged these enormous reports, and summarized them in two large volumes. Finally, he wrote a preface and added a number of critical comments and a discourse: this was an essential complement to the enormous administrative task of providing a description and analysis of the State. The discourse is rather curious, as Boulainvilliers tried to shed light on the current state of France by writing an essay on the ancient governments of France down to the time of Hugh Capet.[21]

Boulainvilliers's text is an attempt to put forward theses favorable to the nobility—and his later works also deal with the same problem.[22] He criticizes the sale of crown offices, which worked to the disadvantage of the impoverished nobility; he protests against the fact that the nobility has been dispossessed of its right of jurisdiction, and of the profits that went with it; he insists that the nobility has a right to sit in the Conseil du roi; he is critical of the role played by the intendants in the administration of the provinces. But the most important feature of Boulainvilliers's text, and of this recoding of the reports [presented] to the king, is the protest against the fact that the knowledge given to the king, and then to the prince, is a knowledge manufactured by the administrative machine itself. It is a protest against the fact that the king's knowledge of his subjects has been completely colonized, occupied, prescribed, and defined by the State's knowledge about the State. The problem is as follows: Must the king's knowledge of his kingdom and his subjects be isomorphic with the State's knowledge of the State? Must the bureaucratic, fiscal, economic, administrative, and juridical expertise that is required to run the monarchy be reinjected into the prince by all the information he is being given, and which will allow him to govern? Basically, the problem is as follows: Because the prince exercises his arbitrary and unrestricted will over an administration that is completely in his hands and completely at his disposal, the administration, or the great administrative apparatus the king had given the monarchy, is in a sense welded to to the prince himself: they are one and the same. That is why it is impossible to resist him. But the prince (and the prince's power means that he and the administration are one and the same) must, whether he likes it or not, be persuaded to become part of the same body as his administration; he must be welded to it by the knowledge that the administration retransmits to him, but this time from above. The administration allows the king to rule the country at will, and subject to no restrictions. And conversely, the administration rules the king thanks to the quality and nature of the knowledge it forces upon him.

I think that the target of Boulainvilliers and those around him at this time—and the target of those who came after him in the mid-seventeenth century (like the comte de Buat-Nançay[23]) or Montlosier[24] (whose problem was much more complicated because he was writing, in the early Restoration period, against the imperial administration)—the real target of all the historians connected to the nobiliary reaction is the mechanism of power-knowledge that had bound the administrative apparatus to State absolutism since the seventeenth century. I think it is as though a nobility that had been impoverished and to some extent excluded from the exercise of power had established as the prime goal of its offensive, of its counteroffensive, not so much the direct and immediate reconquest of its powers, and not the recuperation of its wealth (which was no doubt now forever beyond its reach), as an important link in the system of power that the nobility had always overlooked, even at the time when it was at the height of its might. The strategic position that the nobility overlooked had been physically occupied by the church, by clerks and magistrates, and then by the bourgeoisie, the adminstrators, and even the financiers who collected indirect taxes. The position that had to be reoccupied as a priority, or the strategic objective Boulainvilliers now set the nobility, and the precondition for any possible revenge, was not what was, in the vocabulary of the court, termed "the favor

of the king." What had to be regained and occupied was now the
king's knowledge. It was the knowledge of the king, or a certain
knowledge shared by king and nobility: an implicit law, a mutual
commitment between the king and his aristocracy. What had to be
done was to reawaken both the nobles' memory, which had become
carelessly forgetful, and the monarch's memories, which had been
carefully—and perhaps wickedly—buried, so as to reconstitute the
legitimate knowledge of the king, which would provide legitimate
foundations for a legitimate government. What is required is therefore
a counterknowledge, a whole program of work that will take the form
of absolutely new historical research. I say counterknowledge because
Boulainvilliers and his successors initially define this new knowledge
and these new methods in negative terms by contrasting it with two
scholarly knowledges, with the two knowledges that are the two faces
(and perhaps also the two phases) of administrative knowledge. At
this time, the great enemy of the new knowledge the nobility wishes
to use to get a new grip on the knowledge of the king, the knowledge
that has to be got rid of, is juridical knowledge. It is the knowledge
of the court, of the prosecutor, the jurisconsult, and the clerk of the
court or *greffier*. For the nobility, this was indeed a hateful knowledge,
for this was the knowledge that had tricked them, that had dispossessed them by using arguments they did not understand, that had
stripped them, without their being able to realize it, of their rights
of jurisdiction and then of their very possessions. But it was also a
hateful knowledge because it was in a sense a circular knowledge
which derived knowledge from knowledge. When the king consulted
greffiers and jurisconsults about his rights, what answer could he ob-
tain, if not a knowledge established from the point of view of the
judges and prosecutors he himself had created? The king therefore
quite naturally finds that it contains eulogies to his own power
(though they may also conceal the subtle ways in which power has
been usurped by the prosecutors and *greffiers*). At all events, a circular
knowledge. A knowledge in which the king will encounter only the
image of his own absolutism, which reflects back at him, in the form

of right, all the usurpations the king has committed [against] his nobility.

The nobility wants to use another form of knowledge against the knowledge of the *greffier:* history. A history whose nature will allow it to get outside right, to get behind right and to slip into its interstices. Only, this history will be unlike any previous history, and it will not be a pictorial or dramatized account of the development of public right. On the contrary, it will attempt to attack public right at the roots, to reinsert the institutions of public right into an older network of deeper, more solemn, and more essential commitments. It will undermine the knowledge of the *greffier,* in which the king finds nothing but eulogies to his own absolutism (or in other words, the praise of Rome again), by tapping historic reserves of equity. Whatever the history of right may say, commitments that were not written down, fidelities that were never recorded in words or texts, have to be revived. Theses that have been forgotten have to reactivated, and the noble blood that has been spilled on behalf of the king has to be remembered. It has to be demonstrated that the very edifice of right— even its most valid institutions, its most explicit and widely recognized ordinances—is the product of a whole series of iniquities, injustices, abuses, dispossessions, betrayals, and infidelities committed by royal power, which reneged on its commitment to the nobility, and by the *robins* or legal small fry who usurped both the power of the nobility and, perhaps without really realizing it, royal power.

The history of right will therefore be a denunciation of betrayals, and of all the betrayals that were born of the betrayals. The goal of this history, whose very form is a challenge to the knowledge of the clerks and judges, is to make the prince see usurpations of which he is unaware and to restore to him a strength, and the memory of bonds, even though it was in his interest to forget them and to let them be forgotten. History will be the weapon of a nobility that has been betrayed and humiliated, and it will use it against the knowledge of the clerks, which always explains contemporary events in terms of contemporary events, power in terms of power, and the letter of the law in terms of the will of the king and vice versa. The form of this history will be profoundly antijuridical, and, going beyond what has been written down, it will decipher and recall what lies beneath everything that has fallen into abeyance, and denounce the blatant hostility concealed by this knowledge. That is the first great adversary of the historical knowledge the nobility wants to create so as to reoccupy the knowledge of the king.

The other great adversary is the knowledge not of the judge or the clerk, but of the intendant: not *le greffe* (the clerk of the court's office) but *le bureau* (the office of the intendant). This too is hateful knowledge. And for symmetrical reasons, as it was the knowledge of the intendants that allowed them to eat into the wealth and power of the nobles. This too is a knowledge that can dazzle the king and hoodwink him, as it is thanks to this knowledge that the king can impose his might, command obedience, and ensure that taxes are collected. This is an administrative knowledge, and above all a quantitative economic knowledge: knowledge of actual or potential wealth, knowledge of tolerable levels of taxation and of useful taxes. The nobility wants to use another form of understanding against the knowledge of the intendants and *le bureau:* history. This time, however, it is a history of wealth and not an economic history. This is a history of the displacement of wealth, of exactions, theft, sleight of hand, embezzlement, impoverishment, and ruin. This, then, is a history that digs beneath the problem of the production of wealth so as to demonstrate that it was ruination, debt, and abusive accumulations that created a certain state of wealth that is, ultimately, no more than a combination of crooked deals done by a king who was aided and abetted by the bourgeoisie. The analysis of wealth will, then, be challenged by a history of how the nobles were ruined by endless wars, a history of how the church tricked them into giving it gifts of land and money, a history of how the bourgeoisie got the nobility into debt, and a history of how royal tax-gatherers ate into the income of the nobles.

The two great discourses that the history of the nobility is trying to challenge—that of the courts and that of *le bureau*—do not share the same chronology. The struggle against juridical knowledge was probably at its height, or more active and more intense, in Boulain-villiers's day, or in other words, between the late seventeenth and the early eighteenth centuries; the struggle against economic knowledge was probably much more violent in the mid-eighteenth century, or at the time of the Physiocrats (Physiocracy was Buat-Nançay's great adversary).[25] Whether it is the knowledge of intendants, of *le bureau,* economic knowledge, the knowledge of clerks and courts, what is at issue is the knowledge that is constituted as the State talks to itself, and which has been replaced by another form of knowledge. Its general profile is that of history. The history of what?

Up to this point, history had never been anything more than the history of power as told by power itself, or the history of power that power had made people tell: it was the history of power, as recounted by power. The history that the nobility now begins to use against the State's discourse about the State, and power's discourse about power, is a discourse that will, I believe, destroy the very workings of historical knowledge. It is at this point, I think, that we see the breakdown—and this is important—of both the close relationship between the narrative of history on the one hand and, on the other hand, the exercise of power, its ritual reinforcement and the picture-book formulation of public right. With Boulainvilliers and the reactionary nobility of the late eighteenth century, a new subject of history appears. This means two things. On the one hand, there is a new speaking subject: someone else begins to speak in history, to recount history; someone else begins to say "I" and "we" as he recounts history; someone else begins to tell the story of his own history; someone else begins to reorganize the past, events, rights, injustices, defeats, and victories around himself and his own destiny. The subject who speaks in history is therefore displaced, but the subject of history is also displaced in the sense that the very object of the narrative is modified: its subject, in the sense of its theme, or object, if you like. The modification of the first, earlier or deeper element now allows rights, institutions, the monarchy, and even the land itself to be defined in relation to this new subject. This subject talks about events that occur beneath the State, that ignore right, and that are older and more profound than institutions.

So what is this new subject of history, which is both the subject that speaks in the historical narrative and what the historical narrative is talking about, this new subject that appears when we get away from the State's juridical or administrative discourse about the State? It is what a historian of the period calls a "society." A society, but in the sense of an association, group, or body of individuals governed by a statute, a society made up of a certain number of individuals, and which has its own manners, customs, and even its own law. The something that begins to speak in history, that speaks of history, and of which history will speak, is what the vocabulary of the day called a "nation."

At this time, the nation is by no means something that is defined by its territorial unity, a definite political morphology, or its systematic subordination to some imperium. The nation has no frontiers, no definite system of power, and no State. The nation circulates behind frontiers and institutions. The nation, or rather "nations," or in other words the collections, societies, groupings of individuals who share a status, mores, customs, and a certain particular law—in the sense of regulatory statutes rather than Statist laws. History will be about this, about these elements. And it is those elements that will begin to speak: it is the nation that begins to speak. The nobility is one nation, as distinct from the many other nations that circulate within the State and come into conflict with one another. It is this notion, this concept of the nation, that will give rise to the famous revolutionary problem of the nation; it will, of course, give rise to the basic concepts of nineteenth-century nationalism. It will also give rise to the notion of race. And, finally, it will give rise to the notion of class.

Together with this new subject of history—a subject that speaks in a history and a subject of which history speaks—we also have the appearance of a new domain of objects, a new frame of reference, a whole field of processes that had previously been not just obscure, but totally neglected. All the obscure processes that go on at the level where groups come into conflict beneath the State and through the law rise to the surface and become history's primary thematic. This is the dark history of alliances, of group rivalries and of interests that are masked or betrayed; the history of the usurpation of rights, of the displacement of fortunes; the history of fidelities and betrayals, the history of expenditure, exactions, debts, trickery, and of things that have been forgotten, and of stupidity. This is also a knowledge whose methodology is not the ritual reactivation of the acts that founded power, but the systematic interpretation of its evil intentions and the recollection of everything that it has systematically forgotten. Its method is the perpetual denunciation of the evil that has been done in history. This is no longer the glorious history of power; it is the history of its lower depths, its wickedness, and its betrayals.

This new discourse (which has, then, a new subject and a new frame of reference) inevitably brings with it what might be called a new pathos, and it is completely different from the great cere-monial ritual that still obscurely accompanied the discourse of history when it was telling those stories about Trojans, Germans, and so on. History no longer has the ceremonial character of something that reinforces power, but a new pathos will mark with its splendor a school of thought that will, broadly speaking, become French right-wing thought. What I mean by this is, first, an almost erotic passion for historical knowledge; second, the systematic perversion of interpretive understanding; third, relentless denunciations; fourth, the articulation of history around something resembling a plot, an attack on the State, a coup d'état or an assault on the State or against the State.

What I have been trying to show you is not exactly what is known as "the history of ideas." I have not so much been trying to show you how the nobility used historical discourse to express either its de-mands or its misfortunes, as to show how a certain instrument of struggle was actually forged in the struggles that took place around the workings of power—struggles within power and against power. That instrument is a knowledge, a new (or at least partly new) knowledge: the new form of history. The recall of history in this form is basically, I think, the wedge that the nobility will try to drive between the knowledge of the sovereign and the expertise of the administration, and it will do so in order to disconnect the absolute will of the sovereign from the absolute docility of his administration. It is not because they are odes to the freedoms of old that the discourse of history, the old story about Gauls and Germans, or the long tale of Clovis and Charlemagne, become instruments in the struggle against absolutism; it is because they disconnect administrative power-knowledge. That is why this type of discourse—which was originally nobiliary and reactionary—will begin to circulate, with many modifications and many conflicts over its form, precisely whenever a political group wants, for one reason or another, to attack the hinge that connects power to knowledge in the workings of the absolute State of the administrative monarchy. And that is why you quite naturally find this type of discourse (and even its formulations) on both what might be called the Right and the Left, in both the nobiliary reaction and in texts produced by revolutionaries before or after 1789. Let me just quote you one text about an unjust king, about the king of wickedness and betrayals: "What punishment"—at this point, the author is addressing Louis XVI—"do you think befits such a barbarous man, this wretched heir to a heap of plunder? Do you think that God's law does not apply to you? Or are you a man for whom everything must be reduced to your glory and subordinated to your satisfaction? And who are you? For if you are not a God, you are a monster!" This was not written by Marat, but by Buat-Nançay, who was writing to Louis XVI in 1778.[26] Ten years later, this would be repeated word for word by the revolutionaries.

You understand why, although this new type of historical knowledge, this new type of discourse, actually did play this important political role and did act as the hinge between the administrative monarchy's power and its knowledge, royal power had to try to bring it under its control. Just as this discourse circulated from Right to Left, from the nobiliary reaction to a bourgeois revolutionary project, so royal power tried to appropriate or control it. And so, from 1760 onward, we begin to see royal power—and this proves the political value, the vital political issue that is at stake in this historical knowledge—trying to organize this historical knowledge by, so to speak, reintroducing it into the play between knowledge and power, between administrative power and the expertise to which it gave rise. From 1760 onward we see the emergence of institutions that were roughly equivalent to a ministry of history. The process began in about 1760, with the establishment of a Bibliothèque de finances, which had to supply His Majesty's ministers with the reports, information, and clarifications they needed. In 1763, a Dépôt de chartes was established for those who wanted to study the history and public right of France. In 1781, the two institutions were merged to form a Bibliothèque de législation—note the terms carefully—d'administration, histoire et droit public. A slightly later text states that this library is intended for His Majesty's ministers, those who are responsible for departments of the general administration, and for the scholars and jurisconsults who had been appointed by the chancellor or keeper of the seals and who were paid at His Majesty's expense to write books and other work that were of use to legislators, historians, and the public.[27]

This ministry of history had an official in charge of it. His name was Jacob-Nicolas Moreau, and it was he, together with a few collaborators, who assembled the huge collection of medieval and premedieval documents on which historians such as Augustin Thierry and Guizot would work in the early nineteenth century.[28] At the time of its creation at least, the meaning of this institution—of this ministry of history—is quite clear: At the time when the political confrontations of the eighteenth century centered on a historical discourse, or, more specifically, at a deeper level, at the time when historical knowledge was indeed a weapon in the struggle against the absolute monarchy's administrative-style knowledge, the monarchy wanted, so to speak, to recolonize that knowledge. The creation of the ministry of history was, if you like, a concession, a first tacit acceptance on the part of the king that there did indeed exist historical material that might, perhaps, reveal the basic laws of the kingdom. It was the first tacit acceptance of a sort of constitution, ten years before the Estates General. So, a first concession on the part of royal power, a first tacit acceptance that something might slip between its power and its administration: the constitution, basic laws, the representation of the people, and so on. But at the same time, historical knowledge was reinstalled, in an authoritarian way, in the very place where attempts had been made to use it against absolutism. That knowledge was a weapon in the struggle to reoccupy the knowledge of the prince, and it was placed between his power and the expertise and workings of the administration. A ministry of history was established between the prince and the administration as a way of reestablishing the link, of making history part of the workings of monarchic power and its administration. A ministry of history was created between the knowledge of the prince and the expertise of his administration, and in order to establish, between the king and his administration, in a controlled way, the uninterrupted tradition of the monarchy.

That is more or less what I wanted to say to you about the establishment of this new type of historical knowledge. I will try to look later at the way in which this knowledge led to the emergence within this element of the struggle between nations, or in other words what will become the race struggle and the class struggle.

1. There are at least fifty accounts of the Trojan origins of the French, from the Pseudo-Frédégaire's *Historia Francorum* (727) to Ronsard's *Franciade* (1572). It is unclear whether Foucault is referring to this tradition as a whole, or to a specific text. The text in question may be the one referred to by A. Thierry in his *Récit du temps mérovingiens, précédé de considérations sur l'histoire de France* (Paris, 1840), or in other words *Les Grandes Chroniques de Saint-Denis* (which were written in the second half of the twelfth century, published by Paulin Paris in 1836, and reprinted by J. Viard in 1920). Many of these stories can be consulted in Dom. M. Bouquet, *Recueil des historiens de Gaule et de la France* (Paris, 1739-1752), vols. 2 and 3.

2. "Know that he is an emperor in his kingdom, and that he can do all and as much as imperial right permits" (J. Boutillier, *Somme rurale, ou le Grand Coutumier général de pratiques civiles* [fourteenth century] [Bruges, 1479]). The 1611 edition of this text is cited by A. Thierry, *Considérations sur l'histoire de France.*

3. Thierry, p. 41 (1868 ed.).

4. F. Hotman, *Franco-Gallia* (Geneva, 1573) (French translation: *La Gaule françoise* [Cologne, 1574], reprinted as *La Gaule française* [Paris: Fayard, 1981]).

5. Cf. *Beati Rhenani Rerum Germanicorum libri tres* (Basel, 1531). The edition published in Ulm in 1693 should also be consulted; the commentary and notes added by the members of the Imperial Historical College provide a genealogy and eulogy of the "Europa corona" of the Hapsburgs (*Beati Rhenani libri tres Institutionem Rerum Historici Imperialis scopum illustratarum* [Ulm, 1693], and especially pp. 569-600. See also the commentaries appended to the Strasbourg edition: Argentatori, 1610).

6. Cf. Hotman, *Franco-Gallia*, chapter 4, "De ortu Francorum, qui Gallia occupata. eius nomen in Francia, vel Francogalliam mutarunt" (pp. 40-52 of the 1576 ed.).

7. Étienne Pasquier, *Recherches de la France*, 3 vols. (Paris 1560-1567). Pasquier studied under Hotman.

8. Cf. Hotman, *Franco-Gallia*, p. 54: "Semper reges Franci habuerunt . . . non tyrannos, aut carnefices: sed liberatis suae custodes, praefectos, tutores sibi constituerunt."

9. Ibid., p. 62.

10. Julius Caesar, *Commentarii de bello gallico*; see especially books 6, 7, and 8.

11. Hotman, *Franco-Gallia*, pp. 55-62.

12. Cf. ibid., p. 65f, where Hotman describes "the continuity of the powers of the council" through the various dynasties.

13. Jean du Tillet, *Les Mémoires et recherches* (Rouen, 1578); *Recueil des Roys de France* (Paris, 1580); *Remonstrance ou Advertissement à la noblesse tant du parti du Roy que des rebelles* (Paris, 1585). Jean de Serres, *Mémoires de la troisième guerre civile, et des derniers troubles de la France* (Paris, 1570); *Inventaire général de l'histoire de la France* (Paris, 1597).

14. P. Audigier, *De l'origine des François et de leur empire* (Paris, 1676).

15. J.-E. Tarault, *Annales de France, avec les alliances, généalogies, conquêtes, fondations ecclésiastiques et civiles en l'une et l'autre empire et dans les royaumes étrangers, depuis Pharamond jusqu'au roi Louis treizième* (Paris, 1635).

16. P. Audigier, *De l'origine des François*, p. 3.

17. Caesar, *De Bello gallico*, book 1, p. 1.

18. It was in fact Bishop Ragvaldson who, speaking of the question of the "fabrication of the human race" at the Council of Basel in 1434, described Scandinavia as humanity's original cradle. He based his claim on the fourth-century chronicle of Jordanis: "Hac igitur Scandza insula quasi officina gentium aut certe velut *vagina nationum* . . . Gotthi quondam memorantur egressi" (*De origine actibusque Getarum* in *Monumanta Germaniae Historica, Auctorum antiquissimorum*, vol. 5, part 1 (Berolini, 1882), pp. 53-258 (quotation from p. 60). A far-reaching debate on this question began after the rediscovery of Tacitus's *De origine et situ Germaniae*, which was published in 1472.

19. Grégoire de Tours, *Historia Francorum* (575-592) (Paris, 1692).

20. Fénélon, *Les Aventures de Télémaque* (Paris, 1695).

21. The reference is to *Etat de la France dans lequel on voit tout ce que regarde le gouvernement écclesiastique, le militaire, la justice, les finances, le commerce, les manufactures, le nombre des habitants, et en général tout ce qui peut faire comprendre à fond cette monarchie; extrait des mémoires dressés par les intendants du royaume, par ordre du roy Louis XIV à la sollicitation de Monseigneur le duc de Bourgogne, père de Louis XV à présent regnant. Avec des Mémoires historiques sur l'ancient gouvernement de cette monarchie jusqu'à Hugues Capet, par M. le comte de Boulainvilliers*, 2 vols. in folio (London, 1727). In 1728, a third volume appeared under the title *Etat de la France, contenant XIV lettres sur les anciens Parlemens de France, avec l'histoire de ce royaume depuis le commencement de la monarchie jusqu'à Charles VIII. On y a joint des Mémoires présentés à M. le duc d'Orléans* (London, 1728).

22. Foucault is alluding to those of Boulainvilliers's historical works that deal with French political institutions. The most important are: *Mémoire sur la noblesse du roiaume de France fait par le comte de Boulainvilliers* (1719; extracts are published in A. Devyver, *Le Sang épuré. Les préjugés de race chez les gentilhommes français de l'Ancien Régime* [Brussels: Éditions de l'Université, 1973], pp. 500-48); *Mémoire pour la noblesse de France contre les Ducs et Pairs*, s. l. (1717); *Mémoires présentés a Mgr. le duc d'Orléans, Régent de France* (The Hague/Amsterdam, 1727); *Histoire de l'ancient gouvernement de la France avec quatorze lettres historiques sur les Parlements ou Etats Généraux*, 3 vols. (The Hague/Amsterdam, 1727) (this is an abridged and revised edition of the *Mémoires*); *Traité sur l'origine et les droits de la noblesse* (1700), in *Continuation des mémoires de littérature et d'histoire* (Paris, 1730), vol. 9, pp. 3-106 (republished, with numerous modifications, as *Essais sur la noblesse contenant une dissertation sur son origine et abaissement, par le feu M. le Comte de Boulainvilliers, avec des notes historiques, critiques et politiques* [Amsterdam, 1732]); *Abrégé chronologique de l'historie de France*, 3 vols. (Paris, 1733); *Histoire des anciens parlemans de France ou Etats Généraux du royaume* (London, 1737).

23. The historical writings of L. G. comte de Buat-Nançay include *Les Origines ou l'Ancient Gouvernement de la France, de l'Italie, de l'Allemagne* (Paris, 1757); *Histoire ancienne des peuples de l'Europe*, 12 vols. (Paris, 1772); *Eléments de la politique, ou Recerche sur les vrais principes de l'économie sociale* (London, 1773); *Les Maximes du gouvernement monarchique pour servir de suite aux éléments de la politique* (London, 1778).

24. Of the many works by F. de Reynaud, comte de Montlosier, only those that relate to the problems raised by Foucault in his lecture will be mentioned here: *De la monarchie française depuis son établissement jusqu'à nos jours*, 3 vols. (Paris, 1814); *Mémoires sur la Révolution française, le Consulat l'Empire, la Restauration et les principaux événements qui l'ont suivie* (Paris, 1830). On Montlosier, see the lecture of 10 March below.

25. See L. G. comte de Buat-Nançay, *Remarques d'un Français, ou Examen impartial du livre de M. Necker sur les finances* (Geneva, 1785).

26. L. G. comte de Buat-Nançay, *Les Maximes du gouvernement monarchique*, pp. 286-87.

27. On this question, see J.-N. Moreau, *Plan des travaux littéraires ordonnés par Sa Majesté pour la recherche, la collection et l'emploi des monuments d'histoire et du droit public de la monarchie française* (Paris, 1782).

28. Cf. J.-N. Moreau, *Principes de morale, de politique et de droit public puisés dans l'histoire de notre monarchie, ou discourse sur l'histoire de France*, 21 vols. (Paris, 1777-1789).

seven

18 FEBRUARY 1976

> *Nation and nations. ~ The Roman conquest. ~ Grandeur and decadence of the Romans. ~ Boulainvilliers on the freedom of the Germans. ~ The Soissons vase. ~ Origins of feudalism. ~ Church, right, and the language of State. ~ Boulainvilliers: three generalizations about war: law of history and law of nature, the institutions of war, the calculation of forces. ~ Remarks on war.*

LAST TIME, I TRIED to show you how the nobiliary reaction was bound up with, not exactly the invention of historical discourse, but rather the shattering of a preexisting historical discourse whose function had until then been to sing the praises of Rome, as Petrarch puts it.[1] Until then, historical discourse had been inferior to the State's discourse about itself; its function was to demonstrate the State's right, to establish its sovereignty, to recount its uninterrupted genealogy, and to use heroes, exploits, and dynasties to illustrate the legitimacy of public right. The disruption of the praise of Rome in the late seventeenth and early eighteenth centuries came about in two ways. One the one hand, we have the recollection, the reactivation, of the fact of the invasion, which, as you will remember, Protestant historiography had already used as an argument against royal absolutism. The evocation of the invasion introduced a major break in time: the Germanic invasion of the fourth to fifth centuries negates right. This is the moment when public right is destroyed, the moment when the hordes flooding out of Germany put an end to Roman absolutism. The other break, the other disruptive principle—which is, I think, more important—is the introduction of a new subject of history, both in the sense that the historical narrative acquires a new domain of objects, and in the sense that a new subject begins to speak in history. History is no longer the State talking about itself; it is something else talking about itself, and the something else that speaks in history and takes itself as the object of its own historical narrative is a sort of new entity known as the nation. "Nation" is, of course, to be understood in the broad sense of the term. I will try to come back to this point, as it is this notion of a nation that generates or gives rise to notions like nationality, race, and class. In the eighteenth century, this notion still has to be understood in a very broad sense.

It is true that you can find in the *Encyclopédie* what I would call a Statist definition of the nation because the encyclopedists give four criteria for the existence of the nation.[2] First, it must be a great multitude of men; second, it must be a great multitude of men inhabiting a defined country; third, this defined country must be circumscribed by frontiers; fourth, the multitude of men who have settled inside those frontiers must obey the same laws and the same government. So we have here a definition of the nation which, so to speak, settles the nation within the frontiers of the State on the one hand, and within the very form of the State on the other. This is, I think, a polemical definition which was intended, if not to refute, at least to rule out the broad definition that prevailed at this time, and which we can find both in texts produced by the nobility and in texts produced by the bourgeoisie. According to this definition, the nobility was a nation, and the bourgeoisie was also a nation. All this will be of vital importance during the Revolution, and especially in Sieyès's text about the Third Estate, which I will try to discuss.[3] But this vague, fluid, shifting notion of the nation, this idea of a nation that does not stop at the frontiers but which, on the contrary, is a sort of mass of individuals who move from one frontier to another, through States, beneath States, and at an infra-State level, persists long into the nineteenth century—in, for instance, the work of Augustin Thierry,[4] Guizot,[5] and others.

We have, then, a new subject of history, and I will try to show you how and why it was the nobility that introduced into the great Statist organization of historical discourse this disruptive principle: the nation as subject-object of the new history. But what was this new history, what did it consist of, and how did it become established in the early eighteenth century? I think that the reasons why this new type of history is deployed in the discourse of the French nobility become clear if we compare it with the nature of the English problem in the seventeenth century, or about one hundred years earlier.

In the England of the late sixteenth and early seventeenth centuries, both the parliamentary opposition and the popular opposition had, basically, to solve a relatively simple problem. They had to demonstrate that there were both two conflicting systems of right and two nations in the English monarchy. On the one hand, there was a system of right corresponding to the Norman nation: the aristocracy and the monarchy were, so to speak, lumped together. This nation brought with it an absolutist system of right, and it imposed it through the violence of the invasion. So: monarchy and aristocracy (absolutist-type right and invasion). That system had to be challenged by asserting the system of Saxon right: the right to basic freedoms, which just happened to be the right of the earliest inhabitants and, at the same time, the right that was being demanded by the poorest, or at least by those who did not belong to either the royal family or aristocratic families. So, two great systems. And the older and more liberal system had to prevail over the new system that had—thanks to the invasion—introduced absolutism. A simple problem.

A century later, or at the end of the seventeenth and the beginning of the eighteenth centuries, the French nobility was obviously faced with a much more complex problem because it had to fight on two fronts. On the one hand, against the monarchy and its usurpations of power; on the other, against the Third Estate, which was taking advantage of the absolute monarchy so as to trample on the rights of the nobility and to use them to its own advantage. So, a struggle on two fronts, but it cannot be waged in the same way on both fronts. In its struggle against the absolutism of the monarchy, the nobility asserts its right to the basic freedoms which were supposedly enjoyed by the Germanic or Frankish people who invaded France at some point. So, in its struggle against the monarchy, the nobility claims freedoms. But in the struggle against the Third Estate, the nobility lays claim to the unrestricted rights granted to it by the invasion. On the one hand, or in the struggle against the Third Estate, it must, in other words, be an absolute victor with unrestricted rights; on the other hand, or in the struggle against the monarchy, it has to lay claim to an almost constitutional right to basic freedoms. Hence the complexity of the problem and hence, I think, the infinitely more sophisticated nature of the analysis that we find in Boulainvilliers, compared to the analysis we find a few decades earlier.

But I want to take Boulainvilliers simply as an example, because there was in fact a whole nucleus, a whole nebula of noble historians who began to formulate their theories in the second half of the seventeenth century (the comte d'Estaing between about 1660 and 1670),[6] and they went on doing so until the comte de Buat-Nançay[7] and possibly the comte de Montlosier[8] (who was writing at the time of the Revolution), the Empire, and the Restoration. Boulainvillers plays an important role because it was Boulainvilliers who tried to retranscribe the reports produced by the intendants for the duc de Bourgogne, and we can therefore take him as a point of reference and as a representative figure who can, provisionally, stand for all the others.[9] How does Boulainvilliers make his analysis? First question: What did the Franks find when they entered Gaul? They obviously did not find the lost homeland to which they wanted to return because of its wealth and civilization (as the old historico-legendary story of the twelfth century would have it when it described the Franks as Gauls who had left their homeland and then decided to go back to it at some point). The Gaul described by Boulainvilliers is by no means a happy, almost Arcadian Gaul which had forgotten Caesar's violence and had happily merged into a newly constituted unity. When they entered Gaul, the Franks found a land that had been conquered. And the fact that it had been conquered meant that Roman absolutism, or the kingly or imperial right that had been established by the Romans, was not a right that had been acclimatized to Gaul; it was not accepted, and did not fit in with either the land or the people. This right was the result of the conquest; Gaul had been subjugated. The right that prevailed there was in no sense a consensual sovereignty; it was the result of domination. And it is the very mechanism of that domination, which lasted throughout the Roman occupation, that Boulainvilliers is trying to isolate by identifying a number of phases.

When the Romans first entered Gaul, their immediate priority was obviously to disarm the warrior aristocracy, which had been the only military force to put up any real opposition; they disarmed the aristocracy and humiliated it in both political and economic terms by (or at least at the same time as) artificially raising up the common people and, according to Boulainvilliers, using the idea of equality to seduce them. In other words, a device typical of all despotisms (and which had, as it happens, been developed in the Roman Republic from Marius to Caesar) was used to convince inferiors that a little more equality for them would do them more good than much greater freedom for all. And the result of this "equalitarization" was a despotic government. In the same way, the Romans made Gaulish society more egalitarian by humbling the nobility, raising up the common people, and establishing their own Caesarism. This was the first phase, and it ended with Caligula's systematic massacre of the former Gaulish nobles who had resisted both the Romans and their characteristic policy of humiliation. We then see the Romans creating the nobility they needed. This was not a military nobility—which might have opposed them—but an administrative nobility that was designed to help them organize a Roman Gaul and, above all, to assist them with all the dishonest tricks they would use to plunder the wealth of Gaul and to ensure that the tax system worked in their favor. So a new nobility was created, and it was a civilian, juridical, and administrative nobility characterized, first, by its acute, sophisticated, and masterly understanding of Roman right, and second, by its knowledge of the Roman language. It was its knowledge of the language and its understanding of right that allowed a new nobility to emerge.

This description makes it possible to dispel the old seventeenth-century myth of a happy and Arcadian Roman Gaul. The refutation of that myth was obviously a way of telling the king of France: If you claim the rights of Roman absolutism, you are not laying claim to basic and essential right over the land of Gaul, but to a specific and particular history whose tricks are not especially honorable. You are at least inscribing yourself within a mechanism of subjugation. What is more, this Roman absolutism, which was established thanks to a certain number of mechanisms of domination, was finally overthrown, swept away and defeated by the Germans—and that had less to do with the contingencies of a military defeat than with an inevitable internal decay. This is the starting point for the second section of Boulainvilliers's analysis—the moment when he analyzes the real effects of Rome's dominion over Gaul. When they entered Gaul, the Germans (or Franks) found a conquered land that was the military armature of Gaul.* The Romans now had no one to defend them from invasions from across the Rhine. Given that they no longer had a nobility, they had to turn to mercenaries in order to defend the Gaulish land they were occupying. These mercenaries were not fighting their own cause, or to defend their own land, but for money. The existence of a mercenary army, of a paid army, obviously implies a very high level of taxation. Gaul therefore had to supply not only mercenaries but also the means to pay them. This had two effects. First, a considerable increase in taxes paid in cash. Second, an increase in the amount of money in circulation or, as we would say today, devaluation. This leads to two things: Money loses its value because it has been devalued and, curiously enough, because it becomes increasingly scarce. The lack of money then leads to a downturn in business and to general impoverishment. It is this state of general desolation that provides the context for the Frankish conquest or which, rather, makes it possible. Gaul's vulnerability to a Frankish

---

*"that was the military armature of Gaul" does not figure in the manuscript, which reads, "a country ruined by absolutism."

invasion is bound up with the fact that the country was in ruins, and the explanation for that is the existence of mercenary armies.

I will come back later to this type of analysis. But the interesting thing about it—and this should be pointed out straightaway—is that Boulainvilliers's analysis is already very different from the analyses we find only a few decades earlier, when the question that was being raised was essentially that of public right, or in other words: Did Roman absolutism, and its system of right, survive the Frankish invasion? Did the Franks abolish, legitimately or otherwise, a sovereignty of the Roman type? That, broadly speaking, was the historical problem that was being raised in the seventeenth century. For Boulainvilliers, the problem is no longer whether Roman right did or did not still exist, or whether one right had the right to replace another. Those problems are no longer being posed. The problem is understanding the internal reasons for the defeat, or in other words, understanding in what sense the Roman government (legitimate or otherwise; that is not the problem) was logically absurd or politically contradictory. The famous problem of the grandeur and decadence of the Romans, which will become one of the great clichés of the historical or political literature of the eighteenth century,[10] and to which Montesquieu[11] will return long after Boulainvilliers, has a very precise meaning. What is, for the first time, taking shape here is an analysis of the economico-political type. A new model is taking shape, and the problem is no longer simply the problem of the negation of right, of the change of right, or of the transformation of an absolutist right into a Germanic-type right. That is the first set of analyses that can be found in Boulainvilliers. I am systematizing it all a bit, but I'm just trying to save time.

To move on from the problem of Gaul and the Romans, the second problem, or the second set of problems, which I will take as an example of Boulainvilliers's analyses, is the problem he raises with regard to the Franks: Who are these Franks who came to Gaul? This is the other side of the problem I was just talking about: Whence the strength of these people who, although they were uncouth, barbarous, and relatively few in number, could actually invade Gaul and destroy the most powerful empire that history had known until then? It is the strength of the Franks and the weakness of the Romans that have to be explained. To begin with the strength of the Franks: They enjoyed something the Romans believed they had to do without: the existence of a warrior aristocracy. The whole of Frankish society was organized around its warriors, who, although they were backed up by a whole series of people who were serfs (or at least servants dependent on clients), were basically the Frankish people itself, as the German people consists essentially of *Leute* or *leudes*, or people who are all men-at-arms, or the very opposite of mercenaries. What is more, these men-at-arms or aristocratic warriors elect their king, but his only function is to settle disputes and juridical problems in peacetime. Its kings are civil magistrates, and nothing more than that. What is more, these kings are chosen by the general consent of groups of *leudes*, or groups of men-at-arms. It is only in times of war—when a strong organization and one power are needed—that they elect a leader, and his leadership obeys very different principles and is absolute. The leader is a warlord who is not necessarily the king of civil society but who may, in certain circumstances, become its king. Someone such as Clovis—of [. . .] historical importance was both civil judge, the civilian magistrate who had been chosen to resolve disputes, and warlord. At all events, what we have here is a society in which power is minimal, at least in peacetime; it follows that freedom is maximal.

Now, what is this freedom that is enjoyed by the members of this warrior aristocracy? It is certainly not freedom in the sense of independence, nor is it the freedom that, basically, allows one to respect others. The freedom enjoyed by these Germanic warriors was essentially the freedom of egoism, of greed—a taste for battle, conquest, and plunder. The freedom of these warriors is not the freedom of tolerance and equality for all; it is a freedom that can be exercised only through domination. Far from being a freedom based upon respect, it is, in other words, a freedom based upon ferocity. And when he traces the etymology of the word *Franc*, Boulainvilliers's follower

Freret says that it certainly does not mean "free" in the sense in which we now understand the word; essentially, it means "ferocious," *ferox*. The word *franc* has exactly the same connotations as the Latin word *ferox*; according to Freret, it has all its favorable and unfavorable meanings. It means "proud, intrepid, haughty, cruel."[12] Here we have the beginnings of the famous great portrait of the "barbarian" which we will go on finding until the late nineteenth century and, of course, in Nietzsche, [for whom] freedom will be equivalent to a ferocity defined as a taste for power and determined greed, an inability to serve others, and constant desire to subjugate others; "unpolished and rough manners, a hatred of Roman names, the Roman language and Roman customs. Brave lovers of freedom, bold, fickle, faithless, eager for gain, impatient, restless,"*[13] et cetera. These are the epithets Boulainvilliers and his successors use to describe this new great blond barbarian who, thanks to their texts, makes his solemn entry into European history—I mean into European historiography.

This portrait of the great blond ferocity of the Germans makes it possible to explain, first of all, how, when these Frankish warriors came to Gaul, they simply could not and would not be assimilated into the Gallo-Romans and, more specifically, why they completely refused to submit to this imperial right. They were much too free, by which I mean too proud, too arrogant, and so on, not to prevent their warlord from becoming a sovereign in the Roman sense of the word. Their freedom made them far too intent on conquest and domination not to seize the land of Gaul for themselves on an individual basis. The Frankish victory therefore did not make their warlord the owner of the land of Gaul, but each of his warriors benefited, directly and in his own right, from the victory and conquest. Each warrior claimed for himself a piece of the land of Gaul. These are the distant beginnings of feudalism; I will omit the details of Boulainvilliers's analysis, as they are so complicated. Each warrior actually seized a piece of land; the king owned only his own land, and therefore had no Roman-style right of sovereignty over the whole of the land of Gaul. Because

---

*Quotation marks in the manuscript.

they had become independent and individual landowners, there was no reason for them to accept a king who ruled over them and who was, in some sense, the heir to the Roman emperors.

This is the beginning of the story of the vase of Soissons—again, I should say the historiography of the vase of Soissons. What is the story? You probably read it in your school textbooks. It was made up by Boulainvilliers, his predecessors, and his successors. They all borrowed the story from Gregory of Tours, and it became one of the clichés of their interminable historical discussions. When, after some battle or other—I can't remember which[14]—Clovis was sharing out the booty, or rather presiding as a civilian magistrate over the sharing out of the booty, you know, when he saw a certain vase, he said, "I want that," but a warrior got up and said: "You don't have any right to that vase. You might well be king, but you will share the booty with the rest of us. You have no preemptive rights, you have no prior or absolute right over the spoils of war. All the victors have an absolute right to the spoils of war: they have to be shared out, and the king has no preeminent right." This is the first phase of the story of the vase of Soissons. We will look later at the second.

Boulainvilliers's description of a Germanic community therefore allows him to explain why Germans completely rejected the Roman organization of power. But it also allows him to explain how and why a small number of poor people were able to conquer and hold the rich and populous land of Gaul. Once again, the comparison to England is interesting. You will recall that the English were faced with exactly the same problem: How was it that sixty thousand Norman warriors succeeded in settling in and holding England? Boulainvilliers has the same problem. And this is how he resolves it. He says this: The reason why the Franks were able to survive in the land they had conquered is that the first precaution they took was not only not to give the Gauls arms, but to confiscate their weapons. Which left a military caste that was both clearly differentiated from other castes and quite isolated from the rest of the country. It was a military caste, and it was purely Germanic. The Gauls no longer had any weapons, but on the other hand, they were left in actual possession of their lands, precisely because warfare was the only occupation of the Germans or Franks. The Franks fought, and the Gauls remained on their land and farmed it. They were merely required to pay certain taxes to allow the Germans to carry out their military functions. The taxes were certainly not light, but they were much less onerous than the taxes the Romans had tried to levy. They were much less onerous because they were, in quantitative terms, lower, but above all because, when the Romans demanded monetary taxes to pay their mercenaries, the peasants could not pay them. They were now being asked only for taxes that were paid in kind, and they could always pay them. To that extent, there was no longer any hostility between the peasant Gauls, who were merely being asked to pay taxes in kind, and the warrior caste. We therefore have a happy and stable Frankish Gaul which is much less impoverished than Roman Gaul was at the end of the Roman occupation. According to Boulainvilliers, the Franks and the Gauls lived happily side by side. Both were free to enjoy what they had in peace: the Franks were happy because the industrious Gauls provided for their needs, and the Gauls were happy because the Franks gave them security. We have here the sort of nucleus of what Boulainvilliers dreamed up: feudalism as the historico-juridical system characteristic of society, of European societies from the sixth, seventh, and eighth centuries down to almost the fifteenth. Until Boulainvilliers analyzed it, this system of feudalism had been identified by neither historians nor jurists. Such was the climate of the juridico-political unity of feudalism: a contented military caste supported and fed by a peasant population that paid it taxes in kind. That, so to speak, was the climate of the juridico-political unity of feudalism.

I would also like to isolate the third set of facts that Boulainvilliers analyzes, because they are important. I refer to the sequence of events whereby the nobility, or rather the warrior aristocracy, that had settled in France gradually lost most of its wealth and power and, ultimately, found itself being held in check by monarchical power. Boulainvilliers's analysis is roughly as follows: The king of the Franks was originally a temporary king in two senses. On the one hand, he was appointed warlord only for the duration of the war. The absolute character of his power lasted, therefore, only so long as the war itself. On the other hand, and to the extent that he was a civil magistrate, he did not necessarily have to belong to one particular dynasty. There was no right of succession, and he had to be elected. Now this sovereign, who was a temporary king in two senses, gradually became the permanent, hereditary, and absolute monarch with whom most European monarchies—and especially the French monarchy—were familiar. How did this transformation come about? First, because of the conquest itself, because of its military success. Because a small army had settled in an immense country which could be assumed, at least at first, to be hostile to it. It was therefore natural that the Frankish army should remain on a war footing in the Gaul it had just occupied. As a result, the man who had been warlord only for the duration of the war became both warlord and civilian leader. The very fact of the occupation kept the military organization intact. It was kept intact, but not without problems, not without difficulties, and not without rebellions on the part of the Franks themselves—on the part of Frankish warriors who did not agree that a military dictatorship should be maintained in peacetime. In order to retain his power, the king was therefore obliged to turn to mercenaries, and he found them either among the very Gaulish people who should have been left disarmed, or among foreigners. For all these reasons, the warrior aristocracy began to find itself being squeezed between a monarchic power that was trying to preserve its absolute character, and the Gaulish people, who were gradually being asked by the monarch himself to support his absolute power.

Which brings us to the second episode in the story of the Soissons vase. This is the moment when Clovis, who could not stomach being told not to touch the vase, was reviewing a military parade and noticed the warrior who had told him not to touch the said vase. Taking his great ax, the good Clovis smashed the warrior's skull in, telling him: "Remember the Soissons vase." Here we have the precise moment at which the man who should have been nothing more than a civilian magistrate—Clovis—holds on to the military form of his power, but uses it to settle a civil dispute. The absolute monarch is born at the moment when the military form of power and discipline begins to organize civilian right.

The second and more significant operation that allows civil power to take an absolutist form is as follows: On the one hand, then, the civil power appeals to the people of Gaul to recruit a band of mercenaries. But another alliance is also formed, and this time it is an alliance between royal power and the old Gaulish aristocracy. This is how Boulainvilliers analyzes it. He says: When the Franks came, which strata of the population of Gaul were worst affected? It was not so much the peasants (whose monetary taxes were transformed into taxes in kind), as the Gaulish aristocracy, whose lands were, of course, confiscated by the German and Frankish warriors. It was this aristocracy that was effectively dispossessed. It suffered as a result, so what did it do? Given that it no longer had its lands and that the Roman State no longer existed, there was only one refuge left; its only remaining shelter was the church. The Gaulish aristocracy therefore took refuge in the church. It not only developed the apparatus of the church; it also used the church to increase and expand its influence over the people by putting a whole system of beliefs into circulation. It was also the church that allowed it to improve its knowledge of Latin, and third, it was in the church that it studied Roman law, and that was an absolutist form of law. When the Frankish sovereigns had to rely on the support of the people in their struggle against the Germanic aristocracy and at the same time to found a State (or at least a monarchy) of the Roman type, what better allies could they hope to find than these men who had such influence over the people on the one hand, and who, because they spoke Latin, were so familiar with Roman law, on the other? The Gaulish aristocrats, the Gaulish nobility who had taken refuge in the church, quite naturally became the natural allies of the new monarchs once they began to establish their absolutism. And so the State, with its Latin, its Roman law, and its legal knowledge, became the great ally of the absolute monarchy.

So you see, Boulainvilliers ascribes great importance to what might be termed the language of knowledges, or the language-knowledge system. He shows how the warrior aristocracy was completely by-passed by the alliance between the monarchy and the people, and that alliance was based on the State, Latin, and a knowledge of the law. Latin became the language of the State, the language of knowledge, and the language of the law. The nobility lost its power to the extent that it belonged to a different linguistic system. The nobility spoke Germanic languages and did not understand Latin. Which meant that when the new system of right was being established by ordinances in Latin, it did not even understand what was happening to it. And it understood so little—and it was so important that it did not under-stand—that the church on the one hand, and the king on the other, did all they could to ensure that the nobility remained in the dark. Boulainvilliers traces the whole history of how the nobility was ed-ucated by showing that the reason the church placed such emphasis on the afterlife, which it described as the sole reason for being in this world, was basically that it wanted to convince the well-educated that nothing that happened in this world was of any importance, and that their true destiny lay in the next world. And so it was that the Germans, who had been so eager to possess and to dominate, the great blond warriors who had been so attached to the present, were gradually transformed into archetypal knights and archetypal crusad-ers who took no interest in what was going on on their own lands and in their own country, and who found themselves dispossessed of their fortune and their power. The Crusades—those great pilgrimages into the beyond—were, in Boulainvilliers's view, an expression or manifestation of what happened when this nobility's attention was fully concentrated on the next world. What was happening in this world, or in other words, on their lands, while they were in Jerusa-lem? The king, the church, and the old Gaulish aristocracy were manipulating the Latin laws that would dispossess them of their lands and their rights.

Hence Boulainvilliers's call—for what? Essentially—and this runs throughout the whole of his work—he does not, like the *parlementaire* historiographers (and popular historiographers) of seventeenth-century England, call for a rebellion on the part of nobles who have been dispossessed of their rights. What the nobility is being invited to do is, essentially, to open up its knowledge, to reopen its own memory, to become aware and to recuperate both expertise and knowledge. This is what Boulainvilliers is inviting the nobility to do in the first instance: "You will not regain power if you do not regain the status of the knowledges of which you have been dispossessed— or which, rather, you have never tried to possess. The fact is that you have always fought without realizing that there comes a point when the real battle, or at least the battle within society, is no longer fought with weapons, but with knowledge." Our ancestors, says Boulainvilliers, took a perverse pride in not knowing who they were. Their constant ability to forget who they were seems to have bordered on imbecility or bewitchment. Gaining a new self-awareness and tracing the sources of knowledge and memory means denouncing all the mystifications of history. If it reinserts itself into the web of knowledge, the nobility can become a force once more, and can establish itself as the subject of history. So if it wishes to become a historical force, that implies that it must, in the first instance, acquire a new self-awareness and reinsert itself into the order of knowledge.

Those are some of the themes I have identified in the voluminous works of Boulainvilliers, and they appear to me to introduce a type of analysis that will be of fundamental importance for all historico-political analyses from the seventeenth century until the present day. Why are these analyses important? First, because of the general primacy they accord to war. But I think that the really important thing about them, given that the primacy accorded to war by these analyses takes the form of the relationship of war, is the role Boulainvilliers gives to that relationship of war. Now I think that in order to use war as a general social analyzer in the way that he does, Boulainvilliers has to generalize war in three successive or superimposed ways. First, he generalizes it with respect to the foundations of right; second, he generalizes it with respect to the battle form; and third, he generalizes it with respect to the fact of the invasion and a second phenomenon that is the invasion's corollary: rebellion. I would like to look a little at these three generalizations.

First, generalization of war with respect to right and the foundations of right. In the earlier analyses of the French *parlementaires* of
the seventeenth century and the English parliamentarians of the same
period, war is a sort of disruptive episode that suspends and overturns
right. War is the ferryman who makes it possible to move from one
system of right to another. In Boulainvilliers, war does not play that
role; war does not disrupt right. War in fact completely conceals right,
and even natural right, to such an extent that right becomes unreal,
abstract, and, in a sense, fictive. Boulainvilliers advances three arguments to prove that war has completely concealed right, to such an
extent that right becomes no more than a useless abstraction. He
argues this in three ways. He first speaks in the historical mode and
says that you can study history as long as you like, and in any way
that you like, but you will never discover any natural rights. Natural
rights do not exist in any society, no matter what it may be. When
historians think they find in Saxon or Celtic society a sort of little
outcrop, a little island of natural right, they are completely mistaken.
No matter where we look, we find only either war itself (beneath the
French, we find the Frankish invasion; beneath the Gallo-Romans, we
find the Roman invasion) or the inequalities that result from wars
and violence. The Gauls, for example, were divided into aristocrats
and nonaristocrats. We also find an aristocracy and a people among
the Medes and the Persians. Which obviously goes to prove that behind that division there were struggles, violence, and wars. And
whenever we see the differences between the aristocracy and the people diminishing, we can be sure that the State is about to sink into
decadence. Once their aristocracies became decadent, Greece and
Rome lost their status and even ceased to exist as States. Inequality
is everywhere, violence creates inequalities everywhere, and wars are
everywhere. No society can last without this sort of warlike tension
between an aristocracy and the popular masses.

This same idea is now applied at the theoretical level. Boulainvilliers says: It is of course conceivable that a sort of primitive freedom
did exist before there was any domination, any power, any war, or
any servitude, but such freedom is conceivable only if there is no

relationship of domination between any of the individuals concerned.
A freedom in which everyone, in which every individual is the
equal of every other individual, this freedom–equality combination
can, in reality, only be something that has no force and no content.
Because . . . what is freedom? Freedom obviously does not consist in
being prevented from trampling on someone else's freedom, because
at that point it ceases to be freedom. The first criterion that defines
freedom is the ability to deprive others of their freedom. What would
be the point of being free and what, in concrete terms, would it mean,
if one could not trample on the freedom of others? That is the primary
expression of freedom. According to Boulainvilliers, freedom is the
direct opposite of equality. It is something that is enjoyed thanks to
difference, domination, and war, thanks to a whole system of relations
of force. A freedom that cannot be translated into a nonegalitarian
relationship of force can only be a freedom that it is weak, impotent,
and abstract.

This idea is now applied in both historical and theoretical terms.
Boulainvilliers says (and once again, I am being very schematic): Let
us accept the fact that natural right did actually exist at some point,
that at the founding moment of history there did exist a right that
made people both free and equal. The weakness of this freedom is
such that, precisely because it is an abstract, fictive freedom with no
real content, it will inevitably be defeated by the historical force of a
freedom that functions as nonequality. And while it is true that something resembling this natural freedom, this egalitarian freedom or this
natural right, did exist somewhere or at some point, it was powerless
to resist the law of history, which states that freedom is strong, vigorous, and meaningful only when it is the freedom of the few and
when it exists at the expense of others, only when a society can
guarantee an essential nonequality.

The egalitarian law of nature is weaker than the nonegalitarian law
of history. It is therefore natural that the egalitarian law of nature
should have given way—on a permanent basis—to the nonegalitarian
law of history. It was because it was primal that natural right was
not, as the jurists claim, foundational; it was foreclosed by the greater

vigor of history. The law of history is always stronger than the law of nature. This is what Boulainvilliers is arguing when he says that history finally created a natural law that made freedom and equality antithetical, and that this natural law is stronger than the law inscribed in what is known as natural right. The fact that history is stronger than nature explains, ultimately, why history has completely concealed nature. When history begins, nature can no longer speak, because in the war between history and nature, history always has the upper hand. There is a relationship of force between nature and history, and it is definitely in history's favor. So natural right does not exist, or exists only insofar as it has been defeated: it is always history's great loser, it is "the other" (like the Gauls who lost to the Romans, like the Gallo-Romans who lost to the Germans). History is, if you like, Germanity, as opposed to nature. So, a first generalization: Rather than disturbing or interrupting it, war conceals history completely.

Second generalization of war with respect to the battle form: According to Boulainvilliers, it is true that conquests, invasions, and the battles that are lost and won do establish a relationship of force; but the relationship of force that finds its expression in the battle was, basically, already established, and it was established by something other than earlier battles. So what is it that establishes the relationship of force and ensures that one nation will win the battle and that the other will lose it? Well, it is the nature and organization of military institutions ; it is the army; it is military institutions. These are important because, on the one hand, they obviously make it possible to win victories, but also because, on the other hand, they also make it possible to articulate society as a whole. According to Boulainvilliers, the important thing, the thing that makes war both the starting point for an analysis of society and the deciding factor in social organization, is the problem of military organization or, quite simply, this: Who has the weapons? The organization of the Germans was essentially based upon the fact that some—the *leudes*—had weapons and that others did not. The characteristic feature of the regime of Frankish Gaul was that it took the precaution of taking the Gauls' weapons from them and reserving them for the Germans (who, because they were men-at-arms, had to be supported by the Gauls). Things began to change for the worse when the laws governing the social distribution of weapons become confused, when the Romans began to employ mercenaries, when the Frankish kings organized militias, and when Philip Augustus began to use foreign knights, and so on. From this point onward, the simple organization that allowed the Germans, and only the Germans, or the warrior aristocracy to own weapons, collapsed in confusion.

The problem of who has the weapons is of course bound up with certain technical problems, and it is in that sense that it can provide the starting point for a general analysis of society. Knights, for example, are synonymous with lances and heavy armor but also with a numerically small army of rich men. "Archer," in contrast, is synonymous with light armor and a large army. As we can see, this points to a whole series of economic and institutional problems. If there is an army of knights, a heavy and numerically small army of knights, the powers of the king are obviously limited, as a king cannot afford such an expensive army of knights. The knights themselves will be obliged to pay for their own upkeep. An army of foot soldiers, in contrast, is a numerically large army, and a king can afford such an army. Hence the growth of royal power, but hence too the increase in taxation. So you see, this time it is not because it takes the form of an invasion that war leaves its mark on the social body; it is because, through the intermediary of military institutions, it has general effects on the civil order as a whole. It is therefore no longer the simple duality between invaders and invaded or victors and vanquished, the memory of the Battle of Hastings or of the Frankish invasion, that serves as social analyzer. It is no longer the simple binary mechanism that puts the seal of war on the entire social body; it is a war that begins before the battle and continues after it is over. It is war insofar as it is a way of waging war, a way of preparing for and organizing war. War in the sense of the distribution of weapons, the nature of the weapons, fighting techniques, the recruitment and payment of soldiers, the taxes earmarked for the army; war as an internal institution, and not the raw event of a battle. This is the operator in Boulainvilliers's analyses. He succeeds in writing the history of France because he constantly traces the connecting thread that, behind the battle and behind the invasion, brings into being the military institution and, going beyond the military institution, all the country's institutions and its whole economy. War is a general economy of weapons, an economy of armed people and disarmed people within a given State, and with all the institutional and economic series that derive from that. It is this formidable generalization of war, as opposed to what it still meant for the historians of the seventeenth century, that gives Boulainvilliers the important dimension I am trying to show you.

The third and final generalization of war that we find in Boulainvilliers's analysis is made not with respect to the fact of the battle but with respect to the invasion-rebellion system. Invasion and rebellion were the two main elements that were introduced to rediscover the war that goes on within societies (in, for example, the English historiography of the seventeenth century). Boulainvilliers's problem is not then simply to discover when the invasion took place, or what the effects of the invasion were; nor does it simply consist in showing whether there was or was not a rebellion. What he wants to show is how a certain relationship of force, which had been revealed by the battle and the invasion, was gradually, and for obscure reasons, inverted. The problem of the English historiographers was that they had to look everywhere, at all institutions, so as to find out where the strong (the Normans) were, and where the weak (the Saxons) were. Boulainvilliers's problem is to discover how the strong became weak, and how the weak became strong. The greater part of his analysis is devoted to the problem of the transition from strength to weakness, and from weakness to strength.

Boulainvilliers begins to analyze and describe this change by looking at what might be called the determination of the internal mechanisms of the inversion, and examples are easily found. What was it that actually made the Frankish aristocracy so strong at the beginning of what was soon to become known as the Middle Ages? It was the fact that, having invaded and occupied Gaul, the Franks themselves directly appropriated the land. They were therefore landowners in their own right, and they were therefore in receipt of taxes in kind that ensured both that the peasant population remained quiet and that the knights remained strong. And it was precisely this, or in other words, the source of their strength, that gradually became the principle of their weakness. Because the nobles lived on their separate estates, and because the tax system financed their ability to make war, they became separated from the king they had created, and were preoccupied only with war and with fighting among themselves. As a result, they neglected everything that had to do with education, instruction, learning Latin, and acquiring expertise. All these things would lead to their loss of power.

If, conversely, you take the example of the Gaulish aristocracy, it could not have been weaker than it was at the beginning of the Frankish invasion: every Gaulish landowner had been dispossessed of everything. And, in historical terms, their very weakness became the source of their strength, thanks to an inevitable development. The fact that they had been driven off their land and into the arms of the church gave them influence over the people, but also an understanding of right. And that gradually put them in a position to grow closer to the king, to become advisers to the king, and therefore to get their hands on a political power and an economic wealth that had previously eluded them. The form and the elements that constituted the weakness of the Gaulish aristocracy were also, from a certain point onward, the very things that allowed it to reverse the situation.

The problem Boulainvilliers is analyzing is therefore not who won and who lost, but who became strong and who became weak. Why did the strong become weak, and why did the weak become strong? History, in other words, now looks essentially like a calculation of forces. Insofar as a description of the mechanisms of relations of force is required, what will be the inevitable outcome of this analysis? The conclusion that the simple dichotomy between victors and vanquished is no longer strictly pertinent to the description of this whole process. Once the strong become weak and the weak become strong, there will be new oppositions, new divisions, and a new distribution of forces: the weak will form alliances among themselves, and the strong will try to form alliances with some and against others. What was still, at the time of the invasion, a sort of pitched battle in which armies fought armies—Franks against Gauls, and Normans against Saxons— these great national masses will be divided and transformed by multiple channels. And we will see the emergence of a diversity of struggles, shifting front lines, conjunctural alliances, and more or less permanent groupings: monarchical power will form an alliance with the old Gaulish nobility, and they will have the support of the people; the tacit understanding that existed between the Frankish warriors and the peasants will break down when the impoverished Frankish warriors increase their demands and demand higher taxes; and so on. Until the seventeenth century, historians had basically taken the great confrontation of the invasion as their model; this little system of support networks, alliances, and internal conflicts will now, so to speak, develop into a form of generalized warfare.

Until the seventeenth century, a war was essentially a war between one mass and another mass. For his part, Boulainvilliers makes the relationship of war part of every social relationship, subdivides it into thousands of different channels, and reveals war to be a sort of permanent state that exists between groups, fronts, and tactical units as they in some sense civilize one another, come into conflict with one another, or on the contrary, form alliances. There are no more multiple and stable great masses, but there is a multiple war. In one sense, it is a war of every man against every man, but it is obviously not a war of every man against every man in the abstract and—I think—unreal sense in which Hobbes spoke of the war of every man against every man when he tried to demonstrate that it is not the war of every man against every man that is at work in the social body. With Boulainvilliers, in contrast, we have a generalized war that permeates the entire social body and the entire history of the social body; it is obviously not the sort of war in which individuals fight individuals, but one in which groups fight groups. And it is, I

think, this generalization of war that is characteristic of Boulainvilliers's thought.

I would like to end by saying this. What does this threefold generalization of war lead to? It leads to this. It is thanks to this that
Boulainvilliers reaches a point that the historians of right [...]* For
those historians who identified history with public right, with the
State, war was therefore essentially a disruption of right, an enigma,
a sort of dark mass or raw event that had to be accepted as such, and
not, certainly not, a principle of intelligibility. There was no question
of that; on the contrary, it was a disruptive principle. Here, in contrast, war turns the very disruption of right into a grid of intelligibility, and makes it possible to determine the force relationship that
always underpins a certain relationship of right. Boulainvilliers can
thus integrate events such as wars, invasions, and change—which were
once seen simply as naked acts of violence—into a whole layer of
contents and prophecies that covered society in its entirety (because,
as we have seen, they affect right, the economy, taxation, religion,
beliefs, education, the study of languages, and juridical institutions).
A history that takes as its starting point the fact of war itself and
makes its analysis in terms of war can relate all these things—war,
religion, politics, manners, and characters—and can therefore act as a
principle that allows us to understand history. According to Boulainvilliers, it is war that makes society intelligible, and I think that the
same can be said of all historical discourse. When I speak of a grid
of intelligibility, I am obviously not saying that what Boulainvilliers
said is true. One could probably even demonstrate that everything he
said was false. I am simply saying that it could be demonstrated. What
was said in the seventeenth century about the Trojan origins of the

---

*The recording breaks down at this point. The manuscript explicitly states: "In one sense,
it is analogous to the juridical problem: How does sovereignty come into being? But this
time, the historical narrative is not being used to illustrate the continuity of a sovereignty
that is legitimate because it remains within the element of right from beginning to end. It
is being used to explain how the specific institution, or the modern historical figure, of the
absolute state was born of intersecting relations of force that became a sort of generalized
war among nations."

Franks, or about how they emigrated and left France under the leadership of a certain Sigovège at some point and then returned, cannot be said to have anything to do with our regime of truth and error. In our terms, it is neither true nor false. The grid of intelligibility established by Boulainvilliers, in contrast, does, I think, establish a certain regime, a certain division between truth and error, that can be applied to Boulainvilliers's own discourse and that can say that his discourse is wrong—wrong as a whole and wrong about the details. Even that it is all wrong, if you like. The fact remains that it is this grid of intelligibility that has been established for our historical discourse.

The other thing I would like to stress is that by making the force relationship intervene as a sort of war that is constantly going on within society, Boulainvilliers was able to recuperate—this time in historical terms—the whole kind of analysis that we find in Machiavelli. But for Machiavelli, the relationship of force was essentially described as a political technique that had to be put in the hands of the sovereign. The relationship of force now becomes a historical object that someone other than the sovereign—something like a nation (like the aristocracy or, at a later stage, the bourgeoisie)—can locate and determine within its own history. The relationship of force, which was once an essentially political object, becomes a historical object, or rather a historico-political object, because it is by analyzing this relationship of force that the nobility, for example, can acquire a new self-awareness, recover its knowledge, and once more become a political force within the field of political forces. When, in a discourse such as Boulainvilliers's, this relationship of force (which was in a sense the exclusive object of the Prince's preoccupations) became an object of knowledge for a group, a nation, a minority, or a class, it became possible to constitute a historico-political field, and to make history function within the political struggle. This is how the organization of a historico-political field begins. At this point, it all comes together: History functions within politics, and politics is used to calculate historical relations of force.

One further remark. As you can see, this is the origin of the idea that war is basically historical discourse's truth-matrix. "Historical discourse's truth-matrix" means this: What philosophy or right would have us believe notwithstanding, truth does not begin, or truth and the Logos do not begin, when violence ceases. On the contrary, it began when the nobility started to wage its political war against both the Third Estate and the monarchy, and it was in this war and by thinking of history in terms of war that something resembling what we now know as historical discourse could establish itself.

Penultimate remark: You are familiar with the cliché that says that classes in the ascendancy are the bearers of universal values and the power of rationality. An awful lot of effort has gone into trying to demonstrate that it was the bourgeoisie that invented history, because history is—as everyone knows—rational and because the bourgeoisie of the eighteenth century, being a rising class, brought with it both universality and rationality. Well, I think that if we look at things a little more closely, we have an example of a class that, precisely because it was decadent and had been dispossessed of its political and economic power, was able to establish a certain historical rationality that was then taken up by the bourgeoisie and then the proletariat. But I would not say that it was because it was decadent that the French aristocracy invented history. It was precisely because it was waging a war that it was able to take war as an object, war being at once the starting point for the discourse, the condition of possibility for the emergence of a historical discourse, a frame of reference, and the object of that discourse. War was both this discourse's starting point and what it was talking about.

One last remark, finally. The reason Clausewitz could say one day, a hundred years after Boulainvilliers and, therefore, two hundred years after the English historians, that war was the continuation of politics by other means is that, in the seventeenth century, or at the beginning of the eighteenth, someone was able to analyze politics, talk about politics, and demonstrate that politics is the continuation of war by other means.

1. See the lectures of 28 January and 11 February above.
2. "Collective word used to designate a considerable quantity of people inhabiting a certain expanse of territory, contained within certain limits, and obedient to the same government." "Nation" in *Encyclopédie, ou Dictionnaire raisonné des sciences, des arts et des métiers* (Lucques, 1758), vol. 11, pp. 29-30.
3. E.-J. Sieyès, *Qu'est-ce que le Tiers-Etat?* On Sieyès, see the lecture of 10 March below.
4. On Augustin Thierry, see the lecture of 10 March below.
5. On François Guizot, see the lecture of 10 March below.
6. Joachim, comte d'Estaing, *Dissertation sur la noblesse d'extraction.*
7. On Buat-Nançay, see the lecture of 10 March below.
8. On Montlosier, see the lecture of 10 March below.
9. The analysis of Boulainvilliers's historical work undertaken by Foucault in this lecture (and the next) is based upon the texts already mentioned in notes 21-22 to the lecture of 11 February and, more specifically, on *Mémoires de l'histoire du gouvernement de la France,* in *Etat de la France . . .; Histoire de l'ancien gouvernement de la France . . .; Dissertation sur la noblesse française servant de Préface aux Mémoires de la maison de Croi et de Boulainvilliers,* in A. Devyer, *Le Sang épuré . . .; Mémoires présentés à Mgr le duc d'Orléans. . . .*
10. This literature begins with Machiavelli, *Discorsi sopra la prima deca di Tito Livio,* written 1513-1517 (Florence, 1531); continues with Bossuet, *Discours sur l'histoire universelle* (Paris, 1681), E. W. Montagu, *Reflections on the Rise and Fall of the Ancient Republics* (London, 1759), and A. Ferguson, *The History of the Progress and Termination of the Roman Republic* (London, 1783); and ends with Edward Gibbon, *History of the Decline and Fall of the Roman Empire,* 6 vols. (London, 1776-1778).
11. Charles-Louis de Montesquieu, *Considérations sur les causes de la grandeur des Romains et de leur décadence* (Amsterdam, 1734).
12. N. Freret, *De l'origine des Français et de leur établissement dans la Gaule,* in *Oeuvres complètes* (Paris, 1796-1799), vol. 5, an VII, p. 202.
13. Cf. F. Nietzsche, *Zur Genealogie der Moral: eine Streitschrift* (Leipzig, 1887), Erste Abhandlung: "Gut und Böse," "Gut und Schlecht," 11; Zweite Abhandlung: "Schuld," "Schlechtes Gewissen und Verwandtes," 16, 17, 18. See also *Morgenröte: Gedanken über die moralischen vorutheile* (Chemnitz, 1881), Zweite Buch 112. (French translations: *Généalogie de la morale. Un écrit polémique* [Paris: Gallimard, 1971] and *Aurore. Pensées sur les préjugés moraux* [Paris: Gallimard, 1970]; English translations by Francis Golffing, *The Genealogy of Morals,* in *The Birth of Tragedy and the Genealogy of Morals* [New York: Doubleday, 1956], and by R. J. Hollingdale, *Daybreak: Thoughts on the Prejudices of Morality* [Cambridge: Cambridge University Press, 1982]). Cf. the quotation from Boulainvilliers in Devyer, *Le Sang épuré . . .*, p. 508: "they were great lovers of freedom, bold, fickle, unfaithful, avid for gain, restless and impatient: this is how the ancient authors describe them."
14. The reference is to the defeat of the Roman Sygarius and the capture of Soissons in 486.

eight

25 February 1976

[*Boulainvilliers and the constitution of a historico-political continuum. - Historicism. - Tragedy and public right. - The central administration of history. - The problematic of the Enlightenment and the genealogy of knowledges. - The four operations of disciplinary knowledge and their effects. - Philosophy and science. - Disciplining knowledges.*]

WHEN I TALKED TO you about Boulainvilliers, I was certainly not trying to prove to you that something resembling history began with him, because, after all, there is no reason to say that history began with Boulainvilliers rather than with, for example, the sixteenth-century jurists who collated the monuments of public right, with the *parlementaires* who, throughout the seventeenth century, searched the archives and jurisprudence of the State to discover what the basic laws of the kingdom might be, or with the Benedictines, who had been great collectors of charters even since the late sixteenth century. What was in fact established by Boulainvilliers in the early eighteenth century was—I think—a historico-political field. In what sense? First, in this sense: By taking the nation, or rather nations, as his object, Boulainvilliers was able to dig beneath institutions, events, kings and their power, and to analyze something else, namely those societies, as they were called at the time, that were bound together by interests, customs, and laws. By taking them as his object, he changed two things. One the one hand, he began to write (and I think it was the first time this had happened) the history of subjects, or in other words, to look at power from the other side. He thus began to give a historical status to something that would, with Michelet in the nineteenth century, become the history of the people or the history of peoples.[1] He discovered a certain form of history that existed on the other side of the power relationship. But he analyzed this new form of history not as though it were an inert substance, but as a force—or forces; power itself was no more than one of those forces—an unusual kind of force, or the strangest of all the forces that were fighting one another within the social body. Power is the power of the little group that exercises it but has no force; and yet, ultimately, this power becomes the strongest force of all, a force that no other force can resist, except violence or rebellion. What Boulainvilliers was discovering was that history should not be the history of power, but the history of a monstrous, or at least strange, couple whose enigmatic nature could not exactly be reduced or understood by any juridical fiction: the couple formed by the primal forces of the people, and the force that had finally been constituted by something that had no force, but that was power.

By displacing the axis, the center of gravity, of his analysis, Boulainvilliers did something important. First, because he defined the principle of what might be called the relational character of power: power is not something that can be possessed, and it is not a form of might; power is never anything more than a relationship that can, and must, be studied only by looking at the interplay between the terms of that relationship. One cannot, therefore, write either the history of kings or the history of peoples; one can write the history of what constitutes those opposing terms, one of which is never infinity, and the other of which is never zero. By writing that history, by defining the relational character of power, and by analyzing it in history, Boulainvilliers was challenging—and this, I think, is the other side of what he was doing—the juridical model of sovereignty which had, until then, been the only way of thinking of the relationship between people and monarch, or between the people and those who govern. Boulainvilliers describes the phenomenon of power not in juridical terms of sovereignty but in historical terms of domination and the play of relations of force. And he places the object of his historical analysis within that field.

In doing so, in taking as his object a power that was essentially relational and not adequate to the juridical form of sovereignty, and by defining a field of forces in which the power-relationship comes into play, Boulainvilliers is taking as his object the historical knowledge that Machiavelli analyzed, but only in prescriptive strategic terms—or in terms of a strategy seen only through the eyes of power and the Prince.[2] You might object that Machiavelli did not just give the Prince advice—whether it is serious or ironic is a different question—about how to manage and organize power, and that the text of *The Prince* itself is full of historical references. You might say that Machiavelli also wrote the *Discorsi*. But for Machiavelli, history is not the domain in which he analyzes power relations. For Machiavelli, history is simply a source of examples, a sort of collection of jurisprudence or of tactical models for the exercise of power. For Machiavelli, history simply records relations of force and the calculations to which they gave rise.

For Boulainvilliers, on the other hand (and this, I think, is the important point), relations of force and the play of power are the very stuff of history. History exists, events occur, and things that happen can and must be remembered, to the extent that relations of power, relations of force, and a certain play of power operate in relations among men. According to Boulainvilliers, historical narratives and political calculations have exactly the same object. Historical narratives and political calculations may not have the same goal, but there is a definite continuity in what they are talking about, and in what is at stake in both narrative and calculation. In Boulainvilliers, we therefore find—for the first time, I think—a historico-political continuum. One could also say, in a slightly different sense, that Boulainvilliers opens up a historico-political field. Let me explain. As I have already told you—and I think this is of fundamental importance if we are to understand Boulainvilliers's starting point—he was trying to make a critique of the knowledge of the intendants, of the sort of analysis and the projects for government that the intendants or, more generally, the monarchical government was constantly drawing up for power's benefit. It is true that Boulainvilliers was a radical opponent of this knowledge, but he challenges it by reimplanting it within his own discourse, and by using for his own ends the very analyses that we find in the knowledge of the intendants. His goal was to confiscate it and to use it against the system of the absolute monarchy, which was both the birthplace and the field of application of this administrative knowledge, this knowledge of the intendants, and this economic knowledge.

And basically, when Boulainvilliers analyzes the historical evolution of a whole series of specific relations between, if you like, military organization and taxation, he is simply acclimatizing, or using for his own historical analyses, the very form of relationship, the type of intelligibility and the model of relations that had been defined by administrative knowledge, fiscal knowledge, and the knowledge of the intendants. When, for example, Boulainvilliers explains the relation between the employment of mercenaries and increased taxation, or between the debts of the peasantry and the impossibility of marketing the produce of the land, he is simply raising the issues raised by the intendants and financiers of the reign of Louis XIV, but he is doing so within the historical dimension. You will find exactly the same speculations in the work of people such as, for example, Boisguilbert[3] and Vauban.[4] The relation between rural indebtedness and urban prosperity was another important topic of discussion throughout the late seventeenth and early eighteenth centuries. We find, then, the same mode of intelligibility in both the knowledge of the intendants and Boulainvilliers's historical analyses, but he is the first to make this type of relation function in the domain of historical narrative. In other words, Boulainvilliers makes what had until then been no more than State management's principle of rationality function as a principle for understanding history. That a continuity has been established between historical narrative and the management of the State is, I believe, of vital importance. It is the use of the State's model of managerial rationality as a grid for the speculative understanding of history that establishes the historico-political continuum. And that continuum now makes it possible to use the same vocabulary and the same grid of intelligibility to speak of history and to analyze the management of the State.

I think, finally, that Boulainvilliers establishes a historico-political continuum to the extent that, when he writes history, he has a specific and definite project: his specific goal is restore to the nobility both a memory it has lost and a knowledge that it has always neglected. What Boulainvilliers is trying to do by giving it back its memory and its knowledge is to give it a new force, to reconstruct the nobility as a force within the forces of the social field. For Boulainvilliers, beginning to speak in the domain of history, recounting a history, is therefore not simply a matter of describing a relationship of force, or of reutilizing on behalf of, for example, the nobility a calculation of intelligibility that had previously belonged to the government. He is doing so in order the modify the very disposition and the current equilibrium of the relations of force. History does not simply analyze or interpret forces: it modifies them. The very fact of having control over, or the fact of being right in the order of historical knowledge, in short, of telling the truth about history, therefore enables him to occupy a decisive strategic position.

To sum all this up, we can say that the constitution of a historico-political field is an expression of the fact that we have gone from a history whose function was to establish right by recounting the exploits of heroes or kings, their battles and their wars and so on, that we have gone from a history that established right by telling the story of wars to a history that continues the war by deciphering the war and the struggle that are going on within all the institutions of right and peace. History thus becomes a knowledge of struggles that is deployed and that functions within a field of struggles; there is now a link between the political fight and historical knowledge. And while it is no doubt true that confrontations have always been accompanied by recollections, memories, and various rituals of memorialization, I think that from the eighteenth century onward—and it is at this point that political life and political knowledge begin to be inscribed in

society's real struggles—strategy, or the element of calculation inherent in such struggles, will be articulated with a historical knowledge
that takes the form of the interpretation and analysis of forces. We
cannot understand the emergence of this specifically modern dimension of politics unless we understand how, from the eighteenth century onward, historical knowledge becomes an element of the struggle:
it is both a description of struggles and a weapon in the struggle.
History gave us the idea that we are at war; and we wage war through
history.

Having established that, let me make two points before we go back
to the war that is waged throughout the history of peoples. My first
point concerns historicism. Everyone knows of course that historicism
is the most dreadful thing in the world. Any philosophy worthy of
the name, any theory of society, any self-respecting epistemology that
has any claim to distinction obviously has to struggle against the plat-
itudes of historicism. No one would dare to admit to being a histor-
icist. And it can, I think, easily be demonstrated that ever since the
nineteenth century, all the great philosophies have, in one way or
another, been antihistoricist. One could also, I think, demonstrate that
all the human sciences survive, or perhaps even exist, only because
they are antihistoricist.[5] One could also demonstrate that when history, or the historical discipline, has recourse to either a philosophy
of history or a juridical and moral ideality, or to the human sciences
(all of which it finds so enchanting), it is trying to escape its fatal
and secret penchant for historicism.

But what is this historicism that everyone—philosophy, the human
sciences, history—is so suspicious of? What is this historicism that
has to be warded off at all cost, and that philosophical, scientific, and
even political modernity have always tried to ward off? Well, I think
that historicism is nothing other than what I have just been talking
about: the link, the unavoidable connection, between war and history,
and conversely, between history and war. No matter how far back it
goes, historical knowledge never finds nature, right, order, or peace.
However far back it goes, historical knowledge discovers only an
unending war, or in other words, forces that relate to one another

and come into conflict with one another, and the events in which relations of force are decided, but always in a provisional way. History encounters nothing but war, but history can never really look down on this war from on high; history cannot get away from war, or discover its basic laws or impose limits on it, quite simply because war itself supports this knowledge, runs through this knowledge, and determines this knowledge. Knowledge is never anything more than a weapon in a war, or a tactical deployment within that war. War is waged throughout history, and through the history that tells the history of war. And history, for its part, can never do anything more than interpret the war it is waging or that is being waged through it.

Well, then, I think it is this essential connection between historical knowledge and the practice of war—it is this, generally speaking, that constitutes the core of historicism, a core that both is irreducible and always has to be sanitized, because of an idea, which has been in circulation for the last one thousand or two thousand years, and which might be described as "platonic" (though we should always be wary of blaming poor old Plato for everything we want to banish). It is an idea that is probably bound up with the whole Western organization of knowledge, namely, the idea that knowledge and truth cannot not belong to the register of order and peace, that knowledge and truth can never be found on the side of violence, disorder, and war. I think that the important thing (and whether it is or is not platonic is of no importance) about this idea that knowledge and truth cannot belong to war, and can only belong to order and peace, is that the modern State has now reimplanted it in what we might call the eighteenth century's "disciplinarization" of knowledges. And it is this idea that makes historicism unacceptable to us, that means that we cannot accept something like an indissociable circularity between historical knowledge and the wars that it talks about and which at the same time go on in it. So this is the problem, and this, if you like, is our first task: We must try to be historicists, or in other words, try to analyze this perpetual and unavoidable relationship between the war that is recounted by history and the history that is traversed by the war it is recounting. And it is along these lines that I will now try to go on with the little story of the Gauls and the Franks that I started to tell.

So much for my first remark, for my first excursus on historicism. To move on to the second: an objection can be made. There might be another way of approaching the theme I touched upon a moment ago, or in other words the disciplinarization of knowledges in the eighteenth century. If we make history, the history of the wars that go on throughout history, the great discursive apparatus that makes possible the eighteenth-century critique of the State, and if we make the history/war relationship the precondition for the emergence of "politics" [. . .] the function of order was to reestablish a continuity in its discourse.*

[At the time when the jurists were exploring the archives in an attempt to discover the basic laws of the kingdom, a historians' history was taking shape, and it was not power's ode to itself. It should not be forgotten that in the seventeenth century, and not only in France, tragedy was one of the great ritual forms in which public right was displayed and in which its problems were discussed. Well, Shakespeare's "historical" tragedies are tragedies about right and the king, and they are essentially centered on the problem of the usurper and dethronement, of the murder of kings and the birth of the new being who is constituted by the coronation of a king. How can an individual use violence, intrigue, murder, and war to acquire a public might that can bring about the reign of peace, justice, order, and happiness? How can illegitimacy produce law? At a time when the theory and history of right are trying to weave the unbroken continuity of public might, Shakespearean tragedy, in contrast, dwells][6] on the wound, on the repeated injury that is inflicted on the body of the kingdom when kings die violent deaths and when illegitimate sovereigns come to the throne. I think that Shakespearean tragedy is, at least in terms of one of its axes, a sort of ceremony, a sort of rememorialization of the

---

*It is difficult to establish the meaning on the basis of the tape recording. The first eighteen pages of the manuscript were in fact moved to the end in the lecture itself.

problems of public right. The same could be said of French tragedy, of that of Corneille and, of course, especially Racine. Besides, in general terms, isn't Greek tragedy too always, essentially, a tragedy about right? I think that there is a fundamental, essential kinship between tragedy and right, between tragedy and public right, just as there is probably an essential kinship between the novel and the problem of the norm. Tragedy and right, the novel and the norm: perhaps we should look into all this.

Be that as it may, tragedy is a sort of representation of public right, a politico-juridical representation of public might, in seventeenth-century France too. There is, however, one difference—and this (genius aside) is where it basically differs from Shakespeare. On the one hand, French classical tragedy usually deals only with ancient kings. This coding is no doubt a matter of political prudence. But after all, it should not be forgotten that one of the reasons for this reference to antiquity is this: In seventeenth-century France, and especially under Louis XIV, monarchic right was, because of its form and even the continuity of its history, depicted as being directly descended from the monarchies of antiquity. We find the same type of power and the same type of monarchy in Augustus and Nero, or even Pyrrhus,[7] that we find with Louis XIV. It is the same monarchy in both substantive and juridical terms. On the other hand, French classical tragedy contains a reference to antiquity, but we can also see the presence of an institution that appears to restrict in some way the tragic powers of tragedy, and to make it tip over into a theater of gallantry and intrigue: the presence of the court. Ancient tragedy, and courtly tragedy. But what is the court, if not—and this is dazzlingly obvious in the case of Louis XIV—yet another lesson in public right? The court's essential function is to constitute, to organize, a space for the daily and permanent display of royal power in all its splendor. The court is basically a kind of permanent ritual operation that begins again every day and requalifies a man who gets up, goes for a walk, eats, has his loves and his passions, and who is at the same time—thanks to all that, because of all that, and because none of all that is eliminated—a sovereign. The specific operation of court ritual and court ceremonial is to make his love affairs sovereign, to make his food sovereign, to make his levee and his going-to-bed ritual sovereign. And while the court constantly requalifies his daily routine as sovereign in the person of a monarch who is the very substance of monarchy, tragedy does the same thing in reverse; tragedy undoes and, if you like, recomposes what court ritual establishes each day.

What is the point of classical tragedy, of Racinian tragedy? Its function—or at least one of its axes—is to constitute the underside of the ceremony, to show the ceremony in shreds, the moment when the sovereign, the possessor of public might, is gradually broken down into a man of passion, a man of anger, a man of vengeance, a man of love, incest, and so on. In tragedy, the problem is whether or not starting from this decomposition of the sovereign into a man of passion, the sovereign-king can be reborn and recomposed: the death and resurrection of the body of the king in the heart of the monarch. That is the problem (and it is much more juridical than psychological) that is posed by Racinian tragedy. In that sense, you can well understand that when Louis XIV asked Racine to be his historiographer, he was simply being true to the tradition of what the historiography of the monarchy had been until then, or in other words, an ode to power itself. But he is also allowing Racine to go on performing the function he had played when he wrote his tragedies. He was basically asking him to write, as a historiographer, the fifth act of a happy tragedy, or in other words, to trace the rise of the private man—the courtier who had a heart—to the point where he becomes at once warlord, monarch, and the holder of sovereignty. Entrusting his historiography to a tragic poet did not disturb the order of right, nor did it betray history's old function of establishing right, of establishing the right of the sovereign State. It marked—thanks to a necessity that is bound up with the absolutism of the king—a return to the purest and most elementary function of royal historiography in an absolute monarchy. It must not be forgotten that as a result of a sort of strange lapse into archaism, the absolute monarchy made the ceremony of power an intense political moment, or that the court, which was one of power's ceremonies, was a daily lesson in public right, a daily demonstration of public right. We can now understand why Racine's appointment allowed the history of the king to take on its purest form and, in a sense, its magico-poetic form. The history of the king could not but become power's ode to itself. So absolutism, court ceremonial, manifestations of public right, classical tragedy, and the historiography of the king: I think they are all part of the same thing.

Excuse my speculations about Racine and historiography. Let's skip a century (the very century that began with Boulainvilliers) and take the example of the last of the absolute monarchs and the last of his historiographers: Louis XVI and Jacob-Nicolas Moreau, the distant successor to Racine, of whom I have already said a few words, as he was the minister of history appointed by Louis XVI toward the end of the 1780s. Who was Moreau, compared to Racine? This is a dangerous parallel, but you might be surprised who comes off worse. Moreau is the scholarly defender of a king who, obviously, needed to be defended on a number of occasions during his lifetime. Moreau certainly played the role of defender when he was appointed in the 1780s—at the very time when the rights of the monarchy were being attacked in the name of history, and from very different directions— not only by the nobility, but also by the *parlementaires* as well as the bourgeoisie. This was the precise moment when history became the discourse that every "nation"—in quotation marks—or at least every order or every class used to lay claim to its right; this is the moment when, if you like, history became the general discourse of political struggles. It was at this point, then, that a ministry of history was created. And at this point, you will ask me: Did history really escape the State, given that, a hundred years after Racine, we see the emergence of a historiographer who had at least equally close links with power of the State because he actually did, as I have just said, have a ministerial or at least administrative function?

So what was the point of creating this central ministry to administer history? Its purpose was to arm the king for the political battle insofar as he was, after all, no more than one force among others, and was being attacked by other forces. It purpose was also to attempt to impose a sort of enforced peace on those historico-political struggles.

Its purpose was to code this discourse on history once and for all, and in such a way that it could be integrated into the practice of the State. Hence the tasks with which Moreau was entrusted: collating the administration's documents, making them available to the administration itself (beginning with the financial administrators and then the others), and, finally, opening up these documents, this storehouse of documents, to the people who were being paid by the king to carry out this research.[8] Quite apart from the fact that Moreau is not Racine, that Louis XVI is not Louis XIV, and that all this is far removed from the ceremonial description of the crossing of the Rhine, what is the difference between Moreau and Racine, between the old historiography (which was, in a sense, at its purest in the late seventeenth century) and the kind of history the State begins to take in hand and bring under its control in the late eighteenth century? Can we say that history ceases to be the State's discourse about itself, once we have, perhaps, left court historiography? Can we say that we are now involved with an administrative-type historiography? I think that there is a considerable difference between the two things, or in any case that it has to be measured.

So, another new excursus, if you will allow me. The difference between what might be called the history of the sciences and the genealogy of knowledges is that the history of sciences is essentially located on an axis that is, roughly speaking, the cognition-truth axis, or at least the axis that goes from the structure of cognition to the demand for truth. Unlike the history of the sciences, the genealogy of knowledges is located on a different axis, namely the discourse-power axis or, if you like, the discursive practice-clash of power axis. Now it seems to me that if we apply it to what is for a whole host of reasons the privileged period of the eighteenth century, to this domain or this region, the genealogy of knowledge must first—before it does anything else—outwit the problematic of the Enlightenment. It has to outwit what was at the time described (and was still described in the nineteenth and twentieth centuries) as the progress of enlightenment, the struggle of knowledge against ignorance, of reason against chimeras, of experience against prejudices, of reason against error, and so on. All this has been described as, or symbolized by, light gradually dispelling darkness, and it is this, I think, that we have to get rid of [on the contrary,] when we look at the eighteenth century—we have to see, not this relationship between day and night, knowledge and ignorance, but something very different: an immense and multiple battle, but not one between knowledge and ignorance, but an immense and multiple battle between knowledges in the plural—knowledges that are in conflict because of their very morphology, because they are in the possession of enemies, and because they have intrinsic power-effects.

I will take one or two examples that will, for a moment, take us away from history. Take the problem of technical or technological knowledge. It is often said that the eighteenth century was the century that saw the emergence of technical knowledges. What actually happened in the eighteenth century was quite different. First of all, we have the plural, polymorphous, multiple, and dispersed existence of different knowledges, which existed with their differences—differences defined by geographical regions, by the size of the workshops or factories, and so on. The differences among them—I am speaking of technological expertise, remember—were defined by local categories, education, and the wealth of their possessors. And these knowledges were struggling against one another, with one another, in a society where knowing the secret behind technological knowledge was a source of wealth, and in which the mutual independence of these knowledges also made individuals independent. So multiple knowledge, knowledge-as-secret, knowledge functioning as wealth and as a guarantee of independence: technological knowledge functioned within this patchwork. Now, as both the productive forces and economic demand developed, the price of these knowledges rose, and the struggle between them, the need to delineate their independence and the need for secrecy intensified and became, so to speak, more tense. At the same time, we saw the development of processes that allowed bigger, more general, or more industrialized knowledges, or knowledges that circulated more easily, to annex, confiscate, and take over smaller, more particular, more local, and more artisanal knowledges.

There was a sort of immense economico-political struggle around or over these knowledges, their dispersal, or their heterogeneity, an immense struggle over the economic inductions and power-effects that were bound up with the exclusive ownership of a knowledge, its dispersal and its secret. What has been called the development of technological knowledge in the eighteenth century has to be thought of in terms of a form of multiplicity, and not in terms of the triumph of light over darkness or of knowledge over ignorance.

Now, the State will intervene, either directly or indirectly, in these attempts at annexation, which are also attempts at generalization, in four main ways. First, by eliminating or disqualifying what might be termed useless and irreducible little knowledges that are expensive in economic terms: elimination and disqualification, then. Second, by normalizing these knowledges; this makes it possible to fit them together, to make them communicate with one another, to break down the barriers of secrecy and technological and geographical boundaries. In short, this makes not only knowledges, but also those who possess them, interchangeable. The normalization of dispersed knowledges. Third operation: the hierarchical classification of knowledges allows them to become, so to speak, interlocking, starting with the most particular and material knowledges, which are also subordinated knowledges, and ending with the most general forms, with the most formal knowledges, which are also the forms that envelop and direct knowledge. So, a hierarchical classification. And finally, once all this has been done, a fourth operation becomes possible: a pyramidal centralization that allows these knowledges to be controlled, which ensures that they can be selected, and both that the content of these knowledges can be transmitted upward from the bottom, and that the overall directions and the general organizations it wishes to promote can be transmitted downward from the top.

The tendency to organize technological knowledges brings with it a whole series of practices, projects, and institutions. The *Encyclopédie*, for example. The *Encyclopédie* is usually seen only in terms of its political or ideological opposition to the monarchy and at least one form of Catholicism. Its interest in technology is not in fact a reflection of some philosophical materialism; it is actually an attempt to homogenize technological knowledges, and it is at once political and economic. The great studies of handicraft methods, metallurgical techniques, and mining—the great surveys that were made between the middle and the end of the eighteenth century—corresponded to this attempt to nomalize technical knowledges. The existence, foundation, or development of *grandes écoles* such as the École des Mines and the École Ponts et Chaussées, and so on, made it possible to establish both quantitative and qualitative levels, breaks and strata between these different knowledges, and that allowed them to be arranged into a hierarchy. And finally, the corps of inspectors who, throughout the kingdom, advised and counseled people on how to develop and use these different knowledges ensured that knowledge was centralized. I have taken the example of technical knowledges, but the same could be said of medical knowledge. Throughout the whole second half of the eighteenth century we see a huge effort being made to homogenize, normalize, classify, and centralize medical knowledge. How could medical knowledge be given a form and a content, how could homogeneous laws be imposed upon the practice of health care, how could rules be imposed upon the population—not so much to make it share this knowledge, as to make it find it acceptable? All this led to the creation of hospitals, dispensaries, and of the Société royale de médecine, the codification of the medical profession, a huge public hygiene campaign, a huge campaign to improve the hygiene of nurslings and children, and so on.[9]

All these projects—and I have cited only two examples—basically had four goals: selection, normalization, hierarchicalization, and centralization. These are the four operations that we see at work in a fairly detailed study of what we call disciplinary power.[10] The eighteenth century was the century when knowledges were disciplined, or when, in other words, the internal organization of every knowledge became a discipline which had, in its own field, criteria of selection that allowed it to eradicate false knowledge or nonknowledge. We also have forms of normalization and homogenization of knowledge-contents, forms of hierarchicalization, and an internal organization

that could centralize knowledges around a sort of de facto axiomati-
zation. So every knowledge was organized into a discipline. These
knowledges that had been disciplinarized from within were then arranged, made to communicate with one another, redistributed, and
organized into a hierarchy within a sort of overall field or overall
discipline that was known specifically as science. Science in the singular did not exist before the eighteenth century. Sciences existed,
knowledges existed, and philosophy, if you like, existed. Philosophy
was, precisely, the organizational system, the system that allowed
knowledges to communicate with one another—and to that extent it
could play an effective, real, and operational role within the development of technical knowledges. The disciplinarization of knowledges, and its polymorphous singularity, now leads to the emergence
of a phenomenon and a constraint that is now an integral part of our
society. We call it "science." At the same time, and for the same
reason, philosophy loses its foundational and founding role. Philosophy no longer has any real role to play within science and the processes of knowledge. At the same time, and for the same reasons,
mathesis—or the project of a universal science that could serve as both
a formal instrument for every science and a rigorous foundation for
all sciences—also disappears. Science, defined as a general domain, as
the disciplinary policing of knowledges, takes over from both philosophy and *mathesis*. From now on, it will raise specific problems relating
to the disciplinary policing of knowledges: problems of classification,
problems of hierarchicalization, problems of proximity, and so on.

A belief in the progress of reason was the eighteenth century's only
awareness of this far-reaching change in the disciplinarization of
knowledges and the subsequent elimination of both the philosophical
discourse operating within science and the sciences' internal project
for a *mathesis*. I think, however, that if we can grasp what was going
on beneath what is called the progress of reason—namely the disciplinarization of polymorphous and heterogeneous knowledges—we
will be able to understand a certain number of things. First, the appearance of the university. Not of course in the strict sense, as the
universities had their function, role, and existence long before this.

But from the end of the eighteenth and beginning of the nineteenth centuries onward—the Napoleonic university was established at precisely this time—we see the emergence of something like a sort of great uniform apparatus of knowledges, with its different stages, its different extensions, its different levels, and its pseudopodia. The university's primary function is one of selection, not so much of people (which is, after all, basically not very important) as of knowledges. It can play this selective role because it has a sort of de facto—and de jure—monopoly, which means that any knowledge that is not born or shaped within this sort of institutional field—whose limits are in fact relatively fluid but which consists, roughly speaking, of the university and official research bodies—that anything that exists outside it, any knowledge that exists in the wild, any knowledge that is born elsewhere, is automatically, and from the outset, if not actually excluded, disqualified a priori. That the amateur scholar ceased to exist in the eighteenth and nineteenth centuries is a well-known fact. So the university has a selective role: it selects knowledges. Its role is to distinguish between qualitative and quantitative levels of knowledge, and to distribute knowledges accordingly. Its role is to teach, which means respecting the barriers that exist between the different floors of the university apparatus. Its role is to homogenize knowledges by establishing a sort of scientific community with a recognized status; its role is to organize a consensus. Its role is, finally, to use, either directly or indirectly, State apparatuses to centralize knowledge. We can now understand why something resembling a university, with its ill-defined extensions and frontiers, should have emerged at the beginning of the nineteenth century, or in other words at the very time when this disciplinarization of knowledges, this organization of knowledges into disciplines, was going on.

This also allows us to understand a second phenomenon, or what might be termed a change in the form of dogmatism. You see, once the mechanism, or the internal discipline of knowledges, includes controls, and once those controls are exercised by a purpose-built apparatus; once we have this form of control—you must understand this—we can do away with what we might call the orthodoxy of statements. This old orthodoxy was costly, for this principle, which functioned as a religious or ecclesiastical mode of functioning, had resulted in the condemnation and exclusion of a certain number of statements that were scientifically true and scientifically productive. The discipline, the disciplinarization of knowledges established in the eighteenth century, will replace that orthodoxy, which applied to statements themselves and sorted those that were acceptable out from those that were unacceptable, with something else: a control that applies not to the content of statements themselves, to their conformity or nonconformity to a certain truth, but to the regularity of enunciations. The problem is now: Who is speaking, are they qualified to speak, at what level is the statement situated, what set can it be fitted into, and how and to what extent does it conform to other forms and other typologies of knowledge? This allows a liberalism that is, if not boundless, at least more broad-minded in terms of the content of statements and, on the other hand, more rigorous, more comprehensive—and has a much greater wing area—at the level of enunciatory procedures. As a result, and as you might have deduced, statements could rotate much more quickly, and truths became obsolete much more quickly. As a result, a number of epistemological obstacles could be removed. Just as an orthodoxy that concentrated on the content of statements had become an obstacle to the renewal of the stock of scientific knowledges, so, in contrast, disciplinarization at the level of enunciations allowed the stock to be renewed much more quickly. We move, if you like, from the censorship of statements to the disciplinarization of enunciations, or from orthodoxy to what I would call "orthology," to a form of control that is now exercised on a disciplinary basis.

Right! I've strayed away from the point with all this. We have been studying, looking at how the disciplinary techniques of power,[11] taken at their most subtle or elementary level, taken at the level of individual bodies, succeeded in changing the political economy of power, and modified its apparatuses; we have also seen how disciplinary techniques of power applied to bodies not only led to an accumulation of knowledge, but also identified possible domains of knowledge. We then saw how the application of disciplines of power to bodies could extract from those subjugated bodies something like a soul-subject, an "ego," a psyche, et cetera. I tried to look at all this last year.[12] I think that we now have to study the emergence of a different form of disciplining, of disciplinarization, which is contemporary with the first but which applies to knowledges and not bodies. And it can, I think, be demonstrated that this disciplinarization of knowledges resulted in both the removal of certain epistemological obstacles and a new form, a new regularity in the proliferation of disciplines. It can be demonstrated that this disciplinarization established a new mode of relationship between power and knowledge. It can, finally, be demonstrated that the disciplinarization of knowledges gave rise to a new constraint: no longer the constraint of truth, but the constraint of science.

All this is taking us away from the historiography of the king, Racine, and Moreau. We could pick up the analysis (but I will not do so now) and show that at the very moment when history, or historical discourse, was entering a general field of conflict, history found itself, for different reasons, in the same position as the technical knowledges I was talking about a moment ago. These technological knowledges, their dispersal, their very morphology, their localized nature, and the secrecy that surrounded them were both an issue and an instrument in an economic struggle and a political struggle. The State intervened in the struggle that these technological knowledges were waging against one another: its function or role was to disciplinarize them, or in other words, to select and homogenize knowledges, and to arrange them into a hierarchy. For very different reasons, historical knowledge entered a field of struggles and battles at much the same time. Not for directly economic reasons, but for reasons pertaining to a struggle, a political struggle. When historical knowledge, which had until then been part of the discourse that the State or power pronounced on itself, was enucleated from that power, and became an instrument in the political struggle that lasted for the whole eighteenth century, the State attempted, in the same way and for the same reason, to take it in hand and disciplinarize it. The establishment, at the end of the eighteenth century, of a ministry of history, the establishment of the great repository of archives that was to become the École des Chartes in the nineteenth century, which more or less coincided with the establishment of the École des Mines and the École des Ponts et Chaussées—the École des Ponts et Chaussées is a little different, not that it matters—also corresponds to the disciplinarization of knowledge. Royal power's objective was to discipline historical knowledge, or historical knowledges, and thus to establish a State knowledge. The difference between this and technological knowledge is that insofar as history was indeed—I think—an anti-State knowledge, there was a perpetual confrontation between the history that had been disciplinarized by the State and that had become the content of official teaching, and the history that was bound up with struggles because it was the consciousness of subjects involved in a struggle. Disciplinarization did not defuse the confrontation. While it can be said that the disciplinarization introduced in the eighteenth century was broadly effective and successful in the realm of technology, where historical knowledge is concerned, disciplinarization did occur, but it not only failed to block the non-Statist history, the decentered history of subjects in struggle, but actually made it stronger thanks to a whole set of struggles, confiscations, and mutual challenges. And to that extent, you always have two levels of historical knowledge and consciousness, and the two levels obviously drift further and further apart. But the gap between the two never prevents either of them from existing. So we have on the one hand a knowledge that has effectively been disciplinarized to form a historical discipline, and on the other hand, a historical consciousness that is polymorphous, divided, and combative. It is simply the other side, the other face of a political consciousness. I would like to try to say a little about these things by looking at the end of the eighteenth century and the beginning of the nineteenth.

1. Jules Michelet, *Le Peuple* (Paris, 1946).
2. Niccolo Machiavelli, *Il Principe* (Rome, 1532); *Discorsi sopra la prima deca di tito Livio*, op. cit.; *Dell'arte della guerra* (Florence, 1521); *Istorie fiorentini* (Florence, 1531). There are many French translations of *Il Principe* (English translation by George Bull: *The Prince* [Harmondsworth: Penguin, 1961]). The other texts referred to may be consulted in E. Barinou, ed., Machiavel, *Oeuvres complètes* (Paris: Bibliothèque de la Pléiade, 1952); this is a revised and updated version of J. Guiraudet's old translations (1798). English translation by Leslie J. Walker: *The Discourse of Niccolo Machiavelli* (London: Routledge and Kegan Paul, 1950). Foucault discusses Machiavelli in "Omnes et singulatim" (1981) and "The Political Technology of Individuals," and in his lecture "On Governmentality"; cf. note 13 to the lecture of 21 January above.
3. Pierre le Pesant de Boisguilbert, *Le Détail de la France* (s.l. 1695); *Factum de la France* (1707), in *Economistes financiers du XVIIIe siècle* (Paris, 1843); *Testament politique de M. de Vauban, Maréchal de France*, 2 vols. (s.l. 1707); *Dissertation sur la nature des richesses, de l'argent et des tributs* (Paris, n.d.).
4. Sébastien le Prestre de Vauban, *Méthode générale et facile pour faire le dénombrement des peuples* (Paris, 1686); *Projet d'une dixme royale* (s.l. 1707).
5. On the antihistoricism of contemporary knowledge, see in particular chapter 4 of *Les Mots et les choses* (English translation: *The Order of Things*).
6. The passage in brackets has been reconstructed from Foucault's manuscript.
7. Characters in, respectively, Corneille's *Cinna* and Racine's *Britannicus* and *Andromaque*. [Trans.]
8. The results of the enormous task undertaken by Moreau will be found in his *Principes de morale, de politique, et de droit public*; for examples of the criteria used by Moreau in preparation for this work, and for its history, see also his *Plan des travaux littéraires ordonnés par Sa Majesté*.
9. On the procedures of normalization in medical knowledge, the reader is referred to *Naissance de la clinique: une archéologie du regard médical* (Paris: PUF, 1963) (English translation by Alan Sheridan: *Birth of the Clinic: An Archaeology of Medical Preception* [London: Tavistock, 1973]); the lecture given by Foucault in Brazil in 1974 on the history of medicine, "El nacimento de la medicine social" ("La Naissance de la médicine sociale," *Dits et écrits*, vol. 3, pp. 207-27); "Incorpoación del hospital en la tecnologia moderna" ("L'incorporation de l'hôpital dans la technologie moderne," in *Dits et écrits*, vol. 3, pp. 508-21); and the analysis of medical policing made in "La Politique de la santé au XVIIIe siècle," in *Dits et écrits*, vol. 3, pp. 13-27 (English translation: "The Politics of Health in the Eighteenth Century," in *Power/Knowledge*, pp. 166-82); and "La Politique de la santé au XVIIIe siècle," in *Dits et écrits*, vol. 3, pp. 725-41.
10. On disciplinary power and its effects on knowledge, see in particular *Surveiller et punir: Naissance de la prison* (Paris: Gallimard, 1975). English translation by Alan Sheridan: *Discipline and Punish: The Birth of the Prison* (London: Allen Lane, 1977).
11. See in particular the lectures given at the Collège de France in 1971-1972: *Théories et institutions pénales*, and in 1972-1973: *La société punitive*, forthcoming.
12. Michel Foucault, *Les Anormaux: Cours au Collège de France, 1974-1975* (Paris: Gallimard and Le Seuil, 1999).

nine

3 MARCH 1976

[

*Tactical generalization of historical knowledge. ~ Constitution,
Revolution, and cyclical history. ~ The savage and the
barbarian. ~ Three ways of filtering barbarism: tactics of
historical discourse. ~ Questions of method: the epistemological
field and the antihistoricism of the bourgeoisie. ~ Reactivation of
historical discourse during the Revolution. ~ Feudalism and the
gothic novel.*

]

LAST TIME, I SHOWED you how a historico-political discourse, or a
historico-political field, took shape and was constituted around the
nobiliary reaction of the early eighteenth century. I would now like
to move to a different point in time, or in other words, to around the
French Revolution and to a moment where we can, I think, grasp two
processes. We can see, on the one hand, how this discourse, which
was originally bound up with the nobiliary reaction, became generalized not so much, or not only, in the sense that is became, so to
speak, the regular or canonical form of historical discourse, but to the
extent that it became a tactical instrument that could be used not
only by the nobility, but ultimately in various different strategies. In
the course of the eighteenth century, and subject to a certain number
of modifications at the level of its basic propositions, historical discourse eventually became a sort of discursive weapon that could be
used by all the adversaries present within the political field. In short,
I would like to show you how this historical instrument must not be
seen as the ideology or an ideological product of the nobility or its

class position, and that we are not dealing with an ideology here; we are dealing with something else. What I am trying to identify is what might, if you like, be termed a discursive tactic, a deployment of knowledge and power which, insofar as it is a tactic, is transferable and eventually becomes the law governing the formation of a knowledge and, at the same time, the general form of the political battle. So the discourse on history is generalized, but in a tactical sense.

The second process we see taking shape at the time of the Revolution is the way in which this tactic is deployed in three directions which correspond to three different battles and produce three rather different tactics: One is centered on nationalities, and is therefore essentially in continuity with the phenomena of language and, therefore, philology; the second centers on social classes, views economic domination as the central phenomenon, and is therefore closely related to political economy; the third direction, finally, is centered on neither nationalities nor classes, but upon race, and views biological specification and selection as the central phenomenon; there is, then, a continuity between this historical discourse and the biological problematic. Philology, political economy, biology. Language, labor, life.[1] We will see all this being reinvested in or rearticulated around this historical knowledge and the tactics that are bound up with it.

The first thing I would like to talk to you about today is therefore this tactical generalization of historical knowledge; how was it displaced from its place of birth—the nobiliary reaction of the early eighteenth century—and how did it become an instrument that could be used in all the political struggles of the late eighteenth century, no matter how we look at them? Our first question concerns the reasons for this tactical polyvalence: How and why did such a particular instrument, such a singular discourse which sang the praises of invaders, become a general instrument to be used in the political tactics and confrontations of the eighteenth century?

I think the explanation is something along these lines. Boulainvilliers made national duality history's principle of intelligibility. Intelligibility meant three things. Boulainvilliers was primarily interested in finding the initial conflict (battle, war, conquest, invasion, et cet-

3 March 1976 191

era), the nucleus of war from which he could derive all the other battles, struggles, and confrontations because they were either its direct effects or the result of a series of displacements, modifications, or reversals of the relationship of force. So, a sort of great genealogy of the struggles that go on in all the various conflicts recorded by history. How could he find the basic struggle, trace the strategic thread running through all these battles? The historical intelligibility that Boulainvilliers wanted to supply also meant that he not only had to locate that basic kernel of war and the way in which every conflict derived from it; he also had to trace the betrayals, the unnatural alliances, the ruses that were used on all sides, all the negations of right, all the inadmissible calculations, and all the unforgivable lapses of memory that made possible this transformation, and, at the same time, the watering down of that relationship of force and that basic confrontation. He had to undertake a sort of great examination of history ("who's to blame?") and therefore trace not only the strategic thread, but also the line—sometimes sinuous but never broken—of ethical divisions that runs through history. Historical intelligibility also had a third meaning; it meant getting beyond these tactical displacements and all these historico-ethical misappropriations in order to demonstrate that a certain relationship of force was both right and fair. Boulainvilliers was concerned with the true relationship of force—in the sense that he had to rediscover a relationship of force that was not ideal but real, and that had, in this case, been recorded and inscribed by history in the course of a decisive ordeal by strength: the Frankish invasion of Gaul. A relationship of force, then, that was historically true and historically real and which was, secondly, a good relationship of force because it could be extricated from all the distortions to which betrayals and various displacements had subjected it. The theme of his search for historical intelligibility was this: to rediscover a state of affairs that was a state of force in its primal rightness. And you will find that Boulainvilliers and his successors formulate this project very clearly. Boulainvilliers, for example, said: We have to relate our modern customs to their true origins, discover the principles of the nation's common right, and then look at what has changed over time. A few years later, Buat-Nançay would say that if we can understand the primitive spirit of government, we will be able to lend a new vigor to certain laws, moderate those laws that are so vigorous as to shift the balance, and reestablish harmony and social relations.

This project of analyzing the intelligibility of history therefore implies three tasks: finding the strategic thread, tracing the thread of ethical divisions, and reestablishing the rectitude of what might be called the "constituent point" of politics and history, or the constituent moment of the kingdom. I say "constituent point" or "constituent moment" so as to try to avoid, without erasing it altogether, the word "constitution." As you can see, it is indeed a matter of constitution; the point of studying history is to reestablish the constitution, but not at all in the sense of an explicit body of laws that were formulated at some given moment. Nor is the goal to rediscover a sort of foundational juridical convention which, at some point in time—or architime—had been established between the king, the sovereign, and his subjects. The point is to rediscover something that has its own consistency and its own historical situation, and it is not so much of the order of the law as of the order of force, not so much of the order of the written word as of the order of an equilibrium. This something is a constitution, but almost in the sense that a doctor would understand that term, or in other words, in the sense of a relationship of force, an equilibrium and interplay of proportions, a stable dissymmetry or a congruent inequality. When eighteenth-century doctors evoked the notion of "constitution," they were talking about all these things.[2] We can see this idea of a "constitution"—in both the medical and the military sense—taking shape in the historical literature relating to the nobiliary reaction. It designates both a relationship of force between good and evil, and a relationship of force between adversaries. If we are able to understand and reestablish a basic relationship of force, we will be able to get back to this constituent point. We have to establish a constitution, and we will not get back to that constitution by reestablishing the laws of old, but thanks to something resembling a revolution—a revolution in the sense of a transition from night to day, from the lowest point to the highest point. From Boulainvilliers onward—and this is, I think, the important point—it is the linking together of the two notions of constitution and revolution that makes this possible. So long as historico-juridical literature, which had essentially been written by the *parlementaires,* understood "constitution" to mean essentially the basic laws of the kingdom, or in other words, a juridical apparatus or something of the order of a convention, it was obvious that the return of the constitution meant swearing an oath to reestablish the laws that had been revealed. Once "constitution" no longer meant a juridical armature or a set of laws, but a relationship of force, it was quite obvious that such a relationship of force could not be reestablished on the basis of nothing; it could be reestablished only when there existed something resembling a cyclical historical pattern, or at least something that allowed history to revolve around itself and brought it back to its starting point. You can therefore see how this medico-military idea of a constitution, or in other words, a relationship of force, reintroduces something resembling a cyclical philosophy of history, or at least the idea that the development of history is circular. And when I say that his idea "is introduced," I am really saying that it is reintroduced at the point where the old millenarian theme of the return of the past intersects with an articulated historical knowledge.

This philosophy of history as philosophy of cyclical time becomes possible from the eighteenth century onward, or in other words, once the two notions of a constitution and a relationship of force become established. With Boulainvilliers, we see—I think for the first time—the idea of a cyclical history appearing within an articulated historical discourse. Empires, says Boulainvilliers, rise and fall into decadence depending on how the light of the sun shines upon their territory.[3] The revolution of the sun, and the revolution of history: as you can see, the two things are now linked. So we have a pair, a link among three things: constitution, revolution, and cyclical history. That, if you like, is one aspect of the tactical instrument that Boulainvilliers perfected.

Second aspect: When he is looking for the constituent point—which is both good and true—what is Boulainvilliers trying to do? It is quite obvious that he refuses to look for that constituent point in the law, but he also refuses to find it in nature: antijuridicalism (which is what I have just been telling you about), but also naturalism. The great adversary of Boulainvilliers and his successors is nature, or natural man. To put it a different way, the great adversary of this type of analysis (and Boulainvilliers's analyses will become instrumental and tactical in this sense too) is, if you like, natural man or the savage. "Savage" is to be understood in two senses. The savage—noble or otherwise—is the natural man whom the jurists or theorists of right dreamed up, the natural man who existed before society existed, who existed in order to constitute society, and who was the element around which the social body could be constituted. When they look for the constituent point, Boulainvilliers and his successors are not trying to find this savage who, in some sense, exists before the social body. The other thing they are trying to ward off is the other aspect of the savage, that other natural man or ideal element dreamed up by economists: a man without a past or a history, who is motivated only by self-interest and who exchanges the product of his labor for another product. What the historico-political discourse of Boulainvilliers and his successors is trying to ward off is both the savage who emerges from his forests to enter into a contract and to found society, and the savage *Homo economicus* whose life is devoted to exchange and barter. The combination of the savage and exchange is, I think, basic to juridical thought, and not only to eighteenth-century theories of right—we constantly find the savage-exchange couple from the eighteenth-century theory of right to the anthropology of the nineteenth and twentieth centuries. In both the juridical thought of the eighteenth century and the anthropology of the nineteenth and twentieth centuries, the savage is essentially a man who exchanges. He is the exchanger: he exchanges rights and he exchanges goods. Insofar as he exchanges rights, he founds society and sovereignty. Insofar as he exchanges goods, he constitutes a social body which is, at the same time, an economic body. Ever since the eighteenth century, the savage has been the subject of an elementary exchange. Well, the historico-political discourse inaugurated by Boulainvilliers creates another figure, and he is the antithesis of the savage (who was of great importance in eighteenth-century juridical theory). This new figure is just as elementary as the savage of the jurists (who were soon followed by the anthropologists) but is constituted on a very different basis: he is the barbarian.

The barbarian is the opposite of the savage, but in what sense? First, in this sense: The savage is basically a savage who lives in a state of savagery together with other savages; once he enters a relation of a social kind, he ceases to be a savage. The barbarian, in contrast, is someone who can be understood, characterized, and defined only in relation to a civilization, and by the fact that he exists outside it. There can be no barbarian unless an island of civilization exists somewhere, unless he lives outside it, and unless he fights it. And the barbarian's relationship with that speck of civilization—which the barbarian despises, and which he wants—is one of hostility and permanent warfare. The barbarian cannot exist without the civilization he is trying to destroy and appropriate. The barbarian is always the man who stalks the frontiers of States, the man who stumbles into the city walls. Unlike the savage, the barbarian does not emerge from some natural backdrop to which he belongs. He appears only when civilization already exists, and only when he is in conflict with it. He does not make his entrance into history by founding a society, but by penetrating a civilization, setting it ablaze and destroying it. I think that the first point, or the difference between the barbarian and the savage, is this relationship with a civilization, and therefore with a history that already exists. There can be no barbarian without a pre-existing history: the history of the civilization he sets ablaze. What is more, and unlike the savage, the barbarian is not a vector for exchange. The barbarian is essentially the vector for something very different from exchange: he is the vector for domination. Unlike the savage, the barbarian takes possession and seizes; his occupation is not the primitive cultivation of the land, but plunder. His relationship with property is, in other words, always secondary: he always seizes existing property; similarly, he makes other serve him. He makes others cultivate his land, tend his horses, prepare his weapons, and so on. His freedom is based solely upon the freedom others have lost. And in his relationship with power, the barbarian, unlike the savage, never surrenders his freedom. The savage is a man who has in his hands, so to speak, a plethora of freedom which he surrenders in order to protect his life, his security, his property, and his goods. The barbarian never gives up his freedom. And when he does acquire a power, acquire a king or elect a chief, he certainly does not do so in order to diminish his own share of right but, on the contrary, to increase his strength, to become an even stronger plunderer, a stronger thief and rapist, and to become an invader who is more confident of his own strength. The barbarian establishes a power in order to increase his own individual strength. For the barbarian, the model government is, in other words, necessarily a military government, and certainly not one that is based upon the contracts and transfer of civil rights that characterize the savage. The type of history established by Boulainvilliers in the eighteenth century is, I think, that of the figure of the barbarian.

So we can well understand why, in modern juridico-anthropological thought—and even in today's bucolic and American utopias—the savage is, despite it all and even though it has to be admitted that he has done a few bad things and has a few faults, always the noble savage. Indeed, how could he not be noble, given that his specific function is to exchange and to give—in accordance with his own best interests, obviously, but in a form of reciprocity in which we can, if you like, recognize the acceptable—and juridical—form of goodness? The barbarian, in contrast, has to be bad and wicked, even if we have to admit that he does have certain qualities. He has to be full of arrogance and has to be inhuman, precisely because he is not the man of nature and exchange; he is the man of history, the man of pillage and fires, he is the man of domination. "A proud, brutal people, without a homeland, and without laws," said Mably (who was, as it happens, very fond of barbarians); "it tolerates atrocious acts of violence because they are regarded as being publicly acceptable."[4] The soul of the barbarian is great, noble, and proud, but it is always associated with treachery and cruelty (all this is in Mably). Speaking of barbarians, Bonneville said: "[T]hese adventurers lived only for war . . . the sword was their right and they exercised it without remorse."[5] And Marat, another great admirer of barbarians, described them as "poor, uncouth, without trade, without arts, but free."[6] The barbarian as natural man? Yes and no. No, in the sense that he is always bound up with a history (and a preexisting history). The barbarian appears against a backdrop of history. And if he is related to nature, said Buat-Nançay (who was getting at his closest enemy, namely Montesquieu), it is because—well, what is the nature of things? "It is the relationship between the sun and the mud it dries, between the thistle and the donkey that feeds on it."[7]

Within this historico-political field where knowledge of weapons is constantly being used as a political instrument, the great tactics that are developed in the eighteenth century can, I think, be characterized by the way they use the four elements present in Boulainvilliers's analysis: constitution, revolution, barbarism, and domination. The problem is basically this: How can we establish the best possible fit between unfettered barbarism on the one hand, and the equilibrium of the constitution we are trying to rediscover on the other? How can we arrive at the right balance of forces, and how can we make use of the violence, freedom, and so on that the barbarian brings with him? In other words, which of the barbarian's characteristics do we have to retain, and which do we have to reject, if we are to get a fair constitution to work? What is there in barbarism that we can make use of? Basically, the problem is that of filtering of the barbarian and barbarism: how can barbarian domination be so filtered as to bring about the constituent revolution? It is this problem, and the different solutions to the problem of the need to filter barbarism so as to bring about the constituent revolution, that will define—both in the field of historical discourse and in this historico-political field—the tactical positions of different groups and the different interests of the nobility, monarchic power, or different tendencies within the bourgeoisie. It will define where the center of the battle lies.

I think that in the eighteenth century, this whole set of historical discourses is overshadowed by this problem: not revolution *or* barbarism, but revolution *and* barbarism, or the economy of barbarism in the revolution. A text someone gave me the other day as I was leaving the lecture, if not proves, at least confirms my belief that this is the case. It is a text by Robert Desnos, and it shows perfectly how, right up to the twentieth century, the problem of revolution *or* barbarism—I almost said socialism or barbarism[8]—is a false problem, and that the real problem is revolution *and* barbarism. I take as my witness this text by Robert Desnos, which appeared, I assume, in *La Révolution surréaliste*—I don't know because no reference is given here. Here is the text. You'd think it was straight from the eighteenth century.

Having come from the shadowy East, the men who had been civilized continued the same westward march as Attila, Tamburlaine and so many other famous men. Any man who can be described as "civilized" was once a barbarian. They were, in other words, the bastard sons of the adventurers of the night, or those the enemy (the Romans, the Greeks) had corrupted. Driven away from the shores of the Pacific and the slopes of the Himalayas, and unfaithful to their mission, they now found themselves facing those who drove them out in the not so distant times of the invasions. Sons of Kalmouk, grandsons of the Huns, if you just stripped off the robes borrowed from a wardrobe in Athens or Thebes, the breastplates collected in Sparta and Rome, you would look as your fathers looked on their little horses. And you Normans who work the land, who fish for sardines and who drink cider, just get back on those flimsy boats that traced a long wake beyond the Arctic Circle before they reached these damp fields and these woods that teem with game. Mob, recognize your master! You thought you could flee it, flee that Orient that drove you away by vesting you with the right to destroy what you could not preserve, and now that you have traveled around the world, you find it snapping at your heels again. I beg you, do not imitate a dog trying to catch its tail:

you would be running after the West forever. Stop. Say something to explain your mission to us, great oriental army, you
who have now become *The Westerners*.[9]

Right, in an attempt to resituate in concrete terms the various
historical discourses and political tactics from which they derive, Boulainvilliers all at once introduces into history the great blond barbarian, the juridical and historical fact of the invasion, the appropriation
of lands and the enslavement of men, and, finally, a very limited royal
power. Of all the important and interrelated features that constitute
the fact of barbarism's irruption into history, which have to be eliminated? Which have to be retained so as to establish the right relationship of force that will uphold the kingdom? I will look at the
three great models that were used to filter barbarism. There were
many others in the eighteenth century; I will take these examples
because they were, in political terms, and probably in epistemological
terms too, the most important, and because each of them corresponds
to a very different political position.

The first way of filtering it is the most vigorous, the most absolute,
and it tries to allow no aspect of the barbarian into history: this
position is an attempt to show that the French monarchy is not descended from some Germanic invasion which brought it to France or
which, in some sense, gave birth to it. It attempts to show that the
nobility's ancestors were not conquerors from across the Rhine and
that the privileges of the nobility—the privileges that placed it between the sovereign and other subjects—were either granted to it later
or were usurped by it in some obscure way. In a word, the point is
not to relate the privileged nobility to the barbarian horde that
founded it, but to avoid the issue of the horde, to make it disappear
and to leave the nobility in abeyance—to make it look like both a
late and an artificial creation. This thesis is, of course, the thesis of
the monarchy, and you will find it in a whole series of historians from
Dubos[10] to Moreau.[11]

When articulated as a basic proposition, this thesis gives roughly
this: The Franks—says Dubos and then Moreau—are at bottom simply

a myth, an illusion, something that was created from scratch by Boulainvilliers. The Franks never existed, which quite clearly means that
the invasion never took place at all. So what did happen? There were
invasions, but they were the work of others: the Burgundians invaded,
and the Goths invaded, and the Romans could do nothing about it.
And it was in the face of these invasions that the Romans appealed—as
allies—to a small population that had some military virtues. They
were of course the Franks. But the Franks were not greeted as invaders, as great barbarians with a propensity for plunder and domination,
but as a small population of useful allies. As a result, they immediately
received the rights of citizenship; not only were they immediately
made Gallo-Roman citizens; they were also granted the instruments
of political power (and in this connection, Dubos recalls that Clovis
was, after all, a Roman consul). So there was neither an invasion nor
a conquest, but there was immigration and there was an alliance.
There was no invasion, but it cannot even be said that there was a
Frankish people, with its own legislation or customs. First, there were
quite simply too few of them, says Dubos, for them to able to treat
the Gauls "as Turk to Moor"[12] and to force them to adopt their habits
and customs. Being lost in the midst of the Gallo-Roman masses, they
could not even preserve their own habits. So they literally dissolved.
And besides, how could they fail to be dissolved into this Gallo-
Roman political apparatus, given that they really had no understanding of either administration or government? Dubos even claims that
their art of war had been borrowed from the Romans. Be that as it
may, the Franks were careful not to destroy the mechanisms of what
Dubos calls the admirable administration of Roman Gaul. Dubos says
that the Franks did not alter the nature of anything in Roman Gaul.
Order triumphed. So the Franks were absorbed and their king simply
remained, so to speak, at the pinnacle of, on the surface of, a Gallo-
Roman edifice that could scarcely be penetrated by a few immigrants
of Germanic origin. So the king alone remained at the pinnacle of the
edifice, precisely because he was a king who had the Caesarian rights
of the Roman emperor. There was, in other words, no barbarian-type
aristocracy, as Boulainvilliers believed. The absolute monarch ap-

peared immediately. And it was several centuries later that the break occurred, that something like the invasion's analogue took place, but it was a sort of invasion from within.[13]

At this point, Dubos's analysis moves on to the end of the Carolingian period and the beginning of the Capetian period, where he detects a weakening of the central power, of the Caesar-like absolute power that the Merovingians initially enjoyed. The officers appointed by the king, on the other hand, illegitimately acquired more and more power; they treated everything that came within their administrative remit as though it were their fief, as though it were their own property. And so it was that this decomposition of central power gave birth to something known as feudalism. As you can see, this feudalism was a late phenomenon, and it was related not to the invasion, but to the destruction from within of central power. It was an effect, and it had the same effects as an invasion, but it was an invasion that was launched from within by people who had usurped a power that had been delegated to them. "The dismembering of sovereignty and the transformation of offices into seigneuries"—I am citing a text by Dubos—"had very similar effects to a foreign invasion, created a domineering caste between the king and the people, and turned Gaul into a land that really had been conquered."[14] Dubos rediscovers elements that were, according to Boulainvilliers, typical of what happened at the time of the Franks—invasion, conquest, and domination—but he sees them as internal phenomena due—or correlative—to the birth of an aristocracy. And as you see, it was an aristocracy that was artificial, and completely protected from, completely independent of, the Frankish invasion and the barbarism that came with it. And so the struggles against this conquest began: struggles against this usurpation and this invasion from within. The monarch and the towns which had retained the freedom of the Roman *municipes* will fight side by side against the feudal lords.

In the discourse of Dubos, Moreau, and all the monarchist historians, you have a complete inversion of Boulainvilliers's discourse, but they also transform it in one important sense. The focus of the historical analysis is displaced from the fact of the invasion and the early

Merovingians to this other fact: the birth of feudalism and the first Capetians. You can also see—and this is important—that the invasion of the nobility is analyzed not as the effect of a military invasion and of the irruption of barbarism, but as the result of usurpation from within. The fact of the conquest is still there, but it is stripped of its barbarian context and the right-effects that might have resulted from the military victory. The nobles are not barbarians, but they are crooks, political crooks. Here we have the first position, the first tactical—and inverted—use that is made of Boulainvilliers's discourse.

Now for another, different way of filtering barbarism. The goal of this different type of discourse is to dissociate a Germanic freedom, or in other words, a barbarian freedom, from the exclusive nature of the privileges of the aristocracy. Its goal is, in other words—and to this extent, this thesis, this tactic remains very close to Boulainvilliers's—to go on laying claim to the freedoms the barbarians and Franks brought to France by resisting the Roman absolutism of the monarchy. The hairy bands from across the Rhine did indeed enter Gaul, and they did bring their freedoms with them. These hairy bands were not, however, bands of German warriors who made up the nucleus of an aristocracy that remained an aristocracy within the body of Gallo-Roman society. Those who flooded in were certainly warriors, but they were also a whole people in arms. The political and social form that was introduced into Gaul was not that of an aristocracy but, on the contrary, that of a democracy, that of the widest possible democracy. You will find this thesis in Mably,[15] in Bonneville,[16] and even in Marat, in *Les Chaînes de l'esclavage*. So, the barbarian democracy of the Franks, who know no form of aristocracy, and who know only an egalitarian people of soldier-citizens. "A proud, brutal people with no homeland and no law," said Mably,[17] and every citizen-soldier had only his booty to live on, but would not tolerate any kind of punishment. There is no consistent authority over this people, no rational or constituted authority. And according to Mably, it was this brutal, barbarian democracy that was established in Gaul. And its establishment was the basis, the starting point for a series of processes. The avidity and egoism of the barbarian Franks, which were virtues when it was a matter of crossing the Rhine and invading Gaul, become vices once they settled there: the Franks are no long interested in anything but looting and pillage. They neglect both the exercise of power and the yearly March or May gatherings which placed permanent controls on royal power. They allow the king to do as he likes, and they allow a monarchy, which has absolutist tendencies, to establish itself over them. And according to Mably, the clergy—though this was presumably a reflection of its ignorance and not its cunning—interprets Germanic customs in terms of Roman right: they believe themselves to be the subjects of a monarchy, when they are in fact the body of a republic.

The sovereign's officer-officials also acquire more and more power. And so we begin to move away from the general democracy that Frankish barbarism had brought with it, and toward a system which is both monarchic and aristocratic. This is a slow process, and there is a moment of reaction. This occurs when Charlemagne, who felt increasingly dominated and threatened by the aristocracy, once more turns for support to the people his predecessors had neglected. Charlemagne reestablishes the Champ de Mars and the May gatherings; he allows everyone, including nonwarriors, to attend the assemblies. For a brief moment we have, then, a return to Germanic democracy, and the slow process that leads to the disappearance of democracy begins again after this brief interlude. Twin figures now appear. On the one hand, that of a monarchy, [the monarchy of Hugh Capet]. How does the monarchy succeed in establishing itself? It can do so to the extent that the aristocrats reject barbarian and Frankish democracy and agree to choose a king who has increasingly absolutist tendencies; on the other hand, the Capetians reward the nobles for having consecrated Hugh Capet king by putting them in charge of the administration and turning the offices with which they had been entrusted into fiefs. The complicity between the nobles who created the king and the king who created feudalism thus gives birth to the twin figures of a monarchy and an aristocracy, and they dominate a barbarian democracy. Germanic democracy is thus the starting point for a twofold process. The aristocracy and the absolute monarchy will of course eventually come into conflict, but it must not be forgotten that, basically, they are twin sisters.

Third type of discourse, third type of analysis, and, at the same time, third tactic. This is the most subtle tactic and, in historical terms, the most successful, even though, at the time of its formulation, it had much less impact than the theses of Dubos or Mably. The goal of this third tactical operation is to make a distinction between two forms of barbarism: the barbarism of the Germans will become the bad barbarism from which we have to be freed; and then there is a good barbarism, or the barbarism of the Gauls, which is the only real source of freedom. This performs two important operations: on the one hand, freedom and Germanity, which had been linked together by Boulainvilliers, are dissociated; on the other, Romanity and abso-lutism are dissociated. We will, in other words, find in Roman Gaul elements of the freedom which, as all previous theses had more or less accepted, had been imported by the Franks. Broadly speaking, Mably arrived at his thesis by transforming Boulainvilliers's thesis: German freedoms were destroyed democratically. Bréquigny,[18] Chap-sal,[19] and others arrive at this new thesis by intensifying and displac-ing the sort of passing comment Dubos made when he said that the king and then the towns, which had resisted feudal usurpation, re-belled against feudalism.

The Bréquigny-Chapsal thesis, which will, because it is so impor-tant, become that of the bourgeois historians of the nineteenth century (Augustin Thierry, Guizot), basically consists in saying that there were two tiers to the political system of the Romans. At the level of central government, of the great Roman administration, we are, of course—at least from the time of the empire onward—dealing with an absolute power. But the Romans left the Gauls to enjoy their own primal freedoms. As a result, Roman Gaul was indeed in one sense part of a great absolutist empire, but it was also permeated or pen-etrated by a whole series of pockets of freedom: the Gaulish or Celtic freedoms of old. The Romans left them alone, and they continued to function in the towns, or in the famous *municipes* of the Roman Empire where the archaic freedoms, the ancestral freedoms of the Gauls and the Celts, continued to function in forms that were, as it happens, more or less borrowed from the old Roman city. Freedom is therefore a phenomenon that is compatible with Roman absolutism (and this is, I think, the first time this argument appears in these historical analyses); it is a Gaulish phenomenon, but it is above all an urban phenomenon. Freedom belongs to the towns. And it is to the precise extent that it belongs to the towns that freedom can struggle and become a political force. The towns will of course be destroyed when the Frankish and Germanic invasions take place. But, being nomadic peasants or at least barbarians, the Franks and Germans neglect the towns and settle in the countryside. So the towns, which were neglected by the Franks, are rebuilt and enjoy a new prosperity at this point. When feudalism is established at the end of the reign of the Carolingians, the great secular-ecclesiastical lords will of course try to get their hands on the reconstituted wealth of the cities. But at this point, the towns, which had grown historically strong thanks to their wealth and their freedoms, but thanks also to the fact that they formed a community, are able to struggle, resist, and rebel. Hence all the great rebellious movements that develop in the free towns during the reign of the first Capetians. And they eventually forced both royal power and the aristocracy to respect their rights and, to a certain extent, their laws, their type of economy, their forms of life, their customs, and so on. This happened in the fifteenth and sixteenth centuries.

So you see, this time we have a thesis which, much more than previous theses and even more than Mably's thesis, will become the thesis of the Third Estate, because this is the first time that the history of the town, the history of urban institutions, and the history of wealth and its political effects could be articulated within a historical analysis. This history creates, or at least begins to create, a Third Estate that is a product not merely of the concessions granted by the king, but of its own energy, its wealth, its trade, and of a highly sophisticated urban law that is in part borrowed from Roman law, but which is also articulated with the freedom of old, or in other words, the Gaulish barbarism of old. From this point onward, and for the first time, a Romanity which, in the historical and political thought of the eighteenth century, had always been tinged with absolutism and had always been on the side of the king, now becomes tinged with liberalism. And far from being the theatrical form in which royal power reflects its history, Romanity will, thanks to the analyses I am discussing, become an issue for the bourgeoisie itself. The bourgeoisie will be able to recuperate—in the form of the Gallo-Roman *municeps*—a Romanity that supplies, so to speak, its letters of nobility. The Gallo-Roman municipality is the Third Estate's nobility. And it is this municipality, this autonomy, and this form of municipal freedom that the Third Estate will demand. All this must, of course, be seen in the context of the debate that took place in the eighteenth century around, precisely, municipal freedoms and autonomy. I refer you, for example, to a text by Turgot that dates from 1776.[20] But you can also see that on the eve of the Revolution, Romanity can also lose all the monarchist and absolutist connotations it had had throughout the eighteenth century. A liberal Romanity becomes possible, and even those who are not monarchists or absolutists can revert to it. Even the bourgeois can revert to Romanity. And as you know, the Revolution will have no hesitation in doing so.

The other important thing about the discourse of Bréquigny, Chapsal, and the rest of them is that it allows, you see, the historical field to be greatly extended. With the English historians of the seventeenth century, and with Boulainvilliers too, we basically start with the small nucleus of the invasion, with the few decades, or at most the century, during which the barbarian hordes flooded into Gaul. So you see, we have a gradual extension of the field. We have seen, for instance, the importance Mably ascribes to a figure such as Charlemagne; we have also seen how Dubos extended the historical analysis to include the early Capetians and feudalism. With the analyses of Bréquigny, Chapsal, and others, the domain of historically useful and politically productive knowledge can, on the one hand, be extended upward, as it now goes back to the municipal organization of the Romans and, ultimately, to the ancient freedoms of the Gauls and the Celts. On the other hand, history can be extended downward to include all the struggles, all the urban rebellions which, ever since the beginning of feudalism, led to the emergence, or at least the partial emergence, of the bourgeoisie as an economic and political force in the fifteenth and sixteenth centuries. The field of historical and political debate now covers one and a half thousand years of history. The juridical and historical fact of the invasion has now been completely shattered, and we are now dealing with an immense field of generalized struggles covering fifteen hundred years of history and involving a great variety of actors: kings, the nobility, the clergy, soldiers, royal officers, the Third Estate, the bourgeoisie, the peasants, the townspeople, and so on. This is a history that takes as its support institutions such as Roman freedoms, municipal freedoms, the church, education, trade, language, and so on. A general explosion in the field of history; and it is in this precise field that the historians of the nineteenth century will begin their work.

You might ask: Why all the details, why locate these different tactics within the field of history? It is true that I could quite simply have moved directly on to Augustin Thierry, Montlosier, and all the others who used this instrumentation of knowledge to try to think about the revolutionary phenomenon. I lingered over this for two reasons. First, for methodological reasons. As you have seen, one can very easily, from Boulainvilliers onward, trace the constitution of a historical and political discourse whose domain of objects, pertinent elements, concepts, and methods of analysis are all closely interrelated. The eighteenth century saw the formation of a sort of historical discourse which was common to a whole series of historians, even though their theses, hypotheses, and political dreams were very different. One can quite easily, and without any breaks at all, trace the entire network of basic propositions that subtend each type of analysis: all the transformations that take us from a history that [praises] the Franks (such as Mably, such as Dubos) to the very different history of Frankish democracy. One can quite easily move from one of these histories to the next by identifying a few very simple transpositions at the level of their basic propositions. We have then all these historical discourses, and they form a very closely woven web, no matter what their historical theses or political objectives may be. Now the fact that this epistemic web is so tightly woven certainly does not mean that everyone is thinking along the same lines. It is in fact a precondition for not thinking along the same lines or for thinking along different lines; and it is that which makes the differences politically pertinent. If different subjects are to be able to speak, to occupy different tactical positions, and if they are to be able to find themselves in mutually adversarial positions, there has to be a tight field, there has to be a very tightly woven network to regularize historical knowledge. As the field of knowledge becomes more regular, it becomes increasingly possible for the subjects who speak within it to be divided along strict lines of confrontation, and it becomes increasingly possible to make the contending discourses function as different tactical units within overall strategies (which are not simply a matter of discourse and truth, but also of power, status, and economic interests). The tactical reversibility of the discourse is, in other words, directly proportional to the homogeneity of the field in which it is formed. It is the regularity of the epistemological field, the homogeneity of the discourse's mode of formation, that allows it to be used in struggles that are extradiscursive. That, then, is the methodological reason why I emphasized that the different discursive tactics are distributed across a historico-political field that is coherent, regular, and very tightly woven.[21]

I also stress it for a second reason—a factual reason—pertaining to what happened at the time of the Revolution. What I mean is this: Leaving aside the last form of discourse that I have just been telling you about (Bréquigny or Chapsal), you can see that, basically, those who had the least interest in investing their political projects in history were of course the people of the bourgeoisie or the Third Estate, because going back to a constitution or demanding a return to something resembling an equilibrium of forces implies in some way that you know where you stand in that equilibrium of forces. Now it was quite obvious that the Third Estate or the bourgeoisie could scarcely, at least until the middle of the Middle Ages, identify itself as a historical subject within the play of relations of force. So long as history concentrated on the Merovingians, the Carolingians, the Frankish invaders, or even Charlemagne, how could it find anything relating to the Third Estate or the bourgeoisie? Which is why, whatever has been said to the contrary, the bourgeoisie was, in the eighteenth century, certainly the class that was most hostile, most resistant to history. In a profound sense, it was the aristocracy that was historical. The monarch was historical, and so too were the *parlementaires*. But for a long time, the bourgeoisie remained antihistoricist or, if you like, antihistoric.

The antihistoric character of the bourgeoisie manifests itself in two ways. First, throughout the whole of the first half of the eighteenth century, the bourgeoisie tended to be in favor of an enlightened despotism, or in other words, of a way of moderating monarchical power that was not grounded in history but in the restrictions imposed by knowledge, philosophy, technology, and administration. And then in the second half of the eighteenth century, and especially before the Revolution, the bourgeoisie tried to escape the ambient historicism by demanding a constitution which was precisely not a re-constitution and which was essentially, if not antihistorical, at least ahistorical. Hence, as you can understand, the recourse to natural right, the recourse to something like the social contract. The Rousseauism of the bourgeoisie at the end of the eighteenth century, before and during the Revolution, was a direct response to the historicism of the other political subjects who were fighting in the field of theory and historical analysis. Being a Rousseauist, appealing to the savage and appealing to the contract, was a way of escaping an entire landscape that had been defined by the barbarian, his history, and his relationship with civilization.

This antihistoricism of the bourgeoisie obviously did not remain unchanged, and it was no obstacle to a complete rearticulation of history. You will see that at the moment when the Estates General were called, the registers of grievances are full of historical references, but the most important are, of course, those made by the nobility itself. And when the bourgeoisie in its turn reactivated a whole series of historical knowledges, it was simply responding to the multiple references that had been made to the capitulars, to the Edict of Piste,[22] and to the practices of the Merovingians and the Carolingians. It was a sort of polemical reply to the multiplicity of historical references you find in the nobility's register of grievances. And then you have a second reactivation of history, which is probably more important and more interesting. I refer to the reactivation, during the Revolution itself, of a certain number of moments or historical forms that function as, if you like, the splendors of history. Their reappearance in the Revolution's vocabulary, institutions, signs, manifestations, festivals made it possible to visualize it as a cycle and a return.

So the juridical Rousseauism that had long been its main theme led, in some sense, to the reactivation of two great historical forms during the Revolution. On the one hand, you have the reactivation of Rome, or rather of the Roman city, or in other words, of an archaic Rome that was both republican and virtuous, rather than the Gallo-Roman city with its freedoms and its prosperity. Hence the Roman festival, or the political ritualization of a historical form which, in constitutional or basic terms, derived from those freedoms. The other figure to be reactivated is that of Charlemagne; we have seen the role Mably gave him and how he became the point where Frankish and Gallo-Roman freedoms merged; Charlemagne was the man who summoned the people to the Champ de Mars. Charlemagne as sovereign-warrior, but also as the protector of trade and the towns. Charlemagne as both Germanic king and Roman emperor. Right from the beginning of the Revolution, a whole Carolingian dream unfolds, and it goes on unfolding throughout the Revolution, but much less has been said about it than about the Roman festival. The festival held on the Champ de Mars on 14 July 1789 is a Carolingian festival; it takes place on the Champ de Mars itself, and it permits the recon-stitution or reactivation of a certain relationship between the people gathered there and their sovereign. And the modality of that rela-tionship is Carolingian. That kind of implicit historical vocabulary is at least present in the festival of 14 July 1789. The best proof of that is that in June 1789, or a few weeks before the festival, someone in the Jacobin Club demanded that in the course of the festival, Louis

XVI should forfeit the title of king, that the title of king should be replaced by that of emperor, that when he passed by, the cry should not be "Long live the king!" but "Louis the Emperor!" because the man who is emperor *"imperat sed not regit"*: he commands but does not govern, because he is an emperor and not a king. According to this project, Louis XVI should return from the Champ de Mars with the imperial crown on his head.[23] And it is of course at the point where the Carolingian dream (which is not very well known) and the Roman dream meet that we find the Napoleonic empire.

The other form of historical reactivation that we find in the Revolution is the execration of feudalism, or of what Antraigues, a noble who had rallied to the bourgeoisie, called "the most terrible scourge that heaven, in its anger, could have visited upon a free nation."[24] Now, this execration of feudalism takes several forms. First, a straightforward inversion of Boulainvilliers's thesis, or the invasion thesis. And so you find texts which say—this one is by Abbé Proyart: "Listen, you Frankish gentlemen. We outnumber you by a thousand to one; we have been your vassals for long enough, now you become our vassals. It pleases us to come into the heritage of our fathers."[25] That is what Abbé Proyart wanted the Third Estate to say to the nobility. And in his famous text on the Third Estate, to which I will come back next time, Sieyès said: "Why not send them all back to the forests of Franconia, all these families that still make the insane claim that they are descended from a race of conquerors, and that they have inherited the right of conquest?"[26] And in either 1795 or 1796—I can't remember—Boulay de la Meurthe said, after the mass emigration of the nobility: "The émigrés represent the last vestiges of a conquest from which the French nation has gradually liberated itself."[27]

What you see taking shape here will be just as important in the early nineteenth century: the French Revolution—and the political and social struggles that went on during it—are being reinterpreted in terms of the history of races. And it is no doubt this execration of feudalism that supplies the context for the ambiguous celebration of the gothic that we see appearing in the famous medieval novels of the revolutionary period, in those gothic novels that are at once tales of terror, fear, and mystery, and political novels. They are always about the abuse of power and exactions; they are fables about unjust sovereigns, pitiless and bloodthirsty seigneurs, arrogant priests, and so on. The gothic novel is both science fiction and politics fiction: politics fiction in the sense that these novels essentially focus on the abuse of power, and science fiction in the sense that their function is to reactivate, at the level of the imaginary, a whole knowledge about feudalism, a whole knowledge about the gothic—a knowledge that has, basically, a golden age. It was not literature and it was not the imagination that introduced the themes of the gothic and feudalism at the end of the eighteenth century, and they were neither new nor renovated in any absolute sense. They were in fact inscribed in the order of the imaginary to the precise extent that the gothic and feudalism had been an issue in what was now a hundred-year-long struggle at the level of knowledge and forms of power. Long before the first gothic novel, almost a century before it, there had been arguments over what the feudal lords, their fiefs, their powers, and their forms of domination meant in both historical and political terms. The whole of the eighteenth century was obsessed with the problem of feudalism at the level of right, history, and politics. And it was only at the time of the Revolution—or a hundred years after all that work had been done at the level of knowledge and the level of politics—that there was finally a taking up again of these themes, at the level of the imaginary, in these science-fiction and politics-fiction novels. It was in this domain, therefore, that you had the gothic novel. But all this has to be situated in the context of the history of knowledge and of the political tactics that it makes possible. And so, next time, I will talk to you about history as a reworking of the Revolution.

1. This is obviously a reworking and genealogical reformulation of the fields of knowledge and forms of discursivity that Foucault discusses in "archaeological" terms in *Les Mots et les choses* (*The Order of Things*).
2. The medical doctrine of "constitution" has a long history, but Foucault is presumably referring to the anatomo-pathological theory that was formulated in the eighteenth century on the basis of the work of Sydenham, Le Brun, and Bordeu, and which was further developed in the first half of the nineteenth century by Bichat and the Paris school. See *Naissance de la clinique* (*Birth of the Clinic*).
3. In his discussion of the "decline" and "decadence" of ancient Rome in his *Essai sur la noblesse de France contenant une dissertation sur son origine et abaissement* (which was probably written in about 1700, and which was published in 1730 in his *Continuation des mémoires de littérature*, vol. 10), Boulainvilliers accepts that decadence is "the common destiny of all States that exist for a long time," and then adds: "The world is the plaything of a continuous succession; why should the nobility and its privileges be an exception to the general rule?" Nevertheless, he remarks of this succession that "One of our children will no doubt pierce the darkness in which we live and restore its ancient luster to our name" (p. 85). A contemporary version of the idea of a cycle is also to be found in G. B. Vico's *Scienza nuova* (Naples, 1725). In his *Astrologie mondiale* of 1711 (which was published by Renée Simon in 1949), Boulainvilliers formulates what might be called the pre-Hegelian idea of "the transfer of monarchies from one country or nation to another." This, according to Boulainvilliers, involves an "order" in which "nothing is ever fixed, because no society will endure forever and because the greatest and most feared empires are subject to destruction by the same means as those who created them; other societies will be born of them, will wear them down by force and persuasion, will conquer the old societies and subdue them in their turn" (pp. 141-42).
4. "A proud, brutal people without a homeland and without laws... The French could even tolerate atrocious acts of violence on the part of their chief because, for them, they were in keeping with public morals." G. B. de Mably, *Observations sur l'histoire de France* (Paris, 1823), chap. 1, p. 6 (first ed., Geneva, 1765).
5. N. de Bonneville, *Histoire de l'Europe moderne depuis l'irruption des peuples du Nord dans l'Empire romain jusqu'à la paix de 1738* (Geneva, 1789), vol. 1, part 1, p. 20. The quotation ends: "The sword was their right, and they exercised it without remorse, as though it were a natural right."
6. "Poor, uncouth, without trade, without art, without industry, but free." *Les Chaînes de l'esclavage. Ouvrage destiné à développer les noirs attentats des princes contre le peuple* (chapter entitled "Des vices de la constitution politique"), an I (reprinted: Paris: Union génerale des éditions, 1988), p. 30.
7. C. L.G. comte du Buat-Nançay, *Éléments de la politique*, vol. 1, book 1, chaps. 1-11, "De l'égalité des hommes." We have been unable to trace this quotation (if it is a quotation), but this could be its context.
8. Foucault is alluding to the study group which, from 1948 onward, began to gather around Cornelius Castoriadis and which began to publish *Socialisme ou barbarie* in 1949. The journal ceased publication in 1965, with issue 40. Under the leadership of Castoriadis and Claude Lefort, this group of dissident Trotskyists, activists, and intellectuals (who included Edgar Morin, Jean-François Lyotard, Jean Laplanche, and Gérard Genette) developed such themes as the critique of the Soviet regime, the question of direct democracy, and the critique of reformism.
9. Robert Desnos, "Description d'une révolte prochaine," *La Révolution surréaliste*, no. 3, April 1925, p. 25; reprinted in *La Révolution surréaliste (1924-1929)* (Paris, 1975 [facsimile edition]).

10. J.-N. Dubos, *Histoire critique de l'établissement de la monarchie française dans les Gaules* (Paris, 1734).

11. J.-N. Moreau, *Leçons de morale, de politique et de droit public, puisées dans l'histoire de la monarchie* (Versailles, 1773); *Exposé historique des administrations populaires aux plus anciennes époques de notre monarchie* (Paris, 1789); *Défense de notre constitution monarchique française, précédée de l'Histoire de toutes nos assemblées nationales* (Paris, 1789).

12. An old expression meaning "to treat someone as the Turks treat the Moors." Dubos writes: "I ask the reader to pay particular attention to the natural humor of the inhabitants of Gaul, who, in the absence of any proof to the contrary, have never been regarded in any century as being stupid or cowardly: as we shall see, it is impossible for a handful of Franks to treat the one million Romans living in Gaul *de turc à Maure.*" *Histoire critique,* vol. 4, book 6, pp. 212-13.

13. For Dubos's critique of Boulainvilliers, see ibid., chaps. 8 and 9.

14. It seems that only the last sentence is a direct quotation. Having spoken of the usurpation of royal offices and of how the commissions granted to the dukes and counts were converted into hereditary dignities, Dubos writes: "It was at this time that the Gauls became a conquered land." Ibid., book 4, p. 290 (1742 ed.).

15. G.-B. de Mably, *Observations sur l'histoire de France.*

16. N. de Bonneville, *Histoire de l'Europe moderne depuis l'irruption des peuples du Nord.*

17. Mably, *Observations,* p. 6.

18. L. G. O. F. de Bréquigny, *Diplomata, chartae, epistolae et alia monumenta ad res franciscas spectantia* (Paris, 1679-1783); *Ordonnances des rois de France de la troisième race* (Paris, vol. 11, 1769, vol. 12, 1776).

19. J.-F. Chapsal, *Discours sur la féodalité et l'allodialité, suivi de Dissertations sur le france-alleu des coutumes d'Auvergne, du Bourbonnais, du Nivernois, de Champagne* (Paris, 1791).

20. R.-J. Turgot, *Mémoire sur les municipalités* (Paris, 1776).

21. This passage makes a significant contribution to the debates and controversies provoked by the concept of the episteme, which Foucault elaborates in *Les Mots et les choses* and then reworks in *L'Archéologie du savoir,* part 4, chap. 6.

22. A council held in Pistes (or Pistres) in 864 under the influence of Archbishop Hincmar. Its resolutions are known as the Edict of Pistes. The organization of the monetary system was discussed, the destruction of castles built by seigneurs was ordered, and several towns were given the right to mint coins. The assembly put Pipin II of Aquitaine on trial and declared that he had forfeited his position.

23. The reference is to a motion put to the Jacobin Club on 17 June 1789. Cf. F.-A. Aulard, *La Société des jacobins* (Paris, 1889-1897), vol. 1, p. 153.

24. E. L. H. L., comte d'Antraigues, *Mémoires sur la constitution des Etats provinciaux* (Vivarois, 1788), p. 61.

25. L.-B. Proyart, *Vie du Dauphin père de Louis XV* (Paris and Lyon, 1872), vol. 1, pp. 357-58, cited in A. Devyer, *Le Sang épuré,* p. 370.

26. E.-J. Sieyès, *Qu'est-ce que le Tiers-Etat,* chap. 2, pp. 10-11. In the original, the sentence begins: "Why shouldn't it [the Third Estate]..."

27. A.-J. Boulay de la Meurthe, *Rapport présenté le 25 Vendémiaire an VI au Conseil des Cinq-Cents sur les mesures d'ostracisme, d'exil, d'expulsion les plus convenables aux principes de justice et de liberté, et les plus propres à consolider la république,* cited in A. Devyer, *Le Sang épuré,* p. 415.

ten

10 MARCH 1976

[
The political reworking of the idea of the nation during the Revolution: Sieyès. ~ Theoretical implications and effects on historical discourse. ~ The new history's grids of intelligibility: domination and totalization. ~ Montlosier and Augustin Thierry. ~ Birth of the dialectic.
]

I THINK THAT IN the eighteenth century it was essentially, and almost exclusively, the discourse of history that made war the primary, and almost exclusive, analyzer of political relations. The discourse of history, then, and not the discourse of right and not the discourse of political theory (with its contracts, its savages, its men of the prairies and the forests, its states of nature and its war of every man against every man, and so on). It was not that; it was the discourse of history. So I would now like to show you how, in a rather paradoxical way, the element of war, which actually constituted historical intelligibility in the eighteenth century, was from the Revolution onward gradually, if not eliminated from the discourse of history, at least reduced, restricted, colonized, settled, scattered, civilized if you like, and up to a point pacified. This is because it was, after all, history (as written by Boulainvilliers, or Buat-Nançay, not that it matters) that conjured up the great threat: the great danger that we would be caught up in a war without end; the great danger that all our relations, whatever they might be, would always be of the order of domination. And it is this twofold threat—a war without end as the basis of history and the relationship of domination as the explanatory element in history—that will, in the historical discourse of the nineteenth century, be lessened, broken down into regional threats and transitory episodes, and retranscribed in the form of crises and violence. What is more important still is, I think, the fact that this danger is, essentially, destined to fade away in the end, not in the sense that we will achieve the good and true equilibrium that the eighteenth-century historians were trying to find, but in the sense that reconciliation will come about.

I do not think that this inversion of the problem of war within the discourse of history is an effect of its transplantation or, so to speak, of the fact that a dialectical philosophy took control. I think that what occurred was something like an internal dialecticalization, a self-dialecticalization of historical discourse, and that there is an obvious connection between this and its embourgeoisement. The problem we have to understand is this: How, after this displacement (if not decline) of the role of war within historical discourse, does the relationship of war—which has been mastered within historical discourse—reappear, but this time with a negative role, with a sort of external role? Its role is no longer to constitute history but to protect and preserve society; war is no longer a condition of existence for society and political relations, but the precondition for its survival in its political relations. At this point, we see the emergence of the idea of an internal war that defends society against threats born of and in its own body. The idea of social war makes, if you like, a great retreat from the historical to the biological, from the constituent to the medical.

Today I am going to try to describe the process of the auto-dialecticalization, and therefore the embourgeoisement, of history, of historical discourse. Last time, I tried to show you how and why, in the historico-political field that was constituted in the eighteenth century, it was ultimately the bourgeoisie that was in the most difficult position, that found it most difficult to use the discourse of history as a weapon in the political fight. I would now like to show you how certain obstacles were removed. This certainly did not occur because the bourgeoisie at some point somehow acquired a history or recognized its own history, but as a result of something very specific: the reworking—in political and not historical terms—of the famous notion of the "nation," which the aristocracy had made both the subject and the object of history in the eighteenth century. It was that role, that political reworking of the nation, of the idea of the nation, that led to the transformation that made a new type of historical discourse possible. And I will take Sieyès's famous text on the Third Estate as, if not exactly a starting point, an example of this transformation. As you know, the text asks three questions: "What is the Third Estate? Everything. What has it been until now in the political order? Nothing. What is it asking to be? To become something in that order."[1] The text is both famous and hackneyed, but if we look at it a little more closely, it does, I think, bring about a number of essential transformations.

Speaking of the nation, you know in general terms (I am going over things I have already said in order to summarize them) that the absolute monarchy's thesis was that the nation did not exist, or at least that if it did exist, it did so only to the extent that it found its condition of possibility, and its substantive unity, in the person of the king. The nation did not exist simply because there was a group, a crowd, or a multiplicity of individuals inhabiting the same land, speaking the same language, and observing the same customs and the same laws. That is not what makes a nation. What makes a nation is the fact that there exist individuals who, insofar as they exist alongside one another, are no more than individuals and do not even form a unit. But they do all have a certain individual relationship—both juridical and physical—with the real, living, and bodily person of the king. It is the body of the king, in his physico-juridical relationship with each of his subjects, that creates the body of the nation. A jurist of the late eighteenth century said: "Every particular subject represents only a single individual to the king."* The nation does not

---

*The manuscript has "the king represents the entire nation and" before "every particular." The reference for the quotation is given as "P. E. Lemontey, *Oeuvres*, Paris, vol. V, 1829, p. 15."

constitute a body. The nation in its entirety resides in the person of the king. And the nobiliary reaction derived a multiplicity of nations (well, at least two) from this nation—which is in a sense merely a juridical effect of the body of the king, and which is real only because of the unique and individual reality of the king. The nobiliary reaction then establishes relations of war and domination between those nations; it makes the king an instrument that one nation can use to wage war on and dominate another. It is not the king who constitutes the nation; a nation acquires a king for the specific purpose of fighting other nations. And the history written by the nobiliary reaction made those relations the web of historical intelligibility.

We find a very different definition of the nation in Sieyès, or rather a double definition. On the one hand, a juridical state. Sieyès says that if a nation is to exist, it must have two things: a common law and a legislature.[2] So much for the juridical state. This initial definition of the nation (or rather this first set of essential preconditions for the existence of a nation) demands—before we can speak of a nation— much less than was demanded by the definition advanced by the absolute monarchy. The nation does not, in other words, need a king in order to exist. It is not even necessary for there to be a government. Provided that it is endowed with a common law because there is an agency that is qualified to establish laws, the nation exists even before any government is formed, even before the sovereign is born, and even before power is delegated. That agency is the legislature itself. So the nation is much less than what was required by the absolute monarchy's definition. But in another sense, it is much more than what was required by the nobiliary reaction's definition. According to that definition, and according to history as written by Boulainvilliers, all that was required for the nation to exist were men who were brought together by certain interests, and who had a certain number of things in common, such as customs, habits, and possibly a language.

If there is to be a nation, there must, according to Sieyès, be explicit laws, and agencies to formulate them. The law-legislature couple is the formal precondition for the existence of a nation. This is, however, only the first stage of the definition. If a nation is to survive, if its law is to be applied and if its legislature is to be recognized (not only abroad, or by other nations, but also within the nation itself), if its survival and prosperity are to be not only a formal precondition for its juridical existence, but also a historical precondition for its existence *in* history, then there must be something else, other preconditions. Sieyès now turns his attention to these other preconditions. They are in a sense the substantive preconditions for the existence of the nation, and Sieyès divides them into two groups. The first are what he calls "works," or first, agriculture; second, handicrafts and industry; third, trade; and, fourth, the liberal arts. But in addition to these "works," there must also be what he calls "functions": the army, justice, the church, and the administration.[3] "Works" and "functions"; we would no doubt use the more accurate terms "functions" and "apparatuses" to describe these two sets of historical prerequisites for nationhood. The important point is, however, that it is at this level of functions and apparatuses that the nation's historical conditions of existence are defined. By defining them at this level, and by adding historico-functional preconditions to these juridico-formal preconditions for nationhood, Sieyès is, I think (and this is the first thing that has to be pointed out), reversing the direction of all previous analyses, no matter whether they adopted the monarchist thesis or took a Rousseauist line.

Indeed, so long as the juridical definition of the nation prevailed, what were the elements—agriculture, commerce, industry, et cetera—that Sieyès isolates as the substantive preconditions for the existence of the nation? They were not a precondition for the nation's existence; on the contrary, they were effects of the nation's existence. It was precisely when men, or individuals scattered across the surface of the land, on the edges of the forests or on the plains, decided to develop their agriculture, to trade and to be able to have economic relations with one another, that they gave themselves a law, a State, or a government. In other words, all these functions were in fact effects of the juridical constitution of the nation, or at least its consequences. It was only when the juridical constitution of the nation was an established fact that these functions could be deployed. Nor were apparatuses such as the army, justice, and the administration preconditions for the existence of the nation; they were, if not effects, at least its instruments and guarantors. It was only when the nation had been constituted that it could acquire things like an army or a system of justice.

So you see, Sieyès inverts the analysis. His works and functions, or these functions and apparatuses, exist before the nation—if not in historical terms, at least in terms of conditions of existence. A nation can exist as a nation, and can enter history and survive through history, only if it is capable of commerce, agriculture, and handicrafts; only if it has individuals who are capable of forming an army, a magistrature, a church, and an administration. This means that a group of individuals can always come together and can always give itself laws and a legislature; it can give itself a constitution. If that group of individuals does not have the capacity for commerce, handicrafts, and agriculture, or the ability to form an army, a magistrature, and so on, it will never, in historical terms, be a nation. It might be a nation in juridical terms, but never in historical terms. A contract, a law, or a consensus can never really create a nation. Conversely, it is perfectly possible for a group of individuals to have the wherewithal, the historical ability to develop works, to exercise functions, without ever having been given a common law and a legislature. Such people would, in a sense, be in possession of the substantive and functional elements of the nation; they are not in possession of its formal elements. They are capable of nationhood, but they will not be a nation.

On the basis of this, it is possible to analyze—and Sieyès does analyze—what he thought was going on in France at the end of the eighteenth century. Agriculture, commerce, handicrafts, and the liberal arts do exist. Who fulfills these various functions? The Third Estate, and only the Third Estate. Who runs the army, the church, the administration, and the system of justice? We do of course find people belonging to the aristocracy in important positions, but according to Sieyès, it is the Third Estate that runs nine out of ten of these apparatuses. On the other hand, the Third Estate, which has assumed responsibility for the nation's substantive conditions of existence, has not been given the formal status of a nation. There are no common laws in France; there is a series of laws, some applicable to the nobility, some to the Third Estate, and some to the clergy. No common laws. No legislature either, because laws and ordinances are established by what Sieyès calls an "aulic" system,[4] meaning a courtly system, or arbitrary royal power.

This analysis has, I think, a number of implications. Some are obviously of an immediately political order. They are immediately political in this sense: the point is, you see, that France is not a nation, because it lacks the formal, juridical preconditions for nationhood: common laws and a legislature. And yet there is "a" nation in France, or in other words, a group of individuals who have the potential capacity to ensure the substantive and historical existence of the nation. These people supply the historical conditions of existence of both *a* nation and *the* nation. Hence the central formulation of Sieyès's text, which cannot be understood unless we quite specifically see it in terms of its polemical—explicitly polemical—relationship with the theses of Boulainvilliers, Buat-Nançay, and the rest of them: "The Third Estate is a complete nation."[5] The formula means this: This concept of nation, which the aristocracy wanted to reserve for a group of individuals whose only assets were common customs and a common status, is not enough to describe the historical reality of the nation. But, on the other hand, the Statist entity constituted by the kingdom of France is not really a nation to the extent that it does not exactly coincide with the historical conditions that are necessary and sufficient to constitute a nation. Where, then, are we to find the historical core of a nation that can become "the" nation? In the Third Estate, and only in the Third Estate. The Third Estate is in itself the historical precondition for the existence of a nation, but that nation should, by rights, coincide with the State. The Third Estate is a nation. It contains the constituent elements of a nation. Or, to translate the same propositions differently: "All that is national is ours," says the Third Estate, "and all that is ours is the nation."[6]

Sieyès did not invent this political formula, and he was not alone in formulating it, but it obviously becomes the matrix for a whole political discourse which, as you well know, is still not exhausted today. The matrix of this political discourse displays, I think, two characteristics. First, a certain new relationship between particularity and universality, a certain relationship which is precisely the opposite of that which characterized the discourse of the nobiliary reaction. What, basically, did the nobiliary reaction do? It extracted from the social body constituted by the king and his subjects, it extracted from the monarchic unity, a certain singular right that was sealed in blood and asserted by victory: the singular right of the nobles. And it claimed, whatever the constitution of the social body that surrounded it, to reserve the absolute and singular privilege of that right for the nobility; it extracted, then, this particular right from the totality of the social body and made it function in its singularity. And now, something quite different is beginning to be said. It is beginning to be said that, on the contrary (and this is what the Third Estate will say): "We are no more than one nation among other individuals. But the nation that we constitute is the only one that can effectively constitute the nation. Perhaps we are not, in ourselves, the totality of the social body, but we are capable of guaranteeing the totalizing function of the State. We are capable of Statist universality." And so, and this is the second characteristic of this discourse, we have an inversion of the temporal axis of the demand. The demand will no longer be articulated in the name of a past right that was established by either a consensus, a victory, or an invasion. The demand can now be articulated in terms of a potentiality, a future, a future that is immediate, which is already present in the present because it concerns a certain function of Statist universality that is already fulfilled by "a" nation within the social body, and which is therefore demanding that its status as a single nation must be effectively recognized, and recognized in the juridical form of the State.

So much, if you like, for the political implications of this type of analysis and discourse. It has theoretical implications too, and they are as follows. You see, what, in these conditions, defines a nation is not its archaism, its ancestral nature, or its relationship with the past; it is its relationship with something else, with the State. This means several things. First, that the nation is not essentially specified by its relations with other nations. What characterizes "the" nation is not a horizontal relationship with other groups (such as other nations, hostile or enemy nations, or the nations with which it is juxtaposed). What does characterize the nation is, in contrast, a vertical relationship between a body of individuals who are capable of constituting a State, and the actual existence of the State itself. It is in terms of this vertical nation/State axis, or this Statist potentiality/Statist realization axis, that the nation is to be characterized and situated. This also means that what constitutes the strength of a nation is not so much its physical vigor, its military aptitudes, or, so to speak, its barbarian intensity, which is what the noble historians of the early eighteenth century were trying to describe. What does constitute the strength of a nation is now something like its capacities, its potentialities, and they are all organized around the figure of the State: the greater a nation's Statist capacity, or the greater its potential, the stronger it will be. Which also means that the defining characteristic of a nation is not really its dominance over other nations. The essential function and the historical role of the nation is not defined by its ability to exercise a relationship of domination over other nations. It is something else: its ability to administer itself, to manage, govern, and guarantee the constitution and workings of the figure of the State and of State power. Not domination, but State control. The nation is therefore no longer a partner in barbarous and warlike relations of domination. The nation is the active, constituent core of the State. The nation is the State, or at least an outline State. It is the State insofar as it is being born, is being shaped and is finding its historical conditions of existence in a group of individuals.

Those are, if you like, the theoretical implications at the level of what is understood by "nation." Now for its implications for historical discourse. What we now have is a historical discourse which reintroduces the problem of the State and which, up to a point, once more sees it as its central problem. And to that extent, we have a historical discourse which, up to a point, is close to the historical discourse that existed in the seventeenth century and which was, as I have tried to show you, essentially a way of allowing the State to talk about itself. The functions of that discourse were justificatory or liturgical: the State recounted its own past, or in other words, established its own legitimacy by making itself stronger, so to speak, at the level of its basic rights. This was still the discourse of history in the seventeenth century. It was against this discourse that the nobiliary reaction launched its scathing attack, or a different type of discourse in which the nation was, precisely, something that could be used to break down the unity of the State and to demonstrate that, beneath the formal facade of the State, there were other forces and that they were precisely not forces of the State, but the forces of a particular group with its own history, its own relationship with the past, its own victories, its own blood, and its own relations of domination.

We now have a discourse on history that is more sympathetic to the State and which is no longer, in its essential functions, anti-State. The objective of this new history is not, however, to let the State speak its own self-justificatory discourse. It is to write the history of the relations that are forever being woven between nation and State, between the nation's Statist potential and the actual totality of the State. This makes it possible to write a history which will obviously not become trapped in the circle of revolution and reconstitution, of a revolutionary return to the primitive order of things, as was the case in the seventeenth century. What we do now have, or what we may have, is a history of a rectilinear kind in which the decisive moment is the transition from the virtual to the real, the transition from the national totality to the universality of the State. This, therefore, is a history that is polarized toward the present and toward the State, a history that culminates in the imminence of the State, of the total, complete, and full figure of the State in the present. And this will also make it possible—second point—to write a history in which the relations of force that are in play are not of a warlike nature, but completely civilian, so to speak.

I tried to show you how, in Boulainvilliers's analysis, the clash between the different nations that exist within a single social body is of course mediated by institutions (the economy, education, language, knowledge, et cetera). But the use of civil institutions was, in his analysis, purely instrumental, and the war was still basically a war. Institutions were merely the instruments of a domination which was still a domination of the warlike kind, like an invasion. We now have, in contrast, a history in which war—the war for domination—will be replaced by a struggle that is, so to speak, of a different substance: not an armed clash, but an effort, a rivalry, a striving toward the universality of the State. The State, and the universality of the State, become both what is at stake in the struggle, and the battlefield. This will therefore be an essentially civil struggle to the extent that domination is neither its goal nor its expression, and to the extent that the State is both its object and its space. It will take place essentially in and around the economy, institutions, production, and the administration. We will have a civil struggle, and the military struggle or bloody struggle will become no more than an exceptional moment, a crisis or an episode within it. Far from being the real content of every confrontation and every struggle, the civil war will in fact be no more than an episode, a critical phase in a struggle that now has to be seen not in terms of war or domination, but in nonmilitary or civilian terms.

And this, I think, raises one of the basic questions about history and politics, not only in the nineteenth century, but also in the twentieth. How can we understand a struggle in purely civilian terms? Can what we call struggle—the economic struggle, the political struggle, the struggle for the State—actually be analyzed not in terms of war, but in truly economico-political terms? Or do we have to go beyond all that and discover precisely the never-ending substratum of war and domination that the historians of the eighteenth century were trying to locate? From the nineteenth century onward, or after the redefinition of the notion of the nation, we do at least have a new history. It differs from the history written in the eighteenth century in that it is trying to find within the space of the State the civil basis for the struggle that must replace the warlike, military, and bloody basis discovered by the historians of the eighteenth century.

We have here, if you like, the new historical discourse's conditions of possibility. What concrete form will this new history take? I think that if we want to describe it in overall terms, we can say that it will be characterized by the interplay between, the fitting together, of two grids of intelligibility that are juxtaposed, that intersect, and that, up to a point, correct each other. The first is the grid of intelligibility that was constructed and used in the eighteenth century. When Guizot, Augustin Thierry, and Thiers—and Michelet too—write history, they take as their starting point a relationship of force, a relationship of struggle, and it takes a form that had already been recognized in the eighteenth century: a war, a battle, an invasion, or a conquest. And historians of, say, the type that is still aristocratic, such as Montlosier[7] (but also Augustin Thierry, and Guizot too) always assume that this struggle is the matrix of, if you like, a history. Augustin Thierry, for example, says: "We believe ourselves to be a nation, but we are two nations within one land, two nations which are enemies because of what they remember and because their projects are irreconcilable: one once conquered the other." Of course some of the masters have gone over to the side of the vanquished, but the others, or those who remained masters, are "as foreign to our affections and our customs as if they had come among us yesterday, as deaf to our words of freedom and peace as if our language were as unknown to them as that of our ancestors was unknown to theirs. They went their own way, and took no heed of our way."[8] And Guizot said: "For more than thirteen centuries, France contained two peoples: a victorious people and a vanquished people."[9] So even at this time, we still have the same starting point, the same grid of intelligibility, as in the eighteenth century.

In addition to this first grid, there is another, and it both complements and inverts this primal duality. This is a grid which, rather than functioning with a point of origin such as the first war, the first invasion, or the first national duality, works backward and starts with the present. The fundamental moment is no longer the origin, and intelligibility's starting point is no longer the archaic element; it is, on the contrary, the present. And we have here, I think, an important phenomenon: the inversion of the value of the present in historical and political discourse. In the history and the historico-political field of the eighteenth century, the present was, basically, always the negative moment. It was always the trough of the wave, always a moment of apparent calm and forgetfulness. The present was the moment when, thanks to a whole series of displacements, betrayals, and modifications of the relationship of force, the primitive state of war had become, as it were, muddled and unrecognizable. Not just unrecognizable, but completely forgotten by those who should have been able to use it to their advantage. The nobles' ignorance, absentmindedness, laziness, and greed, all that had made them forget the basic force-relations that defined their relationship with the other people living on their lands. And what is more, the discourse of royal power's clerks, jurists, and administrators had covered up this initial relationship of force. For eighteenth-century history, the present was therefore always the moment of a profound forgetfulness. Hence the need to escape the present thanks to a sudden and violent reawakening that must begin, first and foremost, with a great reactivation of the primitive moment in the order of knowledge. The present was a moment of extreme forgetfulness; it was also the moment when a consciousness must be reawakened.

And now we have a very different grid of historical intelligibility. Once history is polarized around the nation/State, virtuality/actuality, functional totality of the nation/real universality of the State, you can see clearly that the present becomes the fullest moment, the moment of the greatest intensity, the solemn moment when the universal makes its entry into the real. It is at this point that the universal comes into contact with the real in the present (a present that has just passed and will pass), in the imminence of the present, and it is this that gives the present both its value and its intensity, and that establishes it as a principle of intelligibility. The present is no longer the moment of forgetfulness. On the contrary, it is the moment when the truth comes out, when what was obscure or virtual is revealed in the full light of day. As a result, the present both reveals the past and allows it to be analyzed.

I think that history, as we see it functioning in the nineteenth century, or at least the first half of the nineteenth century, uses both grids of intelligibility. It uses both the grid that begins with the initial war which runs through all historical processes and impels all their developments, and a different grid of intelligibility which works backward from the topicality of the present, from the totalizing realization of the State to the past, and which reconstitutes its genesis. The two grids in fact never function in isolation: they are always used almost concurrently, always overlap, are more or less superimposed, and to some extent intersect at the edges. Basically, we have on the one hand a history written in the form of domination—with war in the background—and on the other, a history written in the form of totalization—a history in which what has happened and what is going to happen, namely the emergence of the State, exists, or is at least imminent, in the present. A history that is written, then, both in terms of an initial rift and a totalizing completion. And I think that the utility, the political utilizability, of historical discourse is basically defined by the interplay between these two grids, or by the way in which one or the other of them is privileged.

Broadly speaking, if the first grid of intelligibility—the initial rift—is privileged, the result will be a history that can, if you like, be described as reactionary, aristocratic, and rightist. If the second—the present moment of universality—is privileged, we will have a history of the liberal or bourgeois type. But neither of these histories, each of which has its own tactical position, can actually avoid having to use both grids in one way or another. I would like to show you two examples of this. One is borrowed from a typically rightist or aristocratic history which is, up to a point, a direct descendant of eighteenth-century history but which in fact displaces it considerably and does, despite everything, work with the grid of intelligibility that takes the present as its starting point. The other is a converse example: I will, in other words, take a historian who is regarded as liberal and bourgeois, and show the play between the two grids and even the grid of intelligibility that begins with war, even though historians like this do not privilege it in any absolute sense.

So, first example. In the early nineteenth century, Montlosier appears to be writing a history of the rightist type in the tradition of the nobiliary reaction of the eighteenth century. In such a history, we do indeed find that relations of domination are privileged from the outset: throughout history, we find the relationship of national duality, and the relation of domination characteristic of national duality. Montlosier's book is—Montlosier's books are—full of polemics like this one, which is addressed to the Third Estate: "You are an emancipated race, a race of slaves, a tributary people, you were given license to be free, but not to be noble. For us, it is all a matter of right; for you, it is all a matter of grace. We do not belong to your community; we are a whole unto ourselves." Once again, you find the famous theme I told you about when we were discussing Sieyès. Similarly, Jouffroy could write a sentence such as this in some journal or other (I can't remember which): "The northern race seized Gaul without driving out the vanquished; it bequeathed its successors conquered lands to be governed, and conquered men to rule."[10]

The national duality thesis is asserted by all those historians who are, broadly speaking, émigrés who returned to France and who, at the time of the ultrareaction, reconstructed the invasion as a sort of privileged moment. But if we look at it more closely, Montlosier's analysis functions very differently from the analysis we saw in the eighteenth century. Montlosier obviously does speak of a relation of domination that results from a war, or rather a multiplicity of wars, but he does not really try to situate it. And he says that the important thing is not really what happened at the time of the Frankish invasion, because relations of domination existed long before that and because they were multiple. Long before the Romans invaded Gaul, there was already a relation of domination between a nobility and a people that paid it tribute. It was the result of an ancient war. The Romans came,

and brought their war with them, but they also brought the relationship of domination that existed between their aristocracy and people who were no more than the clients of those rich people, those
nobles and aristocrats. That relationship of domination resulted from
an old war too. And then the Germans came along, with their own
internal relationship of subjugation between those who were free warriors and those who were merely subjects. So what happened at the
beginning of the Middle Ages, at the dawn of feudalism, was not just
that a victorious people was superimposed on a vanquished people.
What was established was a combination of three systems of internal
domination: that of the Gauls, that of the Romans, and that of the
Germans.[11] The feudal nobility of the Middle Ages was, at bottom,
no more than a mixture of three aristocracies, and it established itself
as a new aristocracy that exercised a relationship of domination over
people who were themselves a mixture of Gaulish tributaries, Roman
clients, and German subjects. As a result, we have a relationship of
domination between something which was a nobility, which was a
nation, but which was also the nation in its entirety, or in other words
the feudal nobility; and then we have (outside that nation, or as an
object or partner in that relationship of domination) a whole people
of tributaries, serfs, and so on who are not really the other part of
that nation, who exist outside it. Montlosier, then, operates with a
monism at the level of the nation, and with a dualism at the level of
domination.

And what, according to Montlosier, is the monarchy's role in all
this? Well, the role of the monarchy is to forge this extranational
mass—the product, the mixture of German subjects, Roman clients,
and Gaulish tributaries—into a nation, into a different people. That
is the role of royal power. The monarchy freed tributaries, granted
rights to the towns and made them independent of the nobility; it
even freed the serfs and created from scratch what Montlosier calls a
new people. It had the same rights as the old people, or in other
words, the nobility, but it was numerically superior. Royal power,
says Montlosier, created an immense class.[12]

This type of analysis does of course reactivate all the elements we saw being used in the eighteenth century, but with one important modification. The difference is, you see, that in Montlosier's view, the processes of politics—all that had happened between the Middle Ages and the seventeenth and eighteenth centuries—did not simply modify or displace the relations of force that existed between two partners who were there from the outset, and who had been enemies ever since the invasion. What happened was that something new was created within an entity that was once mononational and totally concentrated around the nobility: a new nation, a new people, or what Montlosier calls a new class was created.[13] The making, then, of a class, of classes, within the social body. Now, what will happen once this new class has been created? The king will use this new class to take away the nobility's economic and political privileges. What means does he use? Once again, Montlosier repeats what his predecessors had said: lies, betrayals, unnatural alliances, and so on. The king also used the raw energy of this new class; he uses the rebellions: urban rebellions against feudal lords, and peasant jacqueries against landowners. And what, asks Montlosier, do we see at work in these rebellions? The discontent of the new class, obviously. But above all, the hand of the king. It was the king who inspired all the rebellions, because every rebellion weakened the power of the nobles and therefore strengthened the power of the king, who urged the nobles to make concessions. And thanks to a circular process, every royal act of emancipation made the people stronger and more arrogant. Every concession the king made to this new class led to further rebellions. Monarchy and popular rebellion worked hand in glove. And the weapons that were used to transfer to the monarch all of the political powers the nobility once had were essentially these rebellions, these rebellions that were fomented and inspired, or at least supported and encouraged, by royal power.

Once this has been done, the monarchy itself usurps power, but it can make it function, or can exercise it, only by turning to this new class. It therefore entrusts its justice and administration to this new class, which finds itself in control of all the functions of the State. As a result, the final moment of the process can only be the ultimate rebellion: having fallen into the hands of this new class, or into the hands of the people, the State is no longer under the control of royal power. All that remains is a naked encounter between a king who has in reality only the power he has been given by popular rebellions, and a popular class which has all the instruments of the State in its hands. This is the final episode, the final rebellion. Against whom? Against the man who has forgotten that he was the last aristocrat who still had any power: the king.

In Montlosier's analysis, the French Revolution therefore looks like the final episode in the transferential process that established royal absolutism.[14] The Revolution completes the constitution of monarchic power. But surely the Revolution overthrew the king? Not at all. The Revolution finished what the kings had begun, and literally speaks its truth. The Revolution has to be read as the culmination of the monarchy; a tragic culmination perhaps, but a culmination that is politically true. The king may well have been decapitated during that scene on 21 January 1793; they decapitated the king, but they crowned the monarchy. The Convention is the truth of the monarchy stripped bare, and the sovereignty that the king snatched away from the nobility is now, in a way that is absolutely necessary, in the hands of a people which, according to Montlosier, proves to be the kings' legitimate heir. Montlosier, aristocrat, émigré, and savage opponent of the least attempt at liberalization under the Restoration, can write this: "The sovereign people: we should not condemn it with too much bitterness. It is simply consummating the work of its sovereign predecessors." The people is therefore the heir, and the legitimate heir, of the kings; it is simply completing the work of the sovereigns who preceded it. It followed, point by point, the route traced for it by kings, by *parlementaires*, by men of the law, and by scholars. As you can see, then, Montlosier's historical analysis is framed by the thesis that it all began with a state of war and a relation of domination. The political demands put forward during the Restoration period certainly included the claim that the rights of the nobility must be restored, that the property that had been nationalized should be returned to it, and that the relations of domination it had once exercised over the whole people should be reestablished. Of course that assertion was made, but you can see that the nucleus, the central content of the historical discourse that is being spoken is indeed a historical discourse that makes the present function as the moment of fullness. It is the moment of effectuation, the moment of totalization. From this moment [onward] all the historical processes that established relations between the aristocracy and the monarchy finally reach their culminating point in the constitution of a Statist totality that is in the hands of a national collectivity. And to that extent, we can say that—regardless of the political themes or the elements of the analysis that are borrowed from the history of Boulainvilliers or Buat-Nançay, or which are directly transposed from it—this discourse actually functions in accordance with a different model.

To close, I would like to take a different, a diametrically different, type of history. It is the history of Augustin Thierry, who was Montlosier's explicit adversary. For Thierry, history's privileged point of intelligibility is, of course, the present. He is quite explicit about this. It is the second grid, which begins with the present, with the fullness of the present, so as to reveal the elements and processes of the past, that will be used. Statist totalization; that is what must be projected onto the past. We have to trace the genesis of that totalization. For Augustin Thierry, the present is indeed "that moment of fullness." The Revolution is—he says—the moment of reconciliation. The setting for this reconciliation, for this constitution of the Statist totality, is the famous scene when Bailly, you know, welcomed the representatives of the nobility and the clergy into the very place where the representatives of the Third Estate were meeting, with the words: "Now the family is reunited."[15]

So let us start with the present. The present moment is that of national totalization in the form of the State. But the fact remains that this totalization could occur only through the violent process of the Revolution, and that this full moment of reconciliation still has the features—and bears the scars—of a war. And Augustin Thierry says that the French Revolution was, basically, nothing more than the final episode in a struggle that had been going on for more than thirteen hundred years, and that it was a struggle between the victors and the vanquished.[16] According to Augustin Thierry, the whole problem of historical analysis is to show how a struggle between victors and vanquished that goes on throughout history can lead to a present that no longer takes the form of a war and a dissymmetrical domination which either perpetuates them or takes them in a different direction; the problem is to show how such a war could lead to the genesis of a universality in which struggles, or at least war, inevitably cease.

Why is it that only one of these two parties can be the agent of universality? That, for Augustin Thierry, is the problem of history. And his analysis therefore consists in tracing the origins of a process that was dualistic when it began, but both monist and universalist when it ended. According to Augustin Thierry, the important thing about this confrontation is that what happened obviously has its starting point in something like an invasion. But although the struggle or confrontation went on throughout the Middle Ages and is still going on, that is not because the victors and the vanquished clashed within institutions; it is because two different societies were constituted. They were not of the same economico-juridical type, and they fought over the administration and over who controlled the State. Even before medieval society was established, a rural society did exist: it was organized after the conquest and in a form that very quickly developed into feudalism. And then there emerged a rival urban society based on both a Roman model and a Gaulish model. In one sense, the confrontation was basically the result of the invasion and the conquest, but it was essentially, or in substantive terms, a struggle between two societies. The conflict between the two did at times take the form of armed conflict, but for the most part it took that of a political and economic confrontation. It may well have been a war, but it was a war between right and freedoms on one side, and debt and wealth on the other.

The confrontation between these two types of society over the constitution of a State will become the basic motor of history. Until the ninth or tenth century, the towns were on the losing side in this confrontation, in this struggle for the State and the universality of the State. And then, from the tenth and eleventh centuries onward, the towns underwent a renaissance. Those in the south adopted the Italian model, and the towns of the northern regions adopted the Nordic model. In both cases, a new form of juridical and economic organization came into being. And the reason urban society eventually triumphed is not at all that it won something like a military victory, but quite simply that it had wealth on its side, but also an administrative ability, a morale, a certain way of life, what Augustin Thierry calls innovatory instincts, and its activity. All these things gave it such strength that, one day, its institutions ceased to be local and became the country's institutions of political right and civil right. Universalization therefore began not with a relationship of domination that gradually swung completely in its favor, but with the fact that all the constituent elements of the State were born of it, were in its hands or had come into its hands. Its force was the force of the State and not the force of war, and the bourgeoisie did not make warlike use of it except when it was really obliged to do so.

There are two great episodes, two main phases in this history of the bourgeoisie and the Third Estate. First, when the Third Estate sensed that it was in control of all the forces of the State, what it proposed to the nobility and the clergy was, well, a sort of social pact. Hence the emergence of both the theory and the institutions of the three orders. This was, however, an artificial unity that did not really correspond to either the realities of the relationship of force or the will of the enemy. The Third Estate had in fact the whole State in its hands, and its enemy, or in other words, the nobility, refused to recognize that the Third Estate had any right at all. It was at this point, in the eighteenth century, that a new process began, and it was to be a more violent process of confrontation. And the Revolution itself was to be the final episode in a violent war. It naturally reactivated the old conflicts, but it was, in some sense, nothing more than the military instrument of a conflict and struggle that were not in themselves warlike. They were essentially civil, and the State was both their object and the space in which they took place. The disappearance of the three-order system, and the violent shocks of the Revolution, simply provided a backdrop for a single event: this is the moment when, having become *a* nation and then having become *the* nation by absorbing all the functions of the State, the Third Estate will effectively take sole control of both nation and State. The fact that it alone is the nation and that the State is under its sole control allows it to assume the functions of universality which will automatically do away with both the old duality and all the relations of domination that have hitherto been at work. The bourgeoisie or Third Estate thus becomes the people, and thus becomes the nation. It has the might of the universal. And the present moment—the moment when Augustin Thierry is writing—is precisely the moment when dualities, nations, and even classes cease to exist. "An immense evolution," said Thierry, "which causes all violent or illegitimate inequalities—master and slave, victor and vanquished, lord and serf—to vanish one by one from the land in which we live. In their place, it finally reveals one people, one law that applies to all and one free and sovereign nation."[17]

So you see, with analyses like this we obviously have, first, the elimination of war's function as an analyzer of historico-political processes, or at least its strict curtailment. War is now no more than an ephemeral and instrumental aspect of confrontations which are not of a warlike nature. Second, the essential element is no longer the relationship of domination that exists between one nation and another or one group and another; the fundamental relationship is the State. And you can also see, in analyses like this, the outline of something that can, in my view, be immediately likened, immediately transposed, to a philosophical discourse of a dialectical type.

The possibility of a philosophy of history, or in other words the appearance, at the beginning of the nineteenth century, of a philosophy that finds in history, and in the plenitude of the present, the moment when the universal speaks its truth, you see—I am not saying that the ground is being prepared for this philosophy; I am saying that it is already at work within historical discourse. What took place was a self-dialecticalization of historical discourse, and it occurred independently of any explicit transposition—or any explicit utilization—of a dialectical philosophy into a historical discourse. But the bourgeoisie's utilization of a historical discourse, the bourgeoisie's modification of the basic elements of the historical intelligibility that it had picked up from the eighteenth century, was at the same time a self-dialecticalization of historical discourse. And so you can understand how, from this point onward, relations could be established between the discourse of history and the discourse of philosophy. Basically, the philosophy of history did not exist in the eighteenth century, except in the form of speculations about the general law of history. From the nineteenth century onward something new—and, I think, something fundamental—began to happen. History and philosophy began to ask the same question: What is it, in the present, that is the agent of the universal? What is it, in the present, that is the truth of the universal? That is the question asked by history. It is also the question asked by philosophy. The dialectic is born.

1. E.-J. Sieyès, *Qu'est-ce que le Tiers-Etat?* p. 1.
2. "A common law and a common representation, that is what makes a nation." Ibid., p. 12.
3. "What is required for the survival and prosperity of a Nation? *Particular* works and *public* functions." Ibid., p. 2; cf. chap. 1, pp. 2-9.
4. Ibid., chap. 2, p. 17.
5. Ibid., chap. 1, p. 2.
6. "The Third Estate comprises all that belongs to the nation; and all that is not the Third Estate cannot be regarded as belonging to the nation. What is the Third Estate? Everything." Ibid., p. 9.
7. F. de Reynaud, comte de Montlosier, *De la monarchie française depuis son établissement jusqu'à nos jours* (Paris, 1814), vols. 1-3.
8. Augustin Thierry, "Sur l'antipathie de race qui divise la nation française," *Le Censeur européen*, 2 April 1820, reprinted in *Dix ans d'études historiques* (Paris, 1935), p. 292.
9. F. Guizot, *Du Gouvernement de la France depuis la Restauration et du ministre actuel* (Paris, 1820), p. 1.
10. Foucault is alluding to Achille Jouffroy d'Abbans (1790-1859). He was a supporter of the Bourbons and published articles supporting divine right, absolute power, and ultra-Montanism in *L'Observateur*. After the fall of Charles X, he published a journal called *La Légitimité*, which was banned from being distributed in France. He is the author of, inter alia, a brochure entitled *Des Idées libérales du Français* (1815), a novel about the Revolution entitled *Les Fastes de l'anarchie* (1820), and a historical study of Gaul, *Les Siècles de la monarchie française* (1823). The quotation from Jouffroy is from *L'Observateur des colonies, de la marine, de la politique, de la littérature et des arts*, 9th installment (1820), p. 299. Cf. A. Thierry, "Sur l'antipathie de race . . ."
11. F. de Reynaud, comte de Montlosier, *De la monarchie française*, book 1, chap. 1, p. 150.
12. Ibid., book 3, chap. 2, p. 152f.
13. Ibid.
14. Ibid., book 2, chap. 3, p. 209.
15. A. Thierry, *Essai sur l'histoire de la formation et du progrès du Tiers-Etat*, in *Oeuvres complètes* (Paris, 1868), vol. 5, p. 3. Thierry writes: "The family is complete."
16. See in particular A. Thierry, "Sur l'antipathie de race . . ." and "Histoire véritable de Jacques Bonhomme," *Le Censeur européen*, May 1820, reprinted in *Dix ans d'études historiques*.
17. A. Thierry, *Essai sur l'histoire . . . du Tiers-Etat*, p. 10. The inaccurate quotation has been checked against the original and emended.

eleven

17 MARCH 1976

[
From the power of sovereignty to power over life. ~ Make live and let die. ~ From man as body to man as species: the birth of biopower. ~ Biopower's fields of application. ~ Population. ~ Of death, and of the death of Franco in particular. ~ Articulations of discipline and regulation: workers' housing, sexuality, and the norm. ~ Biopower and racism. ~ Racism: functions and domains. ~ Nazism. ~ Socialism.
]

IT IS TIME TO end then, to try to pull together what I have been saying this year. I have been trying to raise the problem of war, seen as a grid for understanding historical processes. It seemed to me that war was regarded, initially and throughout practically the whole of the eighteenth century, as a war between races. It was that war between races that I wanted to try to reconstruct. And last time, I tried to show you how the very notion of war was eventually eliminated from historical analysis by the principle of national universality.* I would now like to show you how, while the theme of race does not disappear, it does become part of something very different, namely State racism. So today I would like to tell you a little about State racism, or at least situate it for you.

It seems to me that one of the basic phenomena of the nineteenth century was what might be called power's hold over life. What I mean is the acquisition of power over man insofar as man is a living being,

---

*In the manuscript, the sentence continues: "at the time of the Revolution."

that the biological came under State control, that there was at least a certain tendency that leads to what might be termed State control of the biological. And I think that in order to understand what was going on, it helps if we refer to what used to be the classical theory of sovereignty, which ultimately provided us with the backdrop to—a picture of—all these analyses of war, races, and so on. You know that in the classical theory of sovereignty, the right of life and death was one of sovereignty's basic attributes. Now the right of life and death is a strange right. Even at the theoretical level, it is a strange right. What does having the right of life and death actually mean? In one sense, to say that the sovereign has a right of life and death means that he can, basically, either have people put to death or let them live, or in any case that life and death are not natural or immediate phenomena which are primal or radical, and which fall outside the field of power. If we take the argument a little further, or to the point where it becomes paradoxical, it means that in terms of his relationship with the sovereign, the subject is, by rights, neither dead nor alive. From the point of view of life and death, the subject is neutral, and it is thanks to the sovereign that the subject has the right to be alive or, possibly, the right to be dead. In any case, the lives and deaths of subjects become rights only as a result of the will of the sovereign. That is, if you like, the theoretical paradox. And it is of course a theoretical paradox that must have as its corollary a sort of practical disequilibrium. What does the right of life and death actually mean? Obviously not that the sovereign can grant life in the same way that he can inflict death. The right of life and death is always exercised in an unbalanced way: the balance is always tipped in favor of death. Sovereign power's effect on life is exercised only when the sovereign can kill. The very essence of the right of life and death is actually the right to kill: it is at the moment when the sovereign can kill that he exercises his right over life. It is essentially the right of the sword. So there is no real symmetry in the right over life and death. It is not the right to put people to death or to grant them life. Nor is it the right to allow people to live or to leave them to die. It is the right to take life or let live. And this obviously introduces a startling dissymmetry.

And I think that one of the greatest transformations political right underwent in the nineteenth century was precisely that, I wouldn't say exactly that sovereignty's old right—to take life or let live—was replaced, but it came to be complemented by a new right which does not erase the old right but which does penetrate it, permeate it. This is the right, or rather precisely the opposite right. It is the power to "make" live and "let" die. The right of sovereignty was the right to take life or let live. And then this new right is established: the right to make live and to let die.

This transformation obviously did not occur all at once. We can trace it in the theory of right (but here, I will be extraordinarily rapid). The jurists of the seventeenth and especially the eighteenth century were, you see, already asking this question about the right of life and death. The jurists ask: When we enter into a contract, what are individuals doing at the level of the social contract, when they come together to constitute a sovereign, to delegate absolute power over them to a sovereign? They do so because they are forced to by some threat or by need. They therefore do so in order to protect their lives. It is in order to live that they constitute a sovereign. To the extent that this is the case, can life actually become one of the rights of the sovereign? Isn't life the foundation of the sovereign's right, and can the sovereign actually demand that his subjects grant him the right to exercise the power of life and death over them, or in other words, simply the power to kill them? Mustn't life remain outside the contract to the extent that it was the first, initial, and foundational reason for the contract itself? All this is a debate within political philosophy that we can leave on one side, but it clearly demonstrates how the problem of life began to be problematized in the field of political thought, of the analysis of political power. I would in fact like to trace the transformation not at the level of political theory, but rather at the level of the mechanisms, techniques, and technologies of power. And this brings us back to something familiar: in the seventeenth and eighteenth centuries, we saw the emergence of techniques of power that were essentially centered on the body, on the individual body. They included all devices that were used to ensure the spatial distribution of individual bodies (their separation, their alignment, their serialization, and their surveillance) and the organization, around those individuals, of a whole field of visibility. They were also techniques that could be used to take control over bodies. Attempts were made to increase their productive force through exercise, drill, and so on. They were also techniques for rationalizing and strictly economizing on a power that had to be used in the least costly way possible, thanks to a whole system of surveillance, hierarchies, inspections, bookkeeping, and reports—all the technology that can be described as the disciplinary technology of labor. It was established at the end of the seventeenth century, and in the course of the eighteenth.[1]

Now I think we see something new emerging in the second half of the eighteenth century: a new technology of power, but this time it is not disciplinary. This technology of power does not exclude the former, does not exclude disciplinary technology, but it does dovetail into it, integrate it, modify it to some extent, and above all, use it by sort of infiltrating it, embedding itself in existing disciplinary techniques. This new technique does not simply do away with the disciplinary technique, because it exists at a different level, on a different scale, and because it has a different bearing area, and makes use of very different instruments.

Unlike discipline, which is addressed to bodies, the new nondisciplinary power is applied not to man-as-body but to the living man, to man-as-living-being; ultimately, if you like, to man-as-species. To be more specific, I would say that discipline tries to rule a multiplicity of men to the extent that their multiplicity can and must be dissolved into individual bodies that can be kept under surveillance, trained, used, and, if need be, punished. And that the new technology that is being established is addressed to a multiplicity of men, not to the extent that they are nothing more than their individual bodies, but to the extent that they form, on the contrary, a global mass that is affected by overall processes characteristic of birth, death, production, illness, and so on. So after a first seizure of power over the body in an individualizing mode, we have a second seizure of power that is not individualizing but, if you like, massifying, that is directed not at man-as-body but at man-as-species. After the anatomo-politics of the human body established in the course of the eighteenth century, we have, at the end of that century, the emergence of something that is no longer an anatomo-politics of the human body, but what I would call a "biopolitics" of the human race.

What does this new technology of power, this biopolitics, this bio-power that is beginning to establish itself, involve? I told you very briefly a moment ago; a set of processes such as the ratio of births to deaths, the rate of reproduction, the fertility of a population, and so on. It is these processes—the birth rate, the mortality rate, longevity, and so on—together with a whole series of related economic and political problems (which I will not come back to for the moment) which, in the second half of the eighteenth century, become biopol-itics' first objects of knowledge and the targets it seeks to control. It is at any rate at this moment that the first demographers begin to measure these phenomena in statistical terms. They begin to observe the more or less spontaneous, more or less compulsory techniques that the population actually used to control the birth rate; in a word, if you like, to identify the phenomena of birth-control practices in the eighteenth century. We also see the beginnings of a natalist policy, plans to intervene in all phenomena relating to the birth rate. This biopolitics is not concerned with fertility alone. It also deals with the problem of morbidity, but not simply, as had previously been the case, at the level of the famous epidemics, the threat of which had haunted political powers ever since the early Middle Ages (these famous epidemics were temporary disasters that caused multiple deaths, times when everyone seemed to be in danger of imminent death). At the end of the eighteenth century, it was not epidemics that were the issue, but something else—what might broadly be called endemics, or in other words, the form, nature, extension, duration, and intensity of the illnesses prevalent in a population. These were illnesses that were difficult to eradicate and that were not regarded as epidemics that caused more frequent deaths, but as permanent factors which—and that is how they were dealt with—sapped the population's strength, shortened the working week, wasted energy, and cost money, both because they led to a fall in production and because treating them was expensive. In a word, illness as phenomena affecting a population. Death was no longer something that suddenly swooped down on life—as in an epidemic. Death was now something permanent, something that slips into life, perpetually gnaws at it, diminishes it and weakens it.

These are the phenomena that begin to be taken into account at the end of the eighteenth century, and they result in the development of a medicine whose main function will now be public hygiene, with institutions to coordinate medical care, centralize information, and normalize knowledge. And which also takes the form of campaigns to teach hygiene and to medicalize the population. So, problems of reproduction, the birth rate, and the problem of the mortality rate too. Biopolitics' other field of intervention will be a set of phenomena some of which are universal, and some of which are accidental but which can never be completely eradicated, even if they are accidental. They have similar effects in that they incapacitate individuals, put them out of the circuit or neutralize them. This is the problem, and it will become very important in the early nineteenth century (the time of industrialization), of old age, of individuals who, because of their age, fall out of the field of capacity, of activity. The field of biopolitics also includes accidents, infirmities, and various anomalies. And it is in order to deal with these phenomena that this biopolitics will establish not only charitable institutions (which had been in existence for a very long time), but also much more subtle mechanisms that were much more economically rational than an indiscriminate charity which was at once widespread and patchy, and which was essentially under church control. We see the introduction of more subtle, more rational mechanisms: insurance, individual and collective savings, safety measures, and so on.[2]

Biopolitics' last domain is, finally—I am enumerating the main ones, or at least those that appeared in the late eighteenth and early nineteenth centuries; many others would appear later—control over relations between the human race, or human beings insofar as they are a species, insofar as they are living beings, and their environment, the milieu in which they live. This includes the direct effects of the geographical, climatic, or hydrographic environment: the problem, for instance, of swamps, and of epidemics linked to the existence of swamps throughout the first half of the nineteenth century. And also the problem of the environment to the extent that it is not a natural environment, that it has been created by the population and therefore has effects on that population. This is, essentially, the urban problem. I am simply pointing out some of biopolitics' starting points, some of its practices, and the first of its domains of intervention, knowledge, and power: biopolitics will derive its knowledge from, and define its power's field of intervention in terms of, the birth rate, the mortality rate, various biological disabilities, and the effects of the environment.

In all this, a number of things are, I think, important. The first appears to be this: the appearance of a new element—I almost said a new character—of which both the theory of right and disciplinary practice knew nothing. The theory of right basically knew only the individual and society: the contracting individual and the social body constituted by the voluntary or implicit contract among individuals. Disciplines, for their part, dealt with individuals and their bodies in practical terms. What we are dealing with in this new technology of power is not exactly society (or at least not the social body, as defined by the jurists), nor is it the individual-as-body. It is a new body, a multiple body, a body with so many heads that, while they might not be infinite in number, cannot necessarily be counted. Biopolitics deals with the population, with the population as political problem, as a problem that is at once scientific and political, as a biological problem and as power's problem. And I think that biopolitics emerges at this time.

Second, the other important thing—quite aside from the appearance of the "population" element itself—is the nature of the phenomena that are taken into consideration. You can see that they are collective phenomena which have their economic and political effects, and that they become pertinent only at the mass level. They are phenomena that are aleatory and unpredictable when taken in themselves or individually, but which, at the collective level, display constants that are easy, or at least possible, to establish. And they are, finally, phenomena that occur over a period of time, which have to be studied over a certain period of time; they are serial phenomena. The phenomena addressed by biopolitics are, essentially, aleatory events that occur within a population that exists over a period of time.

On this basis—and this is, I think, the third important point—this technology of power, this biopolitics, will introduce mechanisms with a certain number of functions that are very different from the functions of disciplinary mechanisms. The mechanisms introduced by biopolitics include forecasts, statistical estimates, and overall measures. And their purpose is not to modify any given phenomenon as such, or to modify a given individual insofar as he is an individual, but, essentially, to intervene at the level at which these general phenomena are determined, to intervene at the level of their generality. The mortality rate has to be modified or lowered; life expectancy has to be increased; the birth rate has to be stimulated. And most important of all, regulatory mechanisms must be established to establish an equilibrium, maintain an average, establish a sort of homeostasis, and compensate for variations within this general population and its aleatory field. In a word, security mechanisms have to be installed around the random element inherent in a population of living beings so as to optimize a state of life. Like disciplinary mechanisms, these mechanisms are designed to maximize and extract forces, but they work in very different ways. Unlike disciplines, they no longer train individuals by working at the level of the body itself. There is absolutely no question relating to an individual body, in the way that discipline does. It is therefore not a matter of taking the individual at the level of individuality but, on the contrary, of using overall mechanisms and acting in such a way as to achieve overall states of equilibration or regularity; it is, in a word, a matter of taking control of life and the biological processes of man-as-species and of ensuring that they are not disciplined, but regularized.[3]

Beneath that great absolute power, beneath the dramatic and somber absolute power that was the power of sovereignty, and which consisted in the power to take life, we now have the emergence, with this technology of biopower, of this technology of power over "the" population as such, over men insofar as they are living beings. It is continuous, scientific, and it is the power to make live. Sovereignty took life and let live. And now we have the emergence of a power that I would call the power of regularization, and it, in contrast, consists in making live and letting die.

I think that we can see a concrete manifestation of this power in the famous gradual disqualification of death, which sociologists and historians have discussed so often. Everyone knows, thanks in particular to a certain number of recent studies, that the great public ritualization of death gradually began to disappear, or at least to fade away, in the late eighteenth century and that it is still doing so today. So much so that death—which has ceased to be one of those spectacular ceremonies in which individuals, the family, the group, and practically the whole of society took part—has become, in contrast, something to be hidden away. It has become the most private and shameful thing of all (and ultimately, it is now not so much sex as death that is the object of a taboo). Now I think that the reason why death had become something to be hidden away is not that anxiety has somehow been displaced or that repressive mechanisms have been modified. What once (and until the end of the eighteenth century) made death so spectacular and ritualized it so much was the fact that it was a manifestation of a transition from one power to another. Death was the moment when we made the transition from one power—that of the sovereign of this world—to another—that of the sovereign of the next world. We went from one court of law to another, from a civil or public right over life and death, to a right to either eternal life or eternal damnation. A transition from one power to another. Death also meant the transmission of the power of the dying, and that power was transmitted to those who survived him: last words, last recommendations, last wills and testaments, and so on. All these phenomena of power were ritualized.

Now that power is decreasingly the power of the right to take life, and increasingly the right to intervene to make live, or once power begins to intervene mainly at this level in order to improve life by eliminating accidents, the random element, and deficiencies, death becomes, insofar as it is the end of life, the term, the limit, or the end of power too. Death is outside the power relationship. Death is beyond the reach of power, and power has a grip on it only in general, overall, or statistical terms. Power has no control over death, but it can control mortality. And to that extent, it is only natural that death should now be privatized, and should become the most private thing of all. In the right of sovereignty, death was the moment of the most obvious and most spectacular manifestation of the absolute power of the sovereign; death now becomes, in contrast, the moment when the individual escapes all power, falls back on himself and retreats, so to speak, into his own privacy. Power no longer recognizes death. Power literally ignores death.

To symbolize all this, let's take, if you will, the death of Franco, which is after all a very, very interesting event. It is very interesting because of the symbolic values it brings into play, because the man who died had, as you know, exercised the sovereign right of life and death with great savagery, was the bloodiest of all the dictators, wielded an absolute right of life and death for forty years, and at the moment when he himself was dying, he entered this sort of new field of power over life which consists not only in managing life, but in keeping individuals alive after they are dead. And thanks to a power that is not simply scientific prowess, but the actual exercise of the political biopower established in the eighteenth century, we have become so good at keeping people alive that we've succeeded in keeping them alive when, in biological terms, they should have been dead long ago. And so the man who had exercised the absolute power of life and death over hundreds of thousands of people fell under the influence of a power that managed life so well, that took so little heed of death, and he didn't even realize that he was dead and was being kept alive after his death. I think that this minor but joyous event symbolizes the clash between two systems of power: that of sovereignty over death, and that of the regularization of life.

I would now like to go back to comparing the regulatory technology of life and the disciplinary technology of the body I was telling you about a moment ago. From the eighteenth century onward (or at least the end of the eighteenth century onward) we have, then, two technologies of power which were established at different times and which were superimposed. One technique is disciplinary; it centers on the body, produces individualizing effects, and manipulates the body as a source of forces that have to be rendered both useful and docile. And we also have a second technology which is centered not upon the body but upon life: a technology which brings together the mass effects characteristic of a population, which tries to control the series of random events that can occur in a living mass, a technology which tries to predict the probability of those events (by modifying it, if necessary), or at least to compensate for their effects. This is a technology which aims to establish a sort of homeostasis, not by training individuals, but by achieving an overall equilibrium that protects the security of the whole from internal dangers. So, a technology of drilling, as opposed to, as distinct from, a technology of security; a disciplinary technology, as distinct from a reassuring or regulatory technology. Both technologies are obviously technologies of the body, but one is a technology in which the body is individualized as an organism endowed with capacities, while the other is a technology in which bodies are replaced by general biological processes.

One might say this: It is as though power, which used to have sovereignty as its modality or organizing schema, found itself unable to govern the economic and political body of a society that was undergoing both a demographic explosion and industrialization. So much so that far too many things were escaping the old mechanism of the power of sovereignty, both at the top and at the bottom, both at the level of detail and at the mass level. A first adjustment was made to take care of the details. Discipline had meant adjusting power mechanisms to the individual body by using surveillance and training. That, of course, was the easier and more convenient thing to adjust. That is why it was the first to be introduced—as early as the seventeenth century, or the beginning of the eighteenth—at a local level, in intuitive, empirical, and fragmented forms, and in the restricted framework of institutions such as schools, hospitals, barracks, workshops, and so on. And then at the end of the eighteenth century, you have a second adjustment; the mechanisms are adjusted to phenomena of population, to the biological or biosociological processes character- istic of human masses. This adjustment was obviously much more difficult to make because it implied complex systems of coordination and centralization.

So we have two series: the body-organism-discipline-institutions series, and the population-biological processes-regulatory mechanisms- State.* An organic institutional set, or the organo-discipline of the institution, if you like, and, on the other hand, a biological and Statist set, or bioregulation by the State. I am not trying to introduce a complete dichotomy between State and institution, because disciplines in fact always tend to escape the institutional or local framework in which they are trapped. What is more, they easily take on a Statist dimension in apparatuses such as the police, for example, which is both a disciplinary apparatus and a State apparatus (which just goes to prove that discipline is not always institutional). In similar fashion, the great overall regulations that proliferated throughout the nine- teenth century are, obviously enough, found at the State level, but they are also found at the sub-State level, in a whole series of sub- State institutions such as medical institutions, welfare funds, insur- ance, and so on. That is the first remark I would like to make.

What is more, the two sets of mechanisms—one disciplinary and the other regulatory—do not exist at the same level. Which means of course that they are not mutually exclusive and can be articulated with each other. To take one or two examples. Take, if you like, the example of the town or, more specifically, the rationally planned lay-

---

*The manuscript has "assuring" in place of "regulatory."

out of the model town, the artificial town, the town of utopian reality that was not only dreamed of but actually built in the nineteenth century. What were working-class housing estates, as they existed in the nineteenth century? One can easily see how the very grid pattern, the very layout, of the estate articulated, in a sort of perpendicular way, the disciplinary mechanisms that controlled the body, or bodies, by localizing familes (one to a house) and individuals (one to a room). The layout, the fact that individuals were made visible, and the normalization of behavior meant that a sort of spontaneous policing or control was carried out by the spatial layout of the town itself. It is easy to identify a whole series of disciplinary mechanisms in the working-class estate. And then you have a whole series of mechanisms which are, by contrast, regulatory mechanisms, which apply to the population as such and which allow, which encourage patterns of saving related to housing, to the renting of accommodations and, in some cases, their purchase. Health-insurance systems, old-age pensions; rules on hygiene that guarantee the optimal longevity of the population; the pressures that the very organization of the town brings to bear on sexuality and therefore procreation; child care, education, et cetera, so you have [certain] disciplinary measures and [certain] regulatory mechanisms.

Take the very different—though it is not altogether that different— take a different axis, something like sexuality. Basically, why did sexuality become a field of vital strategic importance in the nineteenth century? I think that sexuality was important for a whole host of reasons, and for these reasons in particular. On the one hand, sexuality, being an eminently corporeal mode of behavior, is a matter for individualizing disciplinary controls that take the form of permanent surveillance (and the famous controls that were, from the late eighteenth to the twentieth century, placed both at home and at school on children who masturbated represent precisely this aspect of the disciplinary control of sexuality. But because it also has procreative effects, sexuality is also inscribed, takes effect, in broad biological processes that concern not the bodies of individuals but the element, the multiple unity of the population. Sexuality exists at the point where body and population meet. And so it is a matter for discipline, but also a matter for regularization.

It is, I think, the privileged position it occupies between organism and population, between the body and general phenomena, that explains the extreme emphasis placed upon sexuality in the nineteenth century. Hence too the medical idea that when it is undisciplined and irregular, sexuality also has effects at two levels. At the level of the body, of the undisciplined body that is immediately sanctioned by all the individual diseases that the sexual debauchee brings down upon himself. A child who masturbates too much will be a lifelong invalid: disciplinary sanction at the level of the body. But at the same time, debauched, perverted sexuality has effects at the level of the population, as anyone who has been sexually debauched is assumed to have a heredity. Their descendants also will be affected for generations, unto the seventh generation and unto the seventh of the seventh and so on. This is the theory of degeneracy:[4] given that it is the source of individual diseases and that it is the nucleus of degeneracy, sexuality represents the precise point where the disciplinary and the regulatory, the body and the population, are articulated. Given these conditions, you can understand how and why a technical knowledge such as medicine, or rather the combination of medicine and hygiene, is in the nineteenth century, if not the most important element, an element of considerable importance because of the link it establishes between scientific knowledge of both biological and organic processes (or in other words, the population and the body), and because, at the same time, medicine becomes a political intervention-technique with specific power-effects. Medicine is a power-knowledge that can be applied to both the body and the population, both the organism and biological processes, and it will therefore have both disciplinary effects and regulatory effects.

In more general terms still, we can say that there is one element that will circulate between the disciplinary and the regulatory, which will also be applied to body and population alike, which will make it possible to control both the disciplinary order of the body and the aleatory events that occur in the biological multiplicity. The element that circulates between the two is the norm. The norm is something that can be applied to both a body one wishes to discipline and a population one wishes to regularize. The normalizing society is therefore not, under these conditions, a sort of generalized disciplinary society whose disciplinary institutions have swarmed and finally taken over everything—that, I think, is no more than a first and inadequate interpretation of a normalizing society. The normalizing society is a society in which the norm of discipline and the norm of regulation intersect along an orthogonal articulation. To say that power took possession of life in the nineteenth century, or to say that power at least takes life under its care in the nineteenth century, is to say that it has, thanks to the play of technologies of discipline on the one hand and technologies of regulation on the other, succeeded in covering the whole surface that lies between the organic and the biological, between body and population.

We are, then, in a power that has taken control of both the body and life or that has, if you like, taken control of life in general—with the body as one pole and the population as the other. We can therefore immediately identify the paradoxes that appear at the points where the exercise of this biopower reaches its limits. The paradoxes become apparent if we look, on the one hand, at atomic power, which is not simply the power to kill, in accordance with the rights that are granted to any sovereign, millions and hundreds of millions of people (after all, that is traditional). The workings of contemporary political power are such that atomic power represents a paradox that is difficult, if not impossible, to get around. The power to manufacture and use the atom bomb represents the deployment of a sovereign power that kills, but it is also the power to kill life itself. So the power that is being exercised in this atomic power is exercised in such a way that it is capable of suppressing life itself. And, therefore, to suppress itself insofar as it is the power that guarantees life. Either it is sovereign and uses the atom bomb, and therefore cannot be power, biopower, or the power to guarantee life, as it has been ever since the nineteenth century. Or, at the opposite extreme, you no longer have a sovereign right that is in excess of biopower, but a biopower that is in excess of sovereign right. This excess of biopower appears when it becomes technologically and politically possible for man not only to manage life but to make it proliferate, to create living matter, to build the monster, and, ultimately, to build viruses that cannot be controlled and that are universally destructive. This formidable extension of biopower, unlike what I was just saying about atomic power, will put it beyond all human sovereignty.

You must excuse this long digression into biopower, but I think that it does provide us with a basic argument that will allow us to get back to the problem I was trying to raise.

If it is true that the power of sovereignty is increasingly on the retreat and that disciplinary or regulatory disciplinary power is on the advance, how will the power to kill and the function of murder operate in this technology of power, which takes life as both its object and its objective? How can a power such as this kill, if it is true that its basic function is to improve life, to prolong its duration, to improve its chances, to avoid accidents, and to compensate for failings? How, under these conditions, is it possible for a political power to kill, to call for deaths, to demand deaths, to give the order to kill, and to expose not only its enemies but its own citizens to the risk of death? Given that this power's objective is essentially to make live, how can it let die? How can the power of death, the function of death, be exercised in a political system centered upon biopower?

It is, I think, at this point that racism intervenes. I am certainly not saying that racism was invented at this time. It had already been in existence for a very long time. But I think it functioned elsewhere. It is indeed the emergence of this biopower that inscribes it in the mechanisms of the State. It is at this moment that racism is inscribed as the basic mechanism of power, as it is exercised in modern States. As a result, the modern State can scarcely function without becoming involved with racism at some point, within certain limits and subject to certain conditions.

What in fact is racism? It is primarily a way of introducing a break into the domain of life that is under power's control: the break between what must live and what must die. The appearance within the biological continuum of the human race of races, the distinction among races, the hierarchy of races, the fact that certain races are described as good and that others, in contrast, are described as inferior: all this is a way of fragmenting the field of the biological that power controls. It is a way of separating out the groups that exist within a population. It is, in short, a way of establishing a biological-type caesura within a population that appears to be a biological domain. This will allow power to treat that population as a mixture of races, or to be more accurate, to treat the species, to subdivide the species it controls, into the subspecies known, precisely, as races. That is the first function of racism: to fragment, to create caesuras within the biological continuum addressed by biopower.

Racism also has a second function. Its role is, if you like, to allow the establishment of a positive relation of this type: "The more you kill, the more deaths you will cause" or "The very fact that you let more die will allow you to live more." I would say that this relation ("If you want to live, you must take lives, you must be able to kill") was not invented by either racism or the modern State. It is the relationship of war: "In order to live, you must destroy your enemies." But racism does make the relationship of war—"If you want to live, the other must die"—function in a way that is completely new and that is quite compatible with the exercise of biopower. On the one hand, racism makes it possible to establish a relationship between my life and the death of the other that is not a military or warlike relationship of confrontation, but a biological-type relationship: "The more inferior species die out, the more abnormal individuals are eliminated, the fewer degenerates there will be in the species as a whole, and the more I—as species rather than individual—can live, the stronger I will be, the more vigorous I will be. I will be able to proliferate." The fact that the other dies does not mean simply that I live in the sense that his death guarantees my safety; the death of the other, the death of the bad race, of the inferior race (or the degenerate, or the abnormal) is something that will make life in general healthier: healthier and purer.

This is not, then, a military, warlike, or political relationship, but a biological relationship. And the reason this mechanism can come into play is that the enemies who have to be done away with are not adversaries in the political sense of the term; they are threats, either external or internal, to the population and for the population. In the biopower system, in other words, killing or the imperative to kill is acceptable only if it results not in a victory over political adversaries, but in the elimination of the biological threat to and the improvement of the species or race. There is a direct connection between the two. In a normalizing society, race or racism is the precondition that makes killing acceptable. When you have a normalizing society, you have a power which is, at least superficially, in the first instance, or in the first line a biopower, and racism is the indispensable precondition that allows someone to be killed, that allows others to be killed. Once the State functions in the biopower mode, racism alone can justify the murderous function of the State.

So you can understand the importance—I almost said the vital importance—of racism to the exercise of such a power: it is the precondition for exercising the right to kill. If the power of normalization wished to exercise the old sovereign right to kill, it must become racist. And if, conversely, a power of sovereignty, or in other words, a power that has the right of life and death, wishes to work with the instruments, mechanisms, and technology of normalization, it too must become racist. When I say "killing," I obviously do not mean simply murder as such, but also every form of indirect murder: the fact of exposing someone to death, increasing the risk of death for some people, or, quite simply, political death, expulsion, rejection, and so on.

I think that we are now in a position to understand a number of things. We can understand, first of all, the link that was quickly—I almost said immediately—established between nineteenth-century biological theory and the discourse of power. Basically, evolutionism, understood in the broad sense—or in other words, not so much Darwin's theory itself as a set, a bundle, of notions (such as: the hierarchy of species that grow from a common evolutionary tree, the struggle for existence among species, the selection that eliminates the less fit)—

naturally became within a few years during the nineteenth century not simply a way of transcribing a political discourse into biological terms, and not simply a way of dressing up a political discourse in scientific clothing, but a real way of thinking about the relations between colonization, the necessity for wars, criminality, the phenomena of madness and mental illness, the history of societies with their different classes, and so on. Whenever, in other words, there was a confrontation, a killing or the risk of death, the nineteenth century was quite literally obliged to think about them in the form of evolutionism.

And we can also understand why racism should have developed in modern societies that function in the biopower mode; we can understand why racism broke out at a number of privileged moments, and why they were precisely the moments when the right to take life was imperative. Racism first develops with colonization, or in other words, with colonizing genocide. If you are functioning in the biopower mode, how can you justify the need to kill people, to kill populations, and to kill civilizations? By using the themes of evolutionism, by appealing to a racism.

War. How can one not only wage war on one's adversaries but also expose one's own citizens to war, and let them be killed by the million (and this is precisely what has been going on since the nineteenth century, or since the second half of the nineteenth century), except by activating the theme of racism? From this point onward, war is about two things: it is not simply a matter of destroying a political adversary, but of destroying the enemy race, of destroying that [sort] of biological threat that those people over there represent to our race. In one sense, this is of course no more than a biological extrapolation from the theme of the political enemy. But there is more to it than that. In the nineteenth century—and this is completely new—war will be seen not only as a way of improving one's own race by eliminating the enemy race (in accordance with the themes of natural selection and the struggle for existence), but also as a way of regenerating one's own race. As more and more of our number die, the race to which we belong will become all the purer.

At the end of the nineteenth century, we have then a new racism modeled on war. It was, I think, required because a biopower that wished to wage war had to articulate the will to destroy the adversary with the risk that it might kill those whose lives it had, by definition, to protect, manage, and multiply. The same could be said of criminality. Once the mechanism of biopower was called upon to make it possible to execute or isolate criminals, criminality was conceptualized in racist terms. The same applies to madness, and the same applies to various abnormalities.

I think that, broadly speaking, racism justifies the death-function in the economy of biopower by appealing to the principle that the death of others makes one biologically stronger insofar as one is a member of a race or a population, insofar as one is an element in a unitary living plurality. You can see that, here, we are far removed from the ordinary racism that takes the traditional form of mutual contempt or hatred between races. We are also far removed from the racism that can be seen as a sort of ideological operation that allows States, or a class, to displace the hostility that is directed toward [them], or which is tormenting the social body, onto a mythical adversary. I think that this is something much deeper than an old tradition, much deeper than a new ideology, that it is something else. The specificity of modern racism, or what gives it its specificity, is not bound up with mentalities, ideologies, or the lies of power. It is bound up with the technique of power, with the technology of power. It is bound up with this, and that takes us as far away as possible from the race war and the intelligibility of history. We are dealing with a mechanism that allows biopower to work. So racism is bound up with the workings of a State that is obliged to use race, the elimination of races and the purification of the race, to exercise its sovereign power. The juxtaposition of—or the way biopower functions through—the old sovereign power of life and death implies the workings, the introduction and activation, of racism. And it is, I think, here that we find the actual roots of racism.

So you can understand how and why, given these conditions, the most murderous States are also, of necessity, the most racist. Here, of course, we have to take the example of Nazism. After all, Nazism was in fact the paroxysmal development of the new power mechanisms that had been established since the eighteenth century. Of course, no State could have more disciplinary power than the Nazi regime. Nor was there any other State in which the biological was so tightly, so insistently, regulated. Disciplinary power and biopower: all this permeated, underpinned, Nazi society (control over the biological, of procreation and of heredity; control over illness and accidents too). No society could be more disciplinary or more concerned with providing insurance than that established, or at least planned, by the Nazis. Controlling the random element inherent in biological processes was one of the regime's immediate objectives.

But this society in which insurance and reassurance were universal, this universally disciplinary and regulatory society, was also a society which unleashed murderous power, or in other words, the old sovereign right to take life. This power to kill, which ran through the entire social body of Nazi society, was first manifested when the power to take life, the power of life and death, was granted not only to the State but to a whole series of individuals, to a considerable number of people (such as the SA, the SS, and so on). Ultimately, everyone in the Nazi State had the power of life and death over his or her neighbors, if only because of the practice of informing, which effectively meant doing away with the people next door, or having them done away with.

So murderous power and sovereign power are unleashed throughout the entire social body. They were also unleashed by the fact that war was explicitly defined as a political objective—and not simply as a basic political objective or as a means, but as a sort of ultimate and decisive phase in all political processes—politics had to lead to war, and war had to be the final decisive phase that would complete everything. The objective of the Nazi regime was therefore not really the destruction of other races. The destruction of other races was one aspect of the project, the other being to expose its own race to the absolute and universal threat of death. Risking one's life, being exposed to total destruction, was one of the principles inscribed in the basic duties of the obedient Nazi, and it was one of the essential objectives of Nazism's policies. It had to reach the point at which the entire population was exposed to death. Exposing the entire population to universal death was the only way it could truly constitute itself as a superior race and bring about its definitive regeneration once other races had been either exterminated or enslaved forever.

We have, then, in Nazi society something that is really quite extraordinary: this is a society which has generalized biopower in an absolute sense, but which has also generalized the sovereign right to kill. The two mechanisms—the classic, archaic mechanism that gave the State the right of life and death over its citizens, and the new mechanism organized around discipline and regulation, or in other words, the new mechanism of biopower—coincide exactly. We can therefore say this: The Nazi State makes the field of the life it manages, protects, guarantees, and cultivates in biological terms absolutely coextensive with the sovereign right to kill anyone, meaning not only other people, but also its own people. There was, in Nazism, a coincidence between a generalized biopower and a dictatorship that was at once absolute and retransmitted throughout the entire social body by this fantastic extension of the right to kill and of exposure to death. We have an absolutely racist State, an absolutely murderous State, and an absolutely suicidal State. A racist State, a murderous State, and a suicidal State. The three were necessarily superimposed, and the result was of course both the "final solution" (or the attempt to eliminate, by eliminating the Jews, all the other races of which the Jews were both the symbol and the manifestation) of the years 1942-1943, and then Telegram 71, in which, in April 1945, Hitler gave the order to destroy the German people's own living conditions.[5]

The final solution for the other races, and the absolute suicide of the [German] race. That is where this mechanism inscribed in the workings of the modern State leads. Of course, Nazism alone took the play between the sovereign right to kill and the mechanisms of biopower to this paroxysmal point. But this play is in fact inscribed in the workings of all States. In all modern States, in all capitalist

States? Perhaps not. But I do think that—but this would be a whole new argument—the socialist State, socialism, is as marked by racism as the workings of the modern State, of the capitalist State. In addition to the State racism that developed in the conditions I have been telling you about, a social-racism also came into being, and it did not wait for the formation of socialist States before making its appearance. Socialism was a racism from the outset, even in the nineteenth century. No matter whether it is Fourier at the beginning of the century[6] or the anarchists at the end of it, you will always find a racist component in socialism.

I find this very difficult to talk about. To speak in such terms is to make enormous claims. To prove the point would really take a whole series of lectures (and I would like to do them). But at least let me just say this: In general terms, it seems to me—and here, I am speculating somewhat—that to the extent that it does not, in the first instance, raise the economic or juridical problems of types of property ownership or modes of production—or to the extent that the problem of the mechanics of power or the mechanisms of power is not posed or analyzed—[socialism therefore] inevitably reaffected or reinvested the very power-mechanisms constituted by the capitalist State or the industrial State. One thing at least is certain: Socialism has made no critique of the theme of biopower, which developed at the end of the eighteenth century and throughout the nineteenth; it has in fact taken it up, developed, reimplanted, and modified it in certain respects, but it has certainly not reexamined its basis or its modes of working. Ultimately, the idea that the essential function of society or the State, or whatever it is that must replace the State, is to take control of life, to manage it, to compensate for its aleatory nature, to explore and reduce biological accidents and possibilities ... it seems to me that socialism takes this over wholesale. And the result is that we immediately find ourselves in a socialist State which must exercise the right to kill or the right to eliminate, or the right to disqualify. And so, quite naturally, we find that racism—not a truly ethnic racism, but racism of the evolutionist kind, biological racism—is fully operational in the way socialist States (of the Soviet Union type) deal with the mentally ill, criminals, political adversaries, and so on. So much for the State.

The other thing I find interesting, and which has caused me problems for a long time, is that, once again, it is not simply at the level of the socialist State that we find this racism at work; we also find it in the various forms of socialist analysis, or of the socialist project throughout the nineteenth century, and it seems to me that it relates to this: whenever a socialism insists, basically, that the transformation of economic conditions is the precondition for the transformation, for the transition from the capitalist State to the socialist State (or in other words, whenever it tries to explain the transformation in terms of economic processes), it does not need, or at least not in the immediate, racism. Whenever, on the other hand, socialism has been forced to stress the problem of struggle, the struggle against the enemy, of the elimination of the enemy within capitalist society itself, and when, therefore, it has had to think about the physical confrontation with the class enemy in capitalist society, racism does raise its head, because it is the only way in which socialist thought, which is after all very much bound up with the themes of biopower, can rationalize the murder of its enemies. When it is simply a matter of eliminating the adversary in economic terms, or of taking away his privileges, there is no need for racism. Once it is a matter of coming to terms with the thought of a one-to-one encounter with the adversary, and with the need to fight him physically, to risk one's own life and to try to kill him, there is a need for racism.

Whenever you have these socialisms, these forms of socialism or these moments of socialism that stress the problem of the struggle, you therefore have racism. The most racist forms of socialism were, therefore, Blanquism of course, and then the Commune, and then anarchism—much more so than social democracy, much more so than the Second International, and much more so than Marxism itself. Socialist racism was liquidated in Europe only at the end of the nineteenth century, and only by the domination of social democracy (and, it has to be said, by the reformism that was bound up with it) on the one hand, and by a number of processes such as the Dreyfus affair in France on the other. Until the Dreyfus affair, all socialists, or at least the vast majority of socialists, were basically racists. And I think that they were racists to the extent that (and I will finish here) they did not reevaluate—or, if you like, accepted as self-evident—the mechanisms of biopower that the development of society and State had been establishing since the eighteenth century. How can one both make a biopower function and exercise the rights of war, the rights of murder and the function of death, without becoming racist? That was the problem, and that, I think, is still the problem.

---

1. On the question of disciplinary technology, see *Surveiller et punir*.
2. On all these questions, see *Cours au Collège de France, année 1978-1979: Le Pouvoir psychiatrique*, forthcoming.
3. Foucault comes back to all these disciplines, especially in *Cours au Collège de France 1977-1978: Sécurité, territoire et population* and *1978-1979: Naissance de la biopolitique*, forthcoming.
4. Foucault refers here to the theory elaborated in mid-nineteenth-century France by certain alienists and in particular by B.-A. Morel (*Traité de dégénérescences physiques, intellectuelles et morales de l'espèce humaine* [Paris, 1857], *Traités des maladies mentales* [Paris, 1870]); V. Magnan (*Leçons cliniques sur les maladies mentales* [Paris, 1893]); and M. Legrain and V. Magnan (*Les Dégénérés, état mental et syndrômes épisodiques* [Paris, 1895]). This theory of degeneracy, which is based upon the principle that a so-called hereditary taint can be transmitted, was the kernel of medical knowledge about madness and abnormality in the second half of the nineteenth century. It was quickly adopted by forensic medicine, and it had a considerable effect on eugenicist doctrines and practices, and was not without its influence on a whole literature, a whole criminology, and a whole anthropology.
5. As early as 19 March, Hitler had drawn up plans to destroy Germany's logistic infrastructure and industrial plant. These dispositions were announced in the decrees of 30 March and 7 April. On these decrees, see A. Speer, *Erinnerungen* (Berlin: Proplyäen-Verlag, 1969) (French translation: *Au Coeur du Troisième Reich* [Paris: Fayard, 1971]; English translation by Richard and Clara Winton: *Inside the Third Reich: Memoirs* [London: Weidenfeld and Nicolson, 1970]). Foucault had definitely read J. Fest's book *Hitler* (Frankfurt am Main, Berlin, and Vienna: Verlag Ulstein, 1973) (French translation: *Hitler* [Paris: Gallimard, 1973]; English translation by Richard and Clara Winton, *Hitler* [London: Weidenfeld and Nicolson, 1974]).
6. In this connection, see in particular Charles Fourier, *Théorie des quatre mouvements et des destinées générales* (Leipzig and Lyon, 1808); *Le Nouveau Monde industriel et sociétaire* (Paris, 1829); *La Fausse Industrie morcelée, répugnante, mensongère*, 2 vols. (Paris, 1836).

Course Summary

IN ORDER TO MAKE a concrete analysis of power relations, we must abandon the juridical model of sovereignty. That model in effect presupposes that the individual is a subject with natural rights or primitive powers; it sets itself the task of accounting for the ideal genesis of the State; and finally, it makes the law the basic manifestation of power. We should be trying to study power not on the basis of the primitive terms of the relationship, but on the basis of the relationship itself, to the extent that it is the relationship itself that determines the elements on which it bears: rather than asking ideal subjects what part of themselves or their powers they have surrendered in order to let themselves become subjects, we have to look at how relations of subjugation can manufacture subjects. Similarly, rather than looking for the single form or the central point from which all forms of power derive, either by way of consequence or development, we must begin

First published in *Annuaire du Collège de France, 76ème année, Histoire des systèmes de pensée, année 1975-1976* (1976), pp. 361-66; reprinted in *Dits et ecrits*, vol. 3, pp. 124-30. An alternative translation, by Robert Hurley, appears in *Ethics: The Essential Works*, vol. 1, pp. 59-66.

by letting them operate in their multiplicity, their differences, their specificity, and their reversibility; we must therefore study them as relations of force that intersect, refer to one another, converge, or, on the contrary, come into conflict and strive to negate one another. And, finally, rather than privileging the law as manifestation of power, we would do better to try to identify the different techniques of constraint that it implements.

If we have to avoid reducing the analysis of power to the schema proposed by the juridical constitution of sovereignty, and if we have to think of power in terms of relations of force, do we therefore have to interpret it in terms of the general form of war? Can war serve as as an analyzer of power relations?

This question masks several other questions:

- Must war be regarded as a primal and basic state of affairs, and must all phenomena of social domination, differentiation, and hierarchicalization be regarded as its derivatives?

- Do processes of antagonism, confrontations, and struggles among individuals, groups, or classes derive in the last instance from general processes of war?

- Can a set of notions derived from strategy and tactics constitute a valid and adequate instrument for the analysis of power relations?

- Are military and warlike institutions, and more generally the processes that are implemented to wage war, the nucleus of political institutions in either an immediate or a remote sense, in either a direct or an indirect sense?

- But the first question that has to be asked is perhaps this: How, when, and in what way did people begin to imagine that it is war that functions in power relations, that an uninterrupted conflict undermines peace, and that the civil order is basically an order of battle?

This is the question that has been posed in this year's lectures. How did people begin to perceive a war just beneath the surface of peace? Who tried to find the principle that explained order, institutions, and history in the noise and confusion of war and in the mud of battles? Who was the first to think that war is the continuation of politics by other means?

❖

A paradox appears at first glance. As States evolve from the early Middle Ages onward, the practices and institutions of war appear to have undergone an obvious evolution. On the one hand, they tended to be concentrated in the hands of a central power which alone had the right and the means to wage war; as a result, they tended to disappear, if only gradually, from the individual-to-individual or group-to-group relationship, and increasingly became, as a result of this line of development, a State privilege. What is more, and as a result of this, war tends to become the professional and technical prerogative of a carefully defined and controlled military apparatus. In a word: a society completely permeated by warlike relations was gradually replaced by a State endowed with military institutions.

Now this transformation had no sooner been completed than there appeared a certain type of discourse about relations between society and war. A discourse developed about relations between society and war. A historico-political discourse—which was very different from the philosophico-juridical discourse organized around the problem of sovereignty—made war the permanent basis of all the institutions of power. This discourse appeared shortly after the end of the Wars of Religion and at the beginning of the great political struggles of seventeenth-century England. According to this discourse, which was exemplified in England by Coke or Lilburne and in France by Boulainvilliers and then by Buat-Nançay, it was war that presided over the birth of States: not an ideal war—the war imagined by the philosophers of the state of nature—but real wars and actual battles; the laws were born in the midst of expeditions, conquests, and burning towns; but the war continues to rage within the mechanisms of power, or at least to constitute the secret motor of institutions, laws, and order. Beneath the omissions, the illusions, and the lies of those who would have us believe in the necessities of nature or the functional requirements of order, we have to rediscover war: war is the cipher of peace. It divides the entire social body, and it does so on a permanent basis; it puts all of us on one side or the other. And it is not enough to rediscover this war as an explanatory principle; it has to be reactivated. We have to force it out of the silent, larval forms in which it goes on without anyone realizing it, and we must pursue it until the decisive battle for which we have to prepare if we wish to be the victors.

This thematic, which I have so far characterized in very vague terms, allows us to understand the importance of this form of analysis.

1. The subject who speaks in this discourse cannot occupy the position of the jurist or the philosopher, or in other words, the position of the universal subject. In this general struggle of which he is speaking, he is inevitably on one side or the other. He is caught up in the battle, has adversaries and is fighting to win. No doubt he is trying to assert a right; but it is *his* right that is at issue—and it is a singular right that is marked by a relationship of conquest, domination, or seniority: the rights of a race, the rights of triumphant invasions or of millennial occupations. And while he also speaks about the truth, he is speaking about the perspectival and strategic truth that will allow him to be victorious. We have, then, a political and historical discourse that lays claim to truth and right, but which explicitly excludes itself from juridico-philosophical universality. Its role is not the role that legislators and philosophers, from Solon to Kant, have dreamed of: standing between the adversaries, at the center of and above the fray, imposing an armistice, establishing an order that brings reconciliation. It is a matter of establishing a right that is stamped with dissymmetry and that functions as a privilege that has

to be either maintained or reestablished; it is a matter of establishing a truth that functions as a weapon. For a subject speaking such a discourse, the universal truth and general right are illusions or traps.

2. We are also dealing with a discourse that inverts the traditional values of intelligibility. An explanation from below, which does not explain things in terms of what is simplest, most elementary, and clearest, but in terms of what is most confused, most obscure, most disorganized, and most haphazard. It uses as an interpretive principle the confusion of violence, passions, hatreds, revenge, and the tissue of the minor circumstances that create defeats and victories. The elliptical and dark god of battles must explain the long days of order, work, and peace. Fury must explain harmonies. The beginnings of history and right are traced back to a series of brute facts (physical strength, force, character traits) and a series of accidents (defeats, victories, the success or failure of conspiracies, rebellions, or alliances). A growing rationality—the rationality of calculations and strategies— will emerge, but it does so only on top of this tangle, and as we move upward and as it develops, it becomes more and more fragile, more and more wicked, more and more bound up with illusions, chimeras, and mystification. So we have the very opposite of those traditional analyses that try to find beneath the apparent or superficial confusion, beneath the visible brutality of bodies and passions, a basic rationality which is both permanent and related, by its very essence, to the just and the good.

3. This type of discourse develops entirely within the historical dimension. It does not attempt to gauge history, unjust government, and abuses and violence by the standard of the ideal principle of reason or law; on the contrary, it looks beneath the form of institutions and legislatures, and tries to revive the forgotten past of real struggles, concealed defeats and victories, and the blood that has dried

on the codes. It takes as its field of reference the never-ending movement of history. But it is also possible for it to look for support to
traditional mythical forms (the lost age of the great ancestors, the
coming of the new kingdom that will wipe away the defeats of old):
this is a discourse that is capable of expressing both the nostalgia of
declining aristocracies and the ardor of the people's revenge.

In short, and unlike the philosophico-juridical discourse organized
around the problem of sovereignty and the law, the discourse that
deciphers war's permanent presence within society is essentially a
historico-political discourse, a discourse in which truth functions as
a weapon to be used for a partisan victory, a discourse that is darkly
critical and at the same time intensely mythical.

⚜

This year's course was devoted to the emergence of this form of analysis: how has war (and its different aspects: invasions, battles, conquests, relations between victors and vanquished, pillage and
appropriation, uprisings) been used as an analyzer of history and,
more generally, social relations?

1. We must begin by ruling out certain false paternities. Especially
Hobbes. What Hobbes calls the war of every man against every man
is in no sense a real historical war, but a play of presentations that
allows every man to evaluate the threat that every man represents to
him, to evaluate the willingness of others to fight, and to assess the
risk that he himself would run if he resorted to force. Sovereignty—
be it that of a "commonwealth by institution" or that of a "commonwealth by acquisition"—is established not by the fact of warlike domination but, on the contrary, by a calculation that makes it possible
to avoid war. For Hobbes, it is a nonwar that founds the State and
gives it its form.

2. The history of wars as the wombs of States was no doubt outlined in the sixteenth century, and at the end of the Wars of Religion
(by Hotman, for example, in France). But it was mainly in the sev-

enteenth century that this type of analysis was developed. First in England, by the parliamentarian opposition and the Puritans, with the idea that English society had been a society of conquest ever since the eleventh century: the monarchy and the aristocracy—and their institutions—were Norman imports, while the Saxon people had, not without difficulty, preserved a few traces of their primitive freedoms. With this backdrop of warlike domination, English historians such as Coke or Selden reconstructed the main episodes in the history of England; each episode is analyzed as either an effect or a resumption of the historically primal state of war that exists between two hostile races which have different institutions and different interests. The revolution, of which these historians are the contemporaries, witnesses, and sometimes the protagonists, is seen as the last battle in that old war, and as its revenge.

An analysis of the same type is also found in France, but at a later date, and especially in aristocratic milieus at the end of the reign of Louis XIV. Boulainvilliers supplies its most vigorous formulation; but this time the story is told, and the rights are demanded, in the name of the victor; when it gives itself a Germanic origin, the French aristocracy claims a right of conquest, and therefore the preeminent possession of all the lands of the kingdom and absolute domination over all its Gaulish or Roman inhabitants. But it also claims prerogatives with respect to royal power, which could not originally have been established without its consent, and which must be kept within the limits established at that time. This is no longer, as in England, a history of a perpetual confrontation between vanquished and victors, and its basic categories are not uprisings and the winning of concessions; it is the history of how the king usurped and betrayed the nobility from which he was descended, and of his unnatural collusion with a bourgeoisie of Gallo-Roman descent. When reworked by Freret and especially Buat-Nançay, this schema was the focus of a whole series of polemics, and it stimulated extensive historical research until the Revolution.

The important point is that the principle of historical analysis was sought in racial duality and the war between races. On this basis, and through the intermediary of the works of Augustin and Amédée Thierry, two types of historical interpretation developed in the nineteenth century: one will be articulated with the class struggle, and the other with a biological confrontation.

SITUATING THE LECTURES

Alessandro Fontana and Mauro Bertani

THESE LECTURES WERE DELIVERED between 7 January and 17 March 1976, or between the publication of *Surveiller et punir* (February 1975) and *La Volonté de savoir* (October 1976), and they occupy a specific, one might say strategic, position in Foucault's thought and research. They mark a sort of pause, a momentary halt and no doubt a turning point, in which he evaluates the road that he has traveled and outlines future lines of investigation.

Foucault's course of lectures on "Society Must Be Defended" opens with a sort of survey or summary of the general features of "disciplinary" power—a power that is applied to individual bodies by techniques of surveillance, normalizing sanctions, and the panoptic organization of punitive institutions—and ends with an outline presentation of what he calls "biopower"—a power that is applied in general ways to the population, life, and living beings. In an attempt to establish a "genealogy" for this power, Foucault subsequently investigated "governmentality," or the power that has, since the late sixteenth century, been exercised through the apparatuses and technologies of reason of State and "policing." The question of disciplines was discussed in the lectures of 1972-1973 ("The Punitive Society"), 1973-1974 ("Psychiatric Power"), and 1974-1975 ("The Abnormals"), and in the book *Discipline and Punish;* governmentality and biopower are discussed in the first volume of *The History of Sexuality* (December 1976), and then in the lectures of 1977-1978 ("Security, Territory, and Population") and 1978-1979 ("Birth of Biopolitics") and in the first lecture of the 1979-1980 course ("Of the Government of the Living").

As the question of the two powers, their specificity, and their articulation is central to these lectures—as is that of war as "analyzer" of power relations and that of the birth of the historico-political discourse of race struggle—it seems appropriate to attempt to "situate" them by evoking a number of points which, in our view, have given rise to misunderstandings, errors, false interpretations, and sometimes falsifications. They relate on the one hand to the birth of Foucault's problematic of power, and on the other to the workings of apparatuses and technologies of power in liberal societies and in totalitarianisms, to the "dialogue" with Marx and Freud about processes of production and sexuality, and, finally, to the question of resistance. We will try to deal with these points by using direct quotations, most of them taken from the texts collected in *Dits et écrits.* It should, however, be stressed that the full dossier on the question of power will not be available until the lectures have been published in full, and that we will have to wait until then before we can attempt to give a definitive account.

Foucault never devoted a book to power. He outlined a general theory of power on a number of occasions; he tirelessly explained himself; and he was not stinting when it came to corrections and clarifications. He tended, rather, to study the workings, the effects and the "how" of power in the many historical analyses he made of asylums, madness, medicine, prisons, sexuality, and "policing." The question of power runs through all these analyses, is an integral part of them, is imminent within them, and is therefore indissociable from them. Since the problematic was enriched both by the pressure of events and by its own internal development, it would be futile to try at all cost to make it part of a coherent whole or an unbroken linear continuity. It was, rather, a constant process of reworking. It is typical of Foucault's approach that until the end of his life, he constantly "reread," resituated, and reinterpreted his early work in the light of his later work and, so to speak, constantly updated it. That is why he always denied having tried to formulate a "general theory" of power, even though it was certainly claimed that that was what he was trying to do with, for example, panopticism. Speaking of truth/power and power/knowledge relations in 1977, he said: "[I]t is difficult to grasp this stratum of objects, or rather this stratum of relations; and as we have no general theory to apprehend them, I am, if you like, a blind empiricist or in other words, I am in the worst of all situations. I have no general theory and I have no reliable instruments."[1] He also remarked in 1977 that the question of power "began to be raised in its nudity" in about 1955, and against the backdrop of "two gigantic shadows," of the "two black heritages" that fascism and Stalinism represented for him and his generation. "The nonanalysis of fascism is one of the most important political facts of the last thirty years."[2] If, he said, the nineteenth century's question had been that of poverty, the question raised by fascism and Stalinism was that of power: "too little wealth" on the one hand, and "too much power" on the other.[3] In the 1930s, Trotskyist circles began to analyze the phenomenon of bureaucracy and the bureaucratization of the Party. The question of power was taken up again in the 1950s, in connection with the "black heritages" of fascism and Stalinism, and it is at this point that we begin to see a divergence between the old theory of wealth, which was born of the "scandal" of poverty, and the problematic of power. These were the years of the Khrushchev report, of the beginnings of "de-Stalinization," and of the Algerian war.

Power relations, phenomena of domination, and practices of subjugation are not specific to "totalitarianisms"; they also exist in the societies we describe as "democratic," or those that Foucault studied in his historical analyses. What is the relationship between a totalitarian society and a democratic society? What are the similarities and differences between their political rationalities, and the use they make of the technologies and apparatuses of power? Speaking of the relationship between the two, Foucault remarked in 1978: "Western societies, which are in general the industrial and developed societies of the late nineteenth century, are societies that are haunted by this secret fear, or even by quite explicitly rebellious movements that call into question that sort of overproduction of power that Stalinism and fascisms no doubt demonstrate in a naked, monstrous fashion." And slightly earlier in the same lecture: "Of course fascism and Stalinism were both responses to a precise and very specific situation. Of course fascism and Stalinism expanded their effects to hitherto unknown dimensions, and it is, if not to be rationally expected, at least to be hoped, that we will never see their like again. They are therefore unique phenomena, but it cannot be denied that, in many respects, fascism and Stalinism simply extended a whole series of mechanisms that already existed in the social and political systems of the West. After all, the organization of great parties, the development of political apparatuses, and the existence of techniques of repression such as labor camps, all that is quite clearly the heritage of liberal Western societies, and all Stalinism and fascism had to do was to stoop down and pick it up."[4]

There would therefore appear to be a very strange kinship between "liberal societies" and totalitarian States, or between the normal and the pathological, and sooner or later it must be investigated. Speaking in 1982 of the twin "diseases" of power, of the two "fevers" known as fascism and Stalinism, Foucault wrote: "One of the numerous reasons why they are, for us, so puzzling, is that in spite of their historical uniqueness they are not quite original. They used and extended mechanisms already present in most other societies. More than that: in spite of their own internal madness, they used to a large extent the ideas and devices of our political rationality."[5] A transfer and extension of technology; all that is missing is the madness and the monstrosity. There is also a "continuity" between fascism and Stalinism at the level of the biopolitics of the exclusion and extermination of the politically dangerous and the ethnically impure—the biopolitics established as early as the eighteenth century by medical policing and then taken over in the nineteenth by social Darwinism, eugenics, and medico-legal theories of heredity, degeneracy, and race. The reader is referred to the remarks made by Foucault in the last (17 March) lecture in the *Society Must Be Defended* series. After all, one of the objectives, if not the essential objective, of this course of lectures is to analyze the way fascism in particular (but also Stalinism) could make use of racial biopolitics in the "government of the living" by stressing the importance of racial purity and ideological orthodoxy.

When it comes to relations between power and political economy, Foucault maintained a sort of "uninterrupted dialogue" with Marx. Marx was in fact not unaware of the question of power and its disciplines: one has only to look at the analyses of "The Working Day," "The Division of Labor and Manufacture," and "Machinery and Large-Scale Industry" in the first volume of *Capital* and of "The Process of Circulation of Capital" in volume 2.[6] But in Marx, relations of domination in the factory appear to be established solely by the play and the effects of the "antagonistic" relations between capital and labor. For Foucault, in contrast, that relationship is possible only because of the subjugations, training, and surveillance that have already been produced and administered by disciplines. In this connection, he remarks: "When, because of the division of labor, there was a need for people who were capable of doing this or of doing that, and when there was a fear that popular resistance movements, inertia, or rebellion might upset the entire capitalist order that was being born, every individual had to be under a precise and concrete surveillance, and I think that the medicalization I was talking about is bound up with this."[7] It was therefore not the "capitalist" bourgeoisie of the nineteenth century that invented and imposed relations of domination; it inherited them from the disciplinary mechanisms of the seventeenth and eighteenth centuries, and simply had to use them, to modify them by intensifying some and attenuating others. "All these power relations do not, therefore, emanate from a single source; it is the overall effect of a tangle of power relations that allows one class or group to dominate another."[8] "Basically," wrote Foucault in 1978, "it is true that the question I was asking was being asked of

Marxism and of other conceptions of history and politics, and it was this: With respect to, for example, the relations of production, don't relations of power represent a level of reality that is both complex and relatively—but only relatively—independent?"⁹ And we can then ask ourselves whether "capitalism," or the mode of production in which these power relations are inscribed, might not represent in its turn a great apparatus for coding and intensifying those "relatively autonomous relations"—relations between the labor force and capital that were certainly "economic" and conflictual—thanks to the divisions, the hierarchies, and the division of labor that had been established in manufactures, workshops, and factories, but also and above all by disciplinary rules, the subjugation of bodies, and the sanitary regulations that adapted, intensified, and bent the labor force to the economic constraints of production. It is therefore not labor that introduced the disciplines; it is more a case of disciplines and norms making it possible to organize labor in the way that it is organized in the so-called capitalist economy.

One could say the same of "sexuality" (but this time the dialogue is with nineteenth-century medicine and with Freud in particular, and the tone is sharper). Foucault never denied that sexuality was "central" to medical discourses and practices from the early eighteenth century onward. But he did dismiss the idea, which was prefigured by Freud and then theorized by "Freudo-Marxism," that this sexuality was simply denied, repressed, or suppressed; on the contrary, according to Foucault, it gave rise to a whole proliferation of eminently positive discourses that actually allowed power—biopower—to control and normalize individuals, behavior, and the population. "Sexuality" is therefore not a repository of secrets from which one can, provided one knows how to detect and decode them, extract the truth about individuals; it is, rather, a domain in which, ever since the campaign against childhood onanism suddenly began in England in the first half of the eighteenth century, power over life has been exercised in the twin forms of the "anatomo-politics of the human body" and the "biopolitics of population." Both powers—that of bodily disciplines and that of the government of the population—are thus articulated around sexuality, and they support and reinforce each other. In the introduction to *The History of Sexuality*, Foucault writes: "The disciplines of the body and the regulations of the population constituted the two poles around which the organization of power over life was deployed. The setting up, in the course of the classical age, of this great bipolar technology—anatomic and biological, individualizing and specifying, directed toward the performance of the body, with attention to the processes of life—characterized a power whose highest function was perhaps no longer to kill, but to invest life through and through."[10] Hence the importance of sex, not as a repository of secrets or basic truths about individuals, but rather as a target, as a political issue. "On the one hand it was tied to the disciplines of the body: the harnessing, intensification, and distribution of forces, the adjustment and economy of energies. On the other hand, it was applied to the regulation of populations, through all the far-reaching effects of its activity.... It was employed as a standard for disciplines and as a basis for regulations."[11]

The specificity and the importance of labor and sexuality—and the fact that they are "cathected" or "hypercathected" by the discourse of political economy on the one hand and by medical knowledge on the other—arise from the fact that they are the points where relations of disciplinary power and biopower's normalizing techniques intersect and therefore intensify their effects and strengthen their hold. These two powers therefore do not, as has sometimes been said, constitute two separate "theories" within Foucault's thought. One does not preclude the other; one is not independent of the other. One does not derive from the other; they are, rather, knowledge/power's two conjoint modes of functioning, though it is true that they do have their own specific foci, points of application, finalities, and *enjeux*: the training of bodies on the one hand, and the regulation of the population on the other. For further discussion, the reader is referred to Foucault's analyses of the town, the norm, and sexuality in the lecture of 17 March in *"Society Must Be Defended"* and to the final chapter of the introduction to *The History of Sexuality* ("Right of Death and Power over Life").

Where there is power, there is always resistance, and the two things are coextensive: "As soon as there is a power relation, there is a possibility of resistance. We can never be ensnared by power: we can always modify its grip in determinate conditions and according to a precise strategy."[12] The field in which power is deployed is therefore not that of a doleful and stable domination: "The struggle is everywhere.... at every moment, we move from rebellion to domination, from domination to rebellion, and it is all this perpetual agitation that I would like to try to bring out."[13] The characteristic feature of power, its aims and its maneuvers, is therefore not so much its boundless might as a sort of congenital inefficacy: "Power is not omnipotent or omniscient; on the contrary," Foucault remarked in 1978 of the analyses made in *The History of Sexuality*. "The reason power relations have produced ways of investigating and analyzing models of knowledge is precisely that," he went on, "power is not omniscient, that power is blind, that it finds itself in an impasse. The reason why we have seen the development of so many power relations, so many systems of control, and so many forms of surveillance is precisely that power has always been impotent."[14] In *The History of Sexuality* Foucault asks: History being the ruse of reason, is power the ruse of history, and does it always emerge the winner? Quite the contrary: "This would be to misunderstand the strictly relational character of power relationships. Their existence depends upon a multiplicity of points of resistance: these play the role of adversary, target, support, or handles in power relations. These points of resistance are present everywhere in the power network."[15]

But how is this resistance, how are these resistances manifested, what form do they take, and how can they be analyzed? Here, one thing has to be stressed from the outset. If, as Foucault says in the first two lectures, power is not deployed and is not exercised in the forms of right and law, and if it is not something that can be taken or exchanged; if it does not consist of interests, a will, or an intention; if it does not originate within the State, and if it therefore cannot be deduced from or understood in terms of the juridico-political category of sovereignty (even if right, law, and sovereignty can represent a sort of coding of power, or can even reinforce it), then neither is resistance a matter of right, or of a right. It is therefore always outside the juridical framework of what has, ever since the seventeenth century, been called "the right to resist": it is not based upon the sovereignty of a preexisting subject.[16] Power and resistance confront each other, and use multiple, mobile, and changing tactics, in a field of relations of force whose logic is not so much the regulated and codified logic of right and sovereignty, as the strategic and warlike logic of struggle. The relationship between power and resistance must therefore be analyzed in the strategic form of struggle rather than in the juridical form of sovereignty.

This is a major theme in these lectures, which were delivered at a time when Foucault was taking a close interest in military institutions and the army.[17] The question he was raising is this: Can these struggles, confrontations, and strategies be analyzed in the general binary form of domination (dominant/dominated) and, therefore in the last instance, war? "Should we turn the expression around, then, and say that politics is war pursued by other means? If we still wish to maintain a separation between war and politics, perhaps we should postulate rather that this multiplicity of force relations can be coded—in part but never totally—either in the form of 'war' or in the forms of 'politics'; this would imply two different strategies (but the one always liable to switch into the other) for integrating these unbalanced, heterogeneous, unstable, and tense force relations."[18] Pointing out to Marxists that when they discuss the concept of "class struggle," they concentrate on investigating "class" rather than "struggle,"[19] Foucault states: "What I would like to discuss, starting with Marx, is not the problem of the sociology of classes, but the strategic method concerning struggles. That is the source of my interest in Marx, and it is on that basis that I would like to raise problems."[20]

Foucault had already devoted his lecture of 10 January 1973 ("The Punitive Society") to relations between war and domination. Here he denounces Hobbes's theory of "the war of every man against every man," analyzes the relationship between civil war and power, and describes the defensive measures taken by society against the criminal, who became a "social enemy" from the seventeenth century onward. As Daniel Defert reminds us in his "Chronology," Foucault was reading Trotsky, Guevara, Luxemburg, and Clausewitz in 1967 and 1968.[21] He was also reading the writings of the Black Panthers at that time, and he remarks in a letter that "they are developing a strategic analysis that has emancipated itself from Marxist theory."[22] In a letter written in December 1972, he says that he wants to analyze power relations by looking at "the most disparaged of all wars: neither Hobbes, nor Clausewitz, nor the class struggle: civil war."[23] And in another letter, written in August 1974, he writes: "My marginals are incredibly familiar and repetitive. I feel like looking at something else: political economy, strategy, politics."[24]

Foucault seems, however, to have been very unsure about how useful the strategic model would be for the analysis of power relations: "Aren't processes of domination more complex, more complicated, than war?" he asked in an interview given in December 1977.[25] And in the questions he addressed to the journal *Hérodote* (July-December 1976), he wrote:

The notion of strategy is essential if one wants to analyze power and its relations with knowledge. Does that necessarily imply that we are waging war through the knowledge in question?

Doesn't strategy allow us to analyze power relations as a technique of domination?

Or do we have to say that domination is a continued form of war?[26]

And shortly afterward, he added: "Is the relation between forces in the order of politics a warlike one: I don't personally feel prepared to answer this with a definite yes or no."[27]

The lectures published here are, essentially, devoted to these questions. Foucault analyzes the themes of war and domination in the historico-political discourse of race struggle used by the English Diggers and Levellers, and in Boulainvilliers. Their stories about the Normans' domination of the Saxons after the Battle of Hastings, and of the Germanic Franks' domination of the Gallo-Romans after the conquest of Gaul, are based on the history of the conquest, which they contrast with both "fictions" of natural right and the universalism of the law. It is, according to Foucault, here and not in Machiavelli or Hobbes that we see the birth of a radical form of history which speaks of war, conquest, and domination, and which can be used as a weapon against royalty and the nobility in England, and against royalty and the Third Estate in France. Foucault calls this historico-political discourse on conquest "historicism," and thus picks up, either directly or indirectly, the thesis formulated, in a very different context and for very different purposes, in 1936 by Friedrich Meinecke in his *Die Entstehung des Historismus*. This is a discourse of struggles, a discourse of battles, and a discourse of races. In the nineteenth century, the "dialectic" appears to have coded, and therefore "neutralized," these struggles. Augustin Thierry had already made use of them in his writings on the Norman Conquest and the formation of the Third Estate, and Nazism would use the racial theme in the policies of discrimination and extermination with which we are only too familiar. And while it is true that this historico-political discourse forces the historian to take sides and to abandon the "median position of referee, judge, or universal witness,"[28] which has been that of philosophers from Solon to Kant, and while it is also true that these discourses are born of war and not of peace, the fact remains that the binary relationship which is introduced into these discourses by the phenomena of domination, and which the model of war explains, does not really explain either the multiplicity of the real struggles that are provoked by disciplinary power or the effects government has on the modes of behavior produced by biopower.

After 1976, Foucault's research shifted toward the analysis of this kind of power, and perhaps that is one of the reasons why, while he does not abandon the problematic of war, he does at least begin to discuss it again. It remains a central issue in *"Society Must Be Defended."* When the real is "polemical," *"We all fight each other,"* he said in 1977.[29] We should not, however, be fooled by this seemingly Hobbesian remark. This is not a reference to the great binary confrontation, to the intense and violent form that the struggles take at certain moments, and only at certain moments, in history. It is, rather, a way of saying that the massive fact of domination and the binary logic of war cannot understand either all the episodic or sporadic struggles that take place in the field of power, or the multiplicity of local, unpredictable, and heterogeneous resistances. Toward the end of his life, in 1982 in a text which is in a sense his philosophical "testament" and in which he tried, as he did so often—so much so that it seems to be one of the "figures" of his thought—to rethink all these questions in the light of his latest work and to bring a new perspective to bear on them, Foucault wrote that what he had been trying to do was not "to analyze the phenomena of power, nor to elaborate the foundation of such an analysis," but rather to produce "a history of the different modes by which, in our culture, human beings are made subjects."[30] In his view, the exercise of power consisted primarily in "directing conduct" in the sense that Christian pastoralism and "governmentality" direct conduct. He wrote: "Basically, power is less a confrontation between two adversaries or the linking of the one to the other than a question of government."[31] And he concluded (though the text has to be read in full) that "Every strategy of confrontation dreams of becoming a relationship of power and every relationship of power leans toward the idea that, if it follows its own line of development and comes up against direct confrontation, it may become the winning strategy."[32]

Foucault first began to raise the question of power in *Histoire de la folie,* which looks at the power that is at work in and that is exercised through the administrative and Statist techniques used in the "great confinement" of dangerous individuals (vagabonds, criminals, and the mad). He returned to it in the early 1970s in the lectures given at the Collège de France on the production of truth and truth-regimes in ancient Greece, on the punitive mechanisms used in Europe from the Middle Ages onward, and on the normalizing apparatuses of the disciplinary society. But in the background to all this, there is the politico-military context, or the "historical circumstances," as Canguilhem called them, of international conflicts and social struggles in France after 1968.

It is not possible to retrace the history of those "circumstances" here. For the record, let us briefly recall that these were the years of war in Vietnam, of "Black September" in Jordan (1970), of student protests against the Salazar regime (1971) three years before the Carnation Revolution, of the IRA's terrorist offensive in Ireland (1972), of the resurgence of the Arab-Israeli conflict in the Yom Kippur War, of normalization in Czechoslovakia, of the colonels' regime in Greece, of the fall of Allende in Chile, of fascist terrorism in Italy, of the miners' strike in England, of the terrible death agony of Francoism in Spain, of the Khmer Rouge's seizure of power in Cambodia, and of civil war in Lebanon, Peru, Argentina, Brazil, and many African states.

Foucault's interest in power stems from the vigilance, attention, and interest with which he followed what Nietzsche called *"die grosse Politik"*: the rise of fascisms around the world, civil wars, the establishment of military dictatorships, the oppressive geopolitical aims of the great powers (and especially of the United States in Vietnam). It is also, and above all, rooted in his "political practice" in the 1970s; this allowed him to understand the workings of the carceral system at first hand or on the ground, to observe the fate reserved for prisoners, to study their material living conditions, to denounce the practices of the penitentiary administration, and to support conflicts and rebellions wherever they broke out.

As for racism, this was a theme that appeared and was dealt with in the seminars and lectures on psychiatry, punishment, the abnormals, and all the knowledges and practices associated with the medical theory of "degeneracy," the forensic theory of eugenicism and social Darwinism, and the penal theory of "social defense," which in the nineteenth century developed techniques for identifying, isolating, and normalizing "dangerous" individuals: the early dawn of ethnic cleansings and labor camps (as Foucault himself reminds us, at the end of the nineteenth century, the French criminologist J. Léveillé advised his Russian colleagues to build labor camps in Siberia when he attended an international penitentiary conference held in St. Peterburg).[33] A new racism was born when "knowledge of heredity"—to which Foucault planned to devote his future research, as he explains in his candidacy presentation to the Collège de France[34]—was combined with the psychiatric theory of degeneracy. Addressing his audience in the last (19 March 1975) of the 1974-1975 course of lectures on "The Abnormals," Foucault said: "You see how psychiatry can use this notion of degeneracy, these analyses of heredity to establish a connection with, or rather to give rise to a racism."[35] He added that Nazism had simply linked, in its turn, this new racism to the ethnic racism that was endemic in the nineteenth century, when it was used to provide an internal social defense against the abnormals.

Against this backdrop of war, of the wars, struggles, and rebellions of those years when, as the saying went, "there was red in the air," *"Society Must Be Defended"* might be described as the meeting point, the hinge or the point of articulation of the political problem of power and the historical question of race: the genealogy of racism, beginning with the historical discourse of the eighteenth and nineteenth centuries on the race struggle, and the transformations they underwent in the nineteenth and twentieth centuries. In terms of war, of the war that traverses the field of power, leads to conflict, distinguishes between friend and foe, and generates dominations and rebellions, one might evoke one of Foucault's "childhood memories," which he himself described in an interview given in 1983. He speaks of the "fright" that gripped him when Chancellor Dollfuss was assassinated in 1934: "The menace of war was our background, our framework of existence. Then the war arrived. Much more than the activities of family life, it was these events concerning the world which are the substance of our memory. I say 'our' because I am nearly sure that most boys and girls in France at this moment had the same experience. Our private life was really threatened, maybe that is the reason why I am fascinated by history and those events of which we are a part. I think that is the nucleus of my theoretical desires."[36]

As for the "intellectual conjuncture" of the years leading up to these lectures—years marked by the crisis in Marxism and by the rise of neoliberal discourse—it is difficult, if not impossible, to know which books Foucault is referring to, either directly or indirectly, in

"Society Must Be Defended." Works by Max Weber, Hannah Arendt, Ernst Cassirer, Max Horkheimer, T. W. Adorno, and Aleksandr Solzhenitsyn had been translated and published since 1970. In one lecture, Foucault pays explicit tribute to Gilles Deleuze and Félix Guattari's *Anti-Oedipus.* Foucault did not, it appears, keep any record of the books he read, and he was not fond of debates with individual authors; he preferred problematization to polemic.[37] We can therefore do no more than speculate as to his way of reading books, using documentation, and exploiting sources (all this, or the production of his books, should be the object of a study in its own right). Nor do we know very much about how he prepared his lectures. The lectures published here are written out almost in full, and, thanks to the courtesy and help of Daniel Defert, we have also been able to consult the manuscript. It does not, however, correspond exactly to the words that were actually spoken. The manuscript consists of "blocks of thought" that Foucault used as markers, points of reference, and guidelines. He often improvised around them, developing or expanding on this or that point, anticipating the next lecture and going back to others. One also has the impression that he did not work to a preestablished plan, but tended, rather, to begin with a problem or certain problems, and that the lecture developed "on the spot" through a sort of spontaneous generation. There were digressions and remarks about future lectures, and some things were dropped (such as the promised lecture on "repression," which was never given but which appears in *The History of Sexuality.*) In 1977, Foucault described his work and his way of working thus: "I am neither a philosopher nor a writer. I am not creating an oeuvre. I do research which is at once historical and political; I am often drawn to problems that I have encountered in one book, that I have not been able to resolve in that book, and I therefore try to deal with them in the next book. There are also conjunctural phenomena which, at a given moment, make some problem look like a particularly urgent problem, a politically urgent problem to do with current affairs, and that's why it interests me."[38] As for methodology and *The Archaeology of Knowledge,* he said: "I do not have a methodology that I apply in the same way to different

domains. On the contrary, I would say that I try to isolate a single field of objects, a domain of objects, by using the instruments I can find or that I can forge as I am actually doing my research, but without privileging the problem of methodology in any way."[39]

Twenty years after the event, these lectures have lost nothing of their topicality and urgency. Foucault rejects juridical theories and political doctrines that are incapable of accounting for relations of power and relations of force within confrontations between knowledges and in real struggles. He rereads the age of the Enlightenment, and shows that it reveals not the progress of reason, but how "minor" knowledges were disqualified in order to promote the centralization, normalization, and disciplinarization of dominant knowledges, rather than the progress of reason. He critiques the idea that history is an invention or the heritage of a bourgeoisie that was on the ascendancy in the eighteenth century. He pays an extended tribute to "historicism," to a history that speaks of conquests and dominations, a "history-battle" in the true sense of the word which developed out of the race struggle, as opposed to natural right. And finally, he shows how the transformation of this struggle during the nineteenth century raised a problem: that of the biopolitical regularization of behavior, the problem of recent memory and of the near future, of the birth and development of racism and fascism. Being accustomed to his changes of scenery and the way he alters his perspective with respect to ruling ideas and established knowledges, Foucault's readers will not be surprised. As for the specialists, one can only suggest that they should not forget that this text is not a book, but a set of lectures, and that it has to be read as such: it is not a work of scholarship, but rather a way of posing an "urgent" problem—that of racism—and of opening up lines of investigation, of outlining a genealogical trace in order to rethink it. So how should one read it? One might recall, to conclude, what Foucault said in 1977: "Philosophy's question . . . is the question as to what we ourselves are. That is why contemporary philosophy is entirely political and entirely historical. It is the politics immanent in history and the history indispensable for politics."[40]

❧

As to the studies Foucault may have consulted while preparing these lectures, we can only speculate. The sources are cited in the notes, but it is practically impossible to tell whether Foucault had read the texts in question or was borrowing from secondary works. A "scientific" bibliography could be established only on the basis of the careful notes taken by Foucault, with one quotation per sheet, together with the bibliographical references to the edition and page; but he then filed them thematically, and not as a dossier relating to any particular book or lecture. The task of reconstructing Foucault's "library" remains to be undertaken, and it is certainly far beyond the scope of this note.

In order to open up a few paths and to provide a guide for future readers and researchers, we will for the moment simply signal a few books that relate to the questions raised in the lectures, and which were available at the time when Foucault was preparing them.

The "Trojan Myth" and the History of Races
T. Simar, *Étude critique sur la formation de la doctrine des races* (Brussels: Lamerti, 1922); J. Barzun, *The French Race* (New York: Columbia University Press, 1932); M. Bloch, "Sur les grandes invasions. Quelques positions de problèmes," *Revue de synthèse*, 1940-1945; G. Huppert, *The Idea of a Perfect History; Historical Erudition and Historical Philosophy in Renaissance France* (Urbana: University of Illinois Press, 1970) (tr. *L'Idée de l'histoire parfaite* [Paris: Flammarion, 1973]); L. Poliakov, *Histoire de l'anti-sémitisme, III: De Voltaire à Wagner* (Paris: Calmann-Lévy, 1968) and *Le Mythe aryen* (Paris: Calmann-Lévy, 1971), C.-G. Dubois, *Celtes et Gaulois au XVIe siècle. Le Développement d'un mythe littéraire* (Paris: Vrin, 1972); A. Devyer, *Le Sang épuré. Les Préjugés de race chez les gentilhommes français de l'Ancien Régime, 1560-1720* (Brussels: Éditions de l'Université, 1973); A. Jouanna, *L'Idée de race en France au XVIe siècle et au début du XVIIe siècle,* thesis defended in June 1975 at the Université de Paris II and distributed by Éditions Champion in 1976.

It should also be pointed out that the problem of the historiography of races was raised, after Meinecke, by Georg Lukács in chapter 7 of *Die Zersörung der Vernuft* (Berlin: Aufbau Verlag, 1954. French, *Le Destruction de la raison* [Paris: L'Arche, 1958-1959]) and in *Der historische Roman* (Berlin: Aufbau Verlag, 1956) (*Le Roman historique* [Paris: Payot, 1965]; *The Historical Novel,* tr. Hannah Mitchell and Stanley Mitchell [London: Merlin Press, 1962]).

Two early German studies of the Trojan myth should also be mentioned: E. Luthgen, *Dies Quellen und der historische Wert des fränkischen Trojasage* (Bonn: R. Weber, 1876) and M. Klippel's thesis, *Die Darstellung des fränkischen Trojanersagen* (Marburg: Beyer und Hans Knecht, 1936).

On the Levellers and Diggers

J. Frank, *The Diggers* (Cambridge, Mass.: Harvard University Press, 1955); H. N. Brailsford, *The Levellers and the English Revolution*, ed. C. Hill (London: Cresset Press, 1961); and especially C. Hill, *Puritanism and Revolution* (London: Secker & Warburg, 1961); *Intellectual Origins of the English Revolution* (Oxford: Clarendon Press, 1965); and *The World Turned Upside Down* (London: Temple Smith, 1972).

On the Imperial Roman Theme and the Translation Imperii *from the* Middle Ages to the Renaissance

F. A. Yates, *Astraea: The Imperial Theme in the Sixteenth Century* (London and Boston: Routledge and Kegan Paul, 1975) (*Astraea* [Paris: Boivin, 1989]).

On Boulainvilliers

R. Simon, *Henry de Boulainvilliers, historien, politique, philosophe, astrologue* (Paris: Boivin, 1942) and *Un Révolté du grand siècle: Henry de Boulainvilliers* (Garches: Ed. du Nouvel Humanisme, 1948).

On the Eighteenth-Century Dispute between "Romanists" and "Germanists" over the French Monarchy, Historiography, and "Constitution"

E. Carcassonne, *Montesquieu et le problème de la constutition française au XVIIIe siècle* (Paris: PUF, 1927; Geneva: Slatkine Reprints, 1970);

L. Althusser, *Montesquieu: La Politique et l'histoire* (Paris: PUF, 1959) ("Montesquieu: Politics and History" in *Politics and History* [London: New Left Books, 1972]).

On A. Thierry and Historiography in France during the Restoration and under the July Monarchy
P. Moreau, *L'Histoire de France au XIXe siècle* (Paris: Les Belles Lettres, 1935); K. J. Carroll, *Some Aspects of the Historical Thought of Augustin Thierry* (Washington, D.C.: Catholic University of America Press, 1951); F. Engel-Janosi, *Four Studies in French Romantic Historical Writings* (Baltimore, Md.: Johns Hopkins University Press, 1955); B. Reizov, *L'Historiographie romantique française (1815-1830)* (Éditions de Moscou, 1957); S. Mellon, *The Political Uses of History in the French Restoration* (Stanford, Calif.: Stanford University Press, 1958); M. Seliger, "Augustin Thierry: Race-Thinking during the Restoration," *Journal of the History of Ideas*, vol. 19 (1958), R. N. Smithson, *Augustin Thierry: Social and Political Consciousness in the Evolution of Historical Method* (Geneva: Droz, 1972).

"Anti-Semitism" and the French Left in the Nineteenth Century
R. F. Byrnes, *Antisemitism in Modern France* (1950; reprint, New York: H. Fertig, 1969); Rabi [W. Rabinovitch], *Anatomie du judaïsme français* (Paris: Éditions de Minuit, 1962); L. Poliakov, *Histoire de l'antisémitisme*, vol. 3 (Paris: Calmann-Lévy, 1968). Foucault may also have been familiar with the many works of E. Silberner collected as *Sozialisten zur Judenfrage* (Berlin: Colloquim Verlag, 1962), and with Zosa Szajikowski, *Jews and the French Revolutions of 1789, 1830 and 1848* (New York: Ktav Publishing House, 1970, reprinted 1972).

It should also be pointed out that R. Aron's two-volume *Penser la guerre, Clausewitz* was published by Gallimard in February 1976.

1. "Kenryoku to chi ('Pouvoir et savoir')," *Dits et écrits*, vol. 3, p. 404.
2. "Powers and Strategies," in Colin Gordon, ed., *Power/Knowledge: Selected Writings and Other Writings 1972-1977* (Hemel Hempstead: Harvester, 1980); p. 139; French original: "Pouvoirs et stratégies," *Dits et écrits*, vol. 3, p. 422.
3. "Gendai no Kenryoku no butai ('La Philosophie analytique du pouvoir')," *Dits et écrits*, vol. 3, p. 536.
4. "Gendai no Kenryoku wo tou," pp. 535-36.
5. "Why Study Power: In Quest of the Subject," in Hubert L. Dreyfus and Paul Rabinow, *Michel Foucault: Beyond Structuralism and Hermeneutics*, with an Afterword by Michel Foucault (Hemel Hempstead: Harvester, 1982), p. 209; French version: "Le Sujet et le pouvoir," *Dits et écrits*, vol. 4, p. 224.
6. Cf. "As malhas do poder ('Les Mailles du pouvoir')," *Dits et écrits*, vol. 4, pp. 182-201 and especially p. 186ff.
7. "El poder, una bestia magnifica ('Le Pouvoir, une bête magnifique')," *Dits et écrits*, vol. 3, p. 374.
8. Ibid., p. 379.
9. "Precisazioni sul potere. riposta ad alcuni critici ('Précisions sur le pouvoir. réponses à certaines critiques')," *Dits et écrits*, vol. 3, p. 629.
10. *The History of Sexuality, Volume I: An Introduction*, trans. Robert Hurley (Harmondsworth: Penguin, 1981), p. 139.
11. Ibid., pp. 145, 146.
12. "Power and Sex," trans. David J. Parent, in Lawrence D. Kritzman, ed., *Michel Foucault: Politics, Philosophy, Culture: Interviews and Other Writings, 1977-1984* (New York and London: Routledge, 1988), p. 123; French original: "Non au sexe roi," *Dits et écrits*, vol. 3, p. 267.
13. "Kenryoku to chi," p. 407.
14. "Precisazioni sul potere," p. 629.
15. *The History of Sexuality, Volume I*, p. 95.
16. Cf. "Power and Strategies," pp. 141-42; "Governmentality," p. 102.
17. "Hanzai tosite no chishiki ('Le Savoir comme crime')," *Dits et écrits*, vol. 3, p. 89; "Power and Sex," p. 123; "Vivre autrement le temps," *Dits et écrits*, vol. 3, p. 268; "Incorporación del hospital en la tecnologia moderna (L'Incorporation de l'hôpital dans la technologie moderne)," ibid., p. 515; "Governmentality," p. 97; and later, "As malhas do poder," pp. 182-201.
18. *The History of Sexuality, Volume I*, p. 93.
19. Cf. "Power and Sex," p. 123; "The Confession of the Flesh," p. 208.
20. "Sekhai-ninshiki no hôhô: marx-shusi wo dô shimatsu suruka ('Méthodologie pour la connaissance du monde: comment se débarasser du marxisme')," *Dits et écrits*, vol. 3, p. 606.
21. Daniel Defert, "Chronologie," *Dits et écrits*, vol. 1, pp. 30-32.
22. Ibid., p. 33.
23. Ibid., p. 42.
24. Ibid., p. 45.
25. "Des Questions de Michel Foucault à *Hérodote*," *Dits et écrits*, vol. 3, p. 94.
26. Ibid.
27. "L'Oeil de pouvoir," *Dits et écrits*, vol. 3, p. 206; English translation: "The Eye of Power," in *Power/Knowledge*, p. 164.
28. "Questions à Michel Foucault sur la géographie," *Dits et écrits*, vol. 3, p. 29; "Questions on Geography" in *Power/Knowledge*, p. 65.
29. "Non au sexe roi," *Dits et écrits*, vol. 3, p. 206; "The Confession of the Flesh," in *Power/Knowledge*, p. 208.

30. "The Subject and Power," in Dreyfus and Rabinow, eds., *Michel Foucault*, p. 203; *Dits et écrits*, vol. 4, p. 237.

31. "The Subject and Power," p. 221; *Dits et écrits*, vol. 4, p. 237.

31. Ibid., pp. 25-26; *Dits et écrits*, vol. 4, p. 242.

33. "Le Jeu de Michel Foucault," *Dits et écrits*, vol. 3, p. 325; "The Confession of the Flesh," p. 225.

34. *Dits et écrits*, vol. 1, pp. 842-86; *Ethics: The Essential Works*, vol. 1, pp. 5-10.

35. *Les Anormaux: Cours au Collège de France, 1974-1975* (Paris: Gallimard and Le Seuil, 1999), p. 299.

36. "The Minimalist Self" (interview with Stephen Riggins), in Kritzman, ed., *Michel Foucault*, p. 7; French translation: "Une Interview de Michel Foucault par Stephen Riggins," *Dits et écrits*, vol. 4, p. 528.

37. Cf. "Polemics, Politics and Problematizations" in Paul Rabinow, ed., *The Foucault Reader* (Harmondsworth: Penguin, 1986); pp. 381-90; French version: "Polémique, politique et problématisations," *Dits et écrits*, vol. 4, pp. 591-98.

38. "El poder, una bestia magnifica," pp. 376-77.

39. "Kenryoku to chi," p. 404.

40. "Power and Sex," p. 12; "Non au sexe roi," p. 266.

INDEX